Nick Vandome

MacBook

4th Edition

For MacBook, MacBook Air and MacBook Pro
Covers OS X Yosemite (v10.10)

In easy steps is an imprint of In Easy Steps Limited
16 Hamilton Terrace · Holly Walk · Leamington Spa
Warwickshire · United Kingdom · CV32 4LY
www.ineasysteps.com

Fourth Edition

In Easy Steps Limited supports The Forest Stewardship Council (FSC), the leading international forest certification organisation. All our titles that are printed on Greenpeace approved FSC certified paper carry the FSC logo.

MIX
Paper from responsible sources
FSC® C020837

Printed and bound in the United Kingdom

ISBN 978-1-84078-604-0

Contents

1 Introducing MacBooks

Apple's MacBook range of laptop computers is stylish and user-friendly. This chapter introduces the MacBook range so you can choose the best one for your mobile computing needs.

About MacBooks

iBooks had a lot of media coverage in terms of appearing in popular TV shows and movies. This has continued with the MacBook range.

When Apple Computer, Inc. (renamed Apple Inc. in 1997) introduced their iMac range of desktop computers in 1998 it was a major breakthrough. To try to match the success of the iMac, Apple began working on a new range of notebook computers. They first entered this market seriously with the Macintosh Portable in 1989. In 1991, Apple introduced the PowerBook range of laptops, which was the forerunner to the MacBook range.

In 1999 a new range of Apple laptops was introduced. This was the iBook range, aimed firmly at the consumer market. In May 2006 the MacBook range first appeared. The two main reasons for this consolidation were:

- Simplifying Apple's laptop range under one banner
- It was during this period that Apple Inc. were moving from Power PC processors for their computers to Intel processors

The MacBook range now consists of:

- **MacBook**. The latest MacBook model was launched in March 2015. It has a 12-inch Retina display screen and is designed to be as thin and as light as possible. It also has an innovative trackpad with Force Touch technology that provides extra functionality.
- **MacBook Pro**. This is the most powerful version of the MacBook and is aimed more at the market previously covered by the PowerBook range.

- **MacBook Air**. This range was designed to be the thinnest and lightest on the market. Although this has now been surpassed by the new Macbook, it is still an ultraportable laptop and ideal for mobile computing.

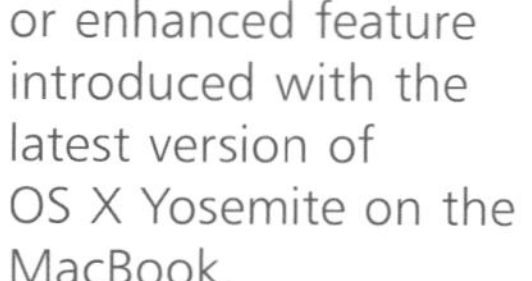

The New icon pictured above indicates a new or enhanced feature introduced with the latest version of OS X Yosemite on the MacBook.

MacBook Specifications

Specifications for all computers change rapidly and for the current MacBook range they are (at the time of printing):

MacBook

- Display: Retina display 12-inch (diagonal) LED backlit display with IPS technology
- Processor: 1.1GHz or 1.2GHz dual-core Intel Core M
- Storage: 256GB or 512GB flash storage
- Memory: 8GB of 1600MHz LPDDR3 onboard memory
- Ports: USB-C which can be used for charging and also as a USB 3.1 port for USB accessories

MacBook Air

- Display: 11.6-inch and 13.3-inch high (diagonal) high-resolution LED-backlit glossy widescreen display
- Processor: 1.6GHz or 2.2GHz dual-core Intel Core i5 or i7
- Storage: 128GB or 256GB flash storage
- Memory: 4GB of 1600MHz LPDDR3 onboard memory
- Ports: Two USB 3 ports and one Thunderbolt port

MacBook Pro

- Display: Retina display 13.3-inch or 15.4-inch (diagonal) LED backlit display with IPS technology – there is also a non-Retina version of the MacBook Pro 13-inch
- Processor: From 2.2GHz to 2.9GHz dual-core Intel Core i7
- Storage: 128GB, 256GB or 512GB of flash storage
- Memory: 8 GB or 16GB of 1600MHz DDR3L onboard memory
- Ports: Two USB 3 ports, two Thunderbolt ports, one HDMI port, one SDXC memory card slot

The MacBook range has different battery usage, for general use, depending on the model. This ranges from 7 hours for the MacBook Pro 13-inch, to 12 hours for the MacBook Air 13-inch.

All MacBooks have a range of energy-saving and environmental features.

The storage and memory on the MacBook range can both be configured to higher levels.

MacBook Air and the MacBook Pro both have flash storage. This is similar in some ways to traditional ROM (Read Only Memory) storage but it generally works faster and results in improved performance. The MacBook Pro Retina display is also designed with a flash architecture throughout to make it one of the most advanced laptops currently on the market.

MacBook Jargon Explained

Since MacBooks are essentially portable computers, a lot of the jargon is the same as for other computers. However, it is worth looking at some of this jargon and the significance it has in terms of MacBooks.

Memory can be thought of as a temporary storage device, as it only keeps information about the currently-open apps. Storage is more permanent, as it keeps the information even when the MacBook has been turned off.

The trackpad on the new MacBook and the MacBook Pro Retina display 13-inch both have Force Touch technology, which provides additional functionality for pressing on the trackpad.

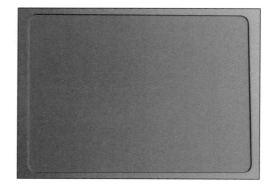

- **Processor**. Also known as the central processing unit, or CPU, this refers to the processing of digital data as it is provided by apps on the computer. The more powerful the processor, the quicker the data is interpreted. As with the rest of Apple's computers, MacBooks use Intel processors.
- **Memory**. This closely relates to the processor and is also known as random-access memory, or RAM. Essentially, this type of memory manages the apps that are being run and the commands that are being executed. The greater the amount of memory there is, the quicker apps will run. With more RAM they will also be more stable and less likely to crash. In the current range of MacBooks, memory is measured in gigabytes (GB) and ranges from 4GB to 16GB.
- **Storage**. This refers to the amount of digital information the MacBook can store. It is frequently referred to in terms of hard disk space and is measured in gigabytes. MacBooks and MacBook Airs have Flash memory.
- **Trackpad**. This is an input device that takes the place of a mouse (although a mouse can still be used with a MacBook, either with a USB cable or wirelessly). Traditionally, trackpads have come with a button that duplicates the function of the buttons on a mouse. However, the trackpad on a MacBook has no button, as the pad itself performs these functions.

- **Graphics card**. This is a device that enables images, video and animations to be displayed on the MacBook. It is also sometimes known as a video card. The faster the graphics card, the better the quality relevant media will be displayed at. In general, very fast graphics cards are really only needed for intensive multimedia applications, such as video games or videos. On a MacBook this is an Intel graphics card.
- **Wireless**. This refers to a MacBook's ability to connect wirelessly to a network, i.e. another computer or an Internet connection. In order to be able to do this, the MacBook must have a wireless card, which enables it to connect to a network or high-speed Internet connection. This is known as the AirPort Extreme Wi-Fi wireless networking card.
- **Bluetooth**. This is a radio technology for connecting devices wirelessly over short distance. It can be used for items such as a wireless mouse, or for connecting to a device, such as an iPhone for downloading photos.
- **Ports**. These are the parts of a MacBook that external devices can be plugged into, using a cable such as a USB or a Thunderbolt port. They are located on the side of the MacBook.

USB stands for Universal Serial Bus and is a popular way of connecting external devices to computers.

The new MacBook has one USB-C port which can be used for charging and external USB devices.

- **USB**. This is a method for connecting a variety of external devices, such as digital cameras, MP3 music players, scanners and printers. The latest range of MacBooks use USB 3.

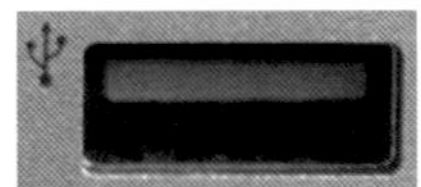

- **Ethernet**. This is for connecting an Ethernet cable to a router, for accessing the Internet, rather than doing it wirelessly.

...cont'd

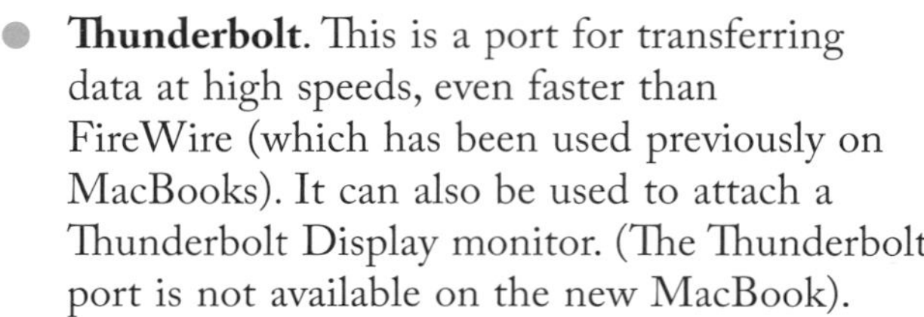

- **Thunderbolt**. This is a port for transferring data at high speeds, even faster than FireWire (which has been used previously on MacBooks). It can also be used to attach a Thunderbolt Display monitor. (The Thunderbolt port is not available on the new MacBook).

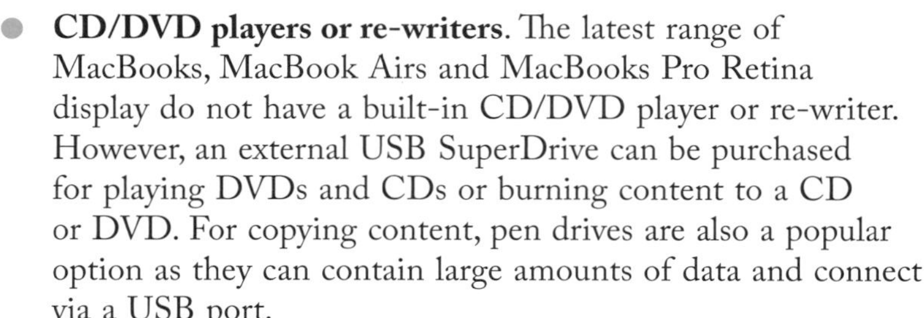

- **CD/DVD players or re-writers**. The latest range of MacBooks, MacBook Airs and MacBooks Pro Retina display do not have a built-in CD/DVD player or re-writer. However, an external USB SuperDrive can be purchased for playing DVDs and CDs or burning content to a CD or DVD. For copying content, pen drives are also a popular option as they can contain large amounts of data and connect via a USB port.

Don't forget

When a USB SuperDrive is attached to a MacBook, it shows up as an external drive in the Finder, see page 34.

- **Webcam (FaceTime)**. This is a type of camera fitted into the MacBook and it can be used to take still photographs or communicate via video with other people. On the MacBook, it is known as the FaceTime camera and it works with the FaceTime app. The FaceTime camera is built-in at the top-middle of the inner casing.

Getting Comfortable

Since you will probably be using your MacBook in more than one location, the issue of finding a comfortable working position can be vital, particularly as you cannot put the keyboard and monitor in different positions, as you can with a desktop computer. Whenever you are using your MacBook, try to make sure that you are sitting in a comfortable position, with your back well supported, and that the MacBook is in a position where you can reach the keyboard easily, and also see the screen, without straining your arms.

If possible, the best place to work on a MacBook is at a dedicated desk or workstation.

Despite the possible temptation to do so, avoid using your MacBook in bed, on your lap or where you have to slouch or strain to reach the MacBook properly.

Seating position

The ideal way to sit at a MacBook is with an office-type chair that offers good support for your back. Even with these types of chairs it is important to maintain a good body position so that your back is straight and your head is pointing forwards.

One of the advantages of office-type chairs is that the height can usually be adjusted, and this can be a great help in achieving a comfortable position.

If you do not have an office-type chair, use a chair with a straight back and place a cushion behind you for extra support and comfort as required.

...cont'd

MacBook position

When working at your MacBook it is important to have it positioned so that both the keyboard and the screen are in a comfortable position. If the keyboard is too low you will have to slouch or strain to reach it.

If the keyboard is too high, your arms will be stretching. This could lead to pain in your tendons.

The ideal setup is to have the MacBook in a position where you can sit with your forearms and wrists as level as possible while you are typing on the keyboard.

Working comfortably at a MacBook involves a combination of a good chair, good posture and good MacBook positioning.

Adjusting the screen

Another factor in working comfortably at a MacBook is the position of the screen. Unlike a desktop computer, it is not feasible to have a MacBook screen at eye level, as this would result in the keyboard being in too high a position. Instead, once you have achieved a comfortable seating position, open the screen so that it is approximately 90 degrees from your eye line.

One potential issue with MacBook screens can be that they reflect glare from sunlight or indoor lighting.

If this happens, either change your position, or block out the light source using some form of blind or shade. Avoid squinting at a screen that is reflecting glare, as this will make you feel uncomfortable and quickly give you a headache.

Input Devices

MacBooks have the same data input devices as most laptops: a keyboard and a trackpad. However, the trackpad has an innovative feature that makes it stand out from the crowd: there is no button – the trackpad itself performs the functions of a button. The trackpad uses multi-touch gestures to replace traditional navigation techniques. These are looked at in detail in Chapter Six. Some of these gestures are:

- **One-finger click**. Click in the middle of the trackpad to perform one-click operations.
- **Scrolling**. This can be done on a page by dragging two fingers on the trackpad either up or down.
- **Zooming on a page or web page**. This can be done by double-clicking with two fingers.

When using the keyboard or trackpad, keep your hands and fingers as flat as possible over the keyboard and trackpad.

Trackpad options

Options for the functioning of the trackpad can be set within the **System Preferences**. To do this:

1. Click on the **Trackpad** button

2. Click on the tabs to set options for pointing and clicking, scrolling and zooming and additional multi-touch gestures with the trackpad

...cont'd

Mouse options

An external mouse can be connected to a MacBook and options for its functioning can be set within the **System Preferences**. To do this:

1. Click on the **Mouse** button

2. Drag the sliders to set the speed at which the cursor moves across the screen and also the speed required for a double-click operation

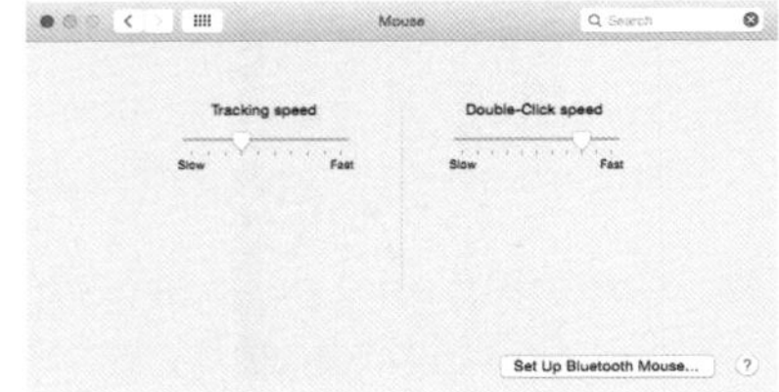

Hot tip

Instead of a traditional mouse, a Magic Mouse can also be connected to a MacBook. This is a mouse that has the same scrolling functionality as the trackpad.

Keyboard options

Options for the functioning of the keyboard can be set within the **System Preferences.** To do this:

1. Click on the **Keyboard** button

2. Click on the **Keyboard** tab to set options for how the keyboard operates, such as the speed for repeating a key stroke

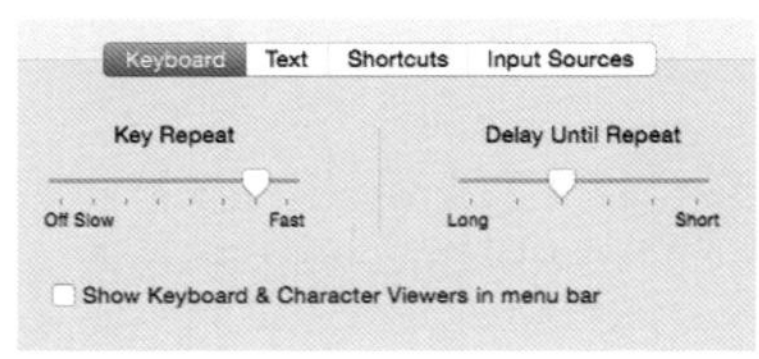

3. Click on the **Text** tab to set keyboard shortcuts for accessing certain words and phrases. Click on this button to add a new shortcut and phrase

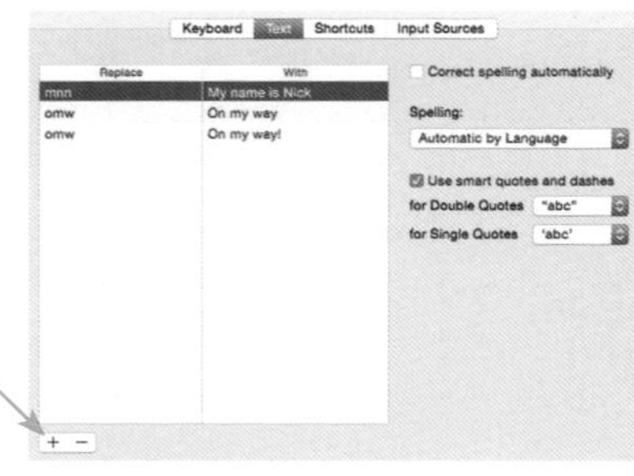

MacBook Power Cable

All MacBooks need a power cable, in the form of an AC Adapter, that can be used to recharge the battery, and it can also be used when the MacBook is not being used in a mobile environment. This can save the battery so, if possible, the adapter should be used instead of battery power.

The MacBook power cable has a light on the end of the magnetic connector. When the cable is plugged in, this appears amber if the MacBook is charging and green when the charging is complete.

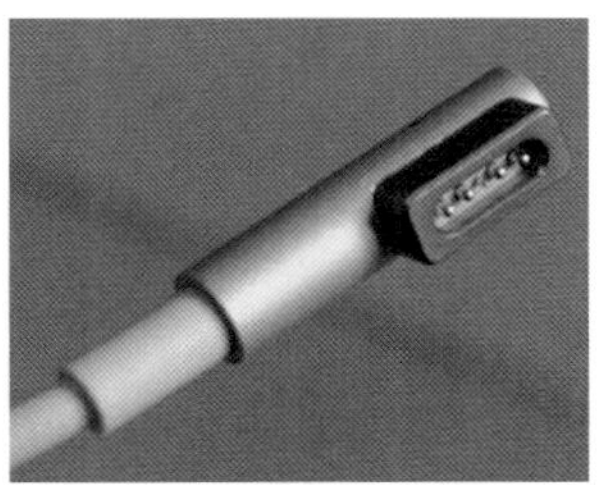

The MacBook adapter also has a built-in safety feature known as the MagSafe power port. This consists of a magnetic connection between the power adapter and the power port on the side of the MacBook. When the connection is made it is a magnetic one rather than a physical one. This means that if the power cord is accidentally pulled or kicked out, the magnetic connection will be broken without dragging the MacBook with it. This is safer for both the user and the MacBook itself.

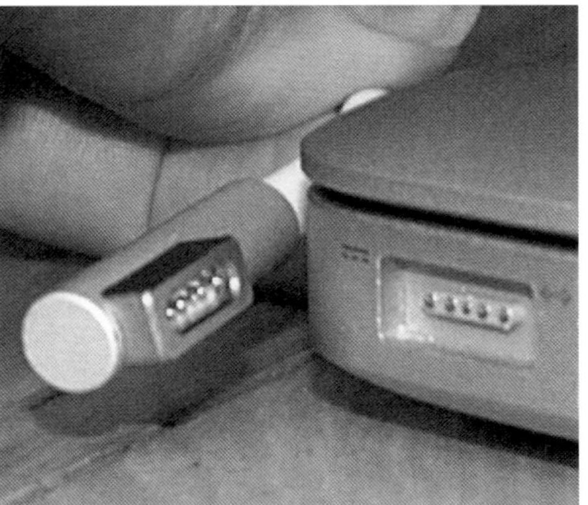

Cleaning a MacBook

Like most things, MacBooks benefit greatly from a little care and attention. The two most important areas to keep clean are the screen and the keyboard.

Cleaning the screen

All computer screens quickly collect dust and fingerprints, and MacBooks are no different. If this is left too long it can make the screen harder to read and cause eye strain and headaches. Clean the screen regularly with the following cleaning materials:

- A lint-free cloth, similar to the type used to clean camera lenses (it is important not to scratch the screen in any way).
- An alcohol-free cleaning fluid recommended for computer screens.
- Screen wipes, that are recommended for use on computer screens.

The outer casing of a MacBook can be cleaned with the same fluid as used for the screen. A duster or a damp (but not wet) cloth and warm water can be equally effective. Keep soap away from MacBooks if possible.

Cleaning the keyboard

Keyboards are notorious for accumulating dust, fluff and crumbs. One way to solve this problem is to turn the MacBook upside down and very gently shake it to loosen any foreign objects. Failing this, a can of compressed air can be used, with a narrow nozzle to blow out any stubborn items that remain lodged between the keys.

Spares and Accessories

Whenever you are going anywhere with your MacBook there are always spares and accessories to consider. Some of these are just nice things to have, while others could be essential in ensuring that you can still use your MacBook if anything goes wrong while you are on your travels. Items to consider putting in your MacBook case include:

Hardware

- **Spare battery**. This is probably the most important spare if you are going to be away from home or work for any length of time, and particularly if you think you may be unable to access a power supply for a long period of time, and be unable to charge your MacBook battery. Like all batteries, MacBook batteries slowly lose power over time and do not keep their charge for as long as when they are new. It is a good idea to always keep an eye on how much battery power you have left and, if you are running low, to try to conserve as much energy as possible.
- **Apple Thunderbolt Display**. The Thunderbolt port enables you to transfer data from peripheral devices to your MacBook at very high speeds. You can also connect a Thunderbolt Display – a 27-inch display that can give stunning clarity to the content on your monitor.
- **Magic Mouse**. This is an external mouse that can be connected to your MacBook and used to perform multi-touch gestures in the same way as the trackpad.
- **External SuperDrive**. The MacBook range does not come with a SuperDrive for using CDs and DVDs but this external one can be used to connect to a MacBook using a USB cable.
- **Wireless Keyboard**. This can be used if you want to have a keyboard that you can move away from your MacBook.
- **USB Ethernet Adapter**. This can be used to connect to an Ethernet network using a USB port.
- **Multi-card reader**. This is a device that can be used to copy data from the cards used in digital cameras. If you have a digital camera, it is possible to download the photographs from it directly onto a MacBook with a cable. However, a multi-card reader can be more efficient and flexible.

MacBook batteries should only be fitted by authorized Apple suppliers for an Apple Store. If you try and fit one yourself it may invalidate the MacBook's warranty.

...cont'd

- **Headphones**. These can be used to listen to music or films if you are in the company of other people and you do not want to disturb them. They can also be very useful if there are distracting noises from other people.
- **Pen drive**. This is a small device that can be used to copy data to and from your MacBook. It connects via a USB port and is about the size of a packet of chewing gum. It is an excellent way of backing up files from your MacBook when you are away from home or the office.
- **Cleaning material**. The materials described on page 18 can be taken to ensure your MacBook is always in tip-top condition for use.
- **DVDs/CDs**. Video or music DVDs and CDs can be taken to provide mobile entertainment, and blank ones can be taken to copy data onto, similar to using a pen drive. An external DVD/CD drive will also be required.

Software

New software programs, or apps, can be downloaded directly from the Mac App Store. There is a huge range on offer, covering over 20 different categories. They can be searched for by **Featured**, **Top Charts** and **Categories** and you can also view and update apps that you have purchased.

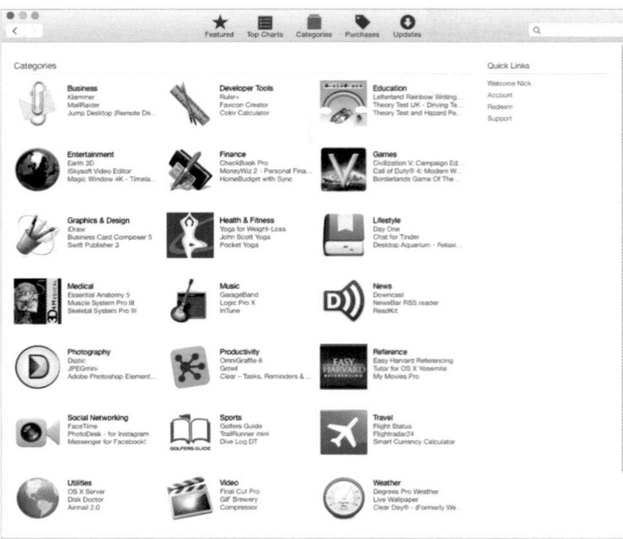

Hot tip

It is important that headphones are comfortable to wear for extended periods of time. In general, the types that fit over the ears are more comfortable than the "bud" variety that are inserted into the ear.

The App Store can be accessed by clicking on this button on the Dock at the bottom of the MacBook screen.

2 Around a MacBook

This chapter looks at getting started with your MacBook: from opening it up and turning it on through to keyboard functions and the System Preferences that are available. It also looks at setting up notifications for a variety of items such as emails and alerts.

Opening Up

The first step towards getting started with a new MacBook is to open it ready for use.

There is no physical latch on the front of a MacBook, just a small groove at the front where the top and bottom parts meet.

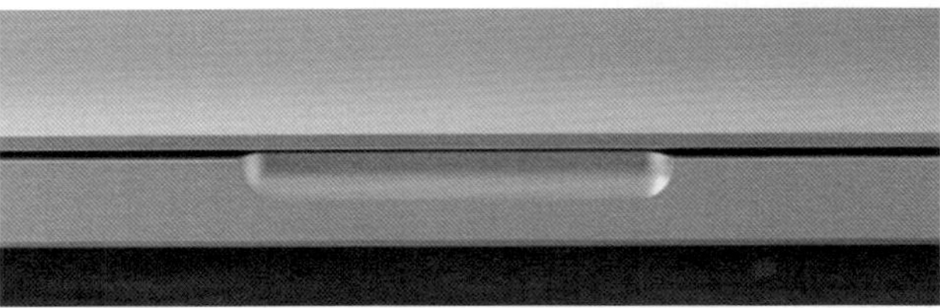

Open the screen of a MacBook carefully, so as not to put any unnecessary pressure on the connection between the screen and the main body of the MacBook.

Instead of a latch, a MacBook has a magnetic closing mechanism, which engages when the monitor screen is closed onto the main body of the MacBook. To open it, raise it firmly upwards from the center, where there is a smooth groove.

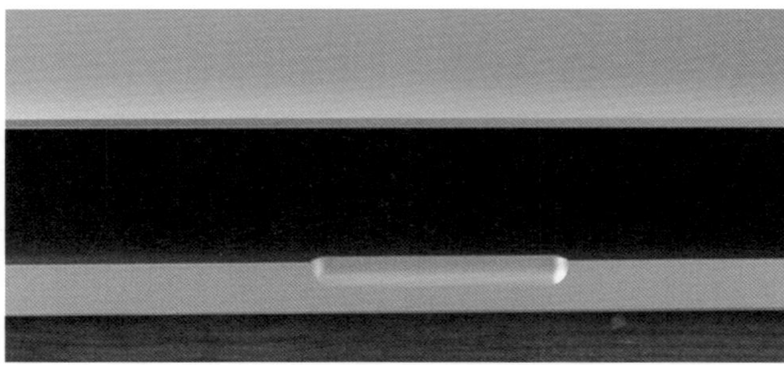

Once the MacBook has been opened the screen should stay in whatever position it is placed.

Turning On

In the latest range of MacBooks, the button for turning on, ready for use, is located at the top-right corner of the keyboard:

The MacBook can be turned on by pushing this button firmly. The MacBook will then make the Apple "chime" to indicate that it has been turned on and has begun the startup process. Once the MacBook has completed this process the opening screen should be displayed. This will include the Desktop and the Dock, which is located at the bottom of the screen. At this point the MacBook is ready for use.

Press the button for turning on with one firm, definite motion. If you accidentally press it twice in quick succession, the MacBook may turn on and then shut down immediately.

MacBook Desktop

The opening view of a MacBook is known as the Desktop. Items, such as apps and files, can be stored on the Desktop but, in general, it is best to try to keep it as clear as possible.

At the top of the Desktop is the Apple Menu and the Menu bar. This contains links to a collection of commonly-used menus and functions, such as Copy and Paste.

At the bottom of the Desktop is the Dock. This is a collection of icons that are shortcuts to frequently-used apps or folders.

One of the items on the Dock is the Finder. This can be used to access the main area for apps, folders and files and also organize the way you work on your MacBook.

The menus on the Menu bar are looked at in detail on page 96.

To specify which items appear on the Desktop, click on **Finder > Preferences** on the Menu bar. Click on the **General** tab and select to show or hide **Hard disks**, **External disks**, **CDs, DVDs and iPods** or **Connected servers**. The selected items will then be displayed as icons on the Desktop.

Apple Menu

The Apple Menu is accessed from the Apple symbol at the left-hand side of the Menu bar:

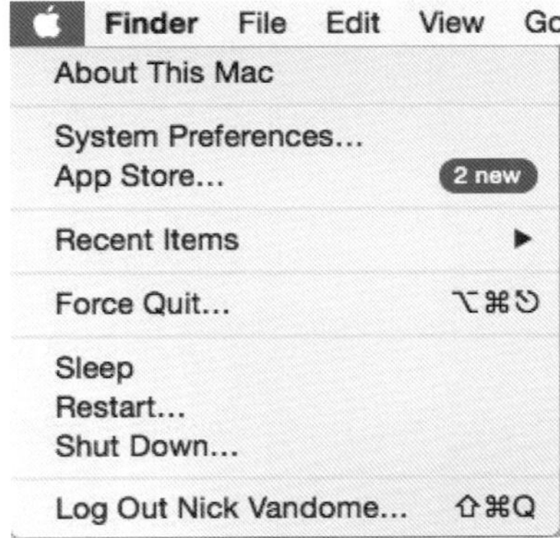

The options on the Apple Menu are:

- **About This Mac**. This provides general information about the processor, the amount of memory and the OS X version.
- **System Preferences**. This is a shortcut to System Preferences. This can be used to access a wide range of options, including those for items such as the Dock.
- **App Store**. This can be used to access the online Mac App Store for downloading apps and also software updates for existing apps and OS X.
- **Recent Items**. This displays the items you have most recently used and viewed.
- **Force Quit**. This can be used to manually quit an app that has frozen or will not close.
- **Sleep**. This puts the MacBook into a state of hibernation.
- **Restart**. This closes down the MacBook and restarts it.
- **Shut Down**. This shuts down the MacBook.
- **Log Out**. This shuts down the currently open apps and logs out the current user.

Force Quit can be used to close down an app that is frozen or is not responding.

Keyboard Buttons

As shown on the previous page, the Apple Menu has options for Sleep, Restart and Shut Down. Sleep saves your current session and puts the MacBook into a state of hibernation. This is useful if your MacBook is going to be inactive for a period but you do not want to close it down.

Don't forget

Restart is most frequently used if there is a problem on your MacBook, such as a frozen app, and you want to turn it off and then back on again to try to resolve the issue.

Shortcut keys can also be used to put the MacBook to sleep.

To do this, press the Alt (Option) and Command keys and the Power button simultaneously. (The Alt and Command keys are located on the left-hand side of the space bar.)

Shortcut Keys

A MacBook keyboard has a number of keys that can be used for shortcuts or specific functions. Four of them are located at the left of the space bar. They are (from left to right):

Contextual menus are ones that have actions that are specific to the item being viewed.

- **The Function key**. This can be used to activate the function (Fn) keys at the top of the keyboard. This is used in conjunction with the F keys on the keyboard: to activate the operation of a function key, hold it down while pressing one of the F keys.
- **The Control key**. This can be used to access contextual menus.
- **The Alt (Option) key**. This is frequently used in conjunction with the Command key to perform specific tasks, such as above with Sleep.
- **The Command key**. As above.

At the top of the keyboard there are keys for changing some of the settings on your MacBook. These are (from left to right):

- F1: Decrease brightness.
- F2: Increase brightness.
- F3: Show all open windows (Mission Control).
- F4: Show/Hide Dashboard widgets.

- F7: Rewind a video.
- F8: Play/Pause a video.
- F9: Fast forward a video (with Fn key, show all open windows, Mission Control).

- F10: Mute volume (with Fn key, displays all open windows for the active app).
- F11: Decrease volume (with Fn key, displays the Desktop and minimizes all windows around the sides of the screen).
- F12: Increase volume (with Fn key, displays the Dashboard).
- Power button. Turns the MacBook on or can be used in conjunction with the Shortcut keys to put it to Sleep.

On some MacBook keyboards, the F5 and F6 keys can be used to adjust the backlighting of the keyboard in low-level light.

The Fn options can also be used without pressing the Fn key. To do this, open **System Preferences** and click on the **Keyboard** button. Under the Keyboard tab, check on the box that says **Use all F1, F2, etc. keys as standard function keys**.

System Preferences

In OS X there are preferences that can be set for just about every aspect of the operating system. This gives you great control over how the interface looks and how the operating system functions. To access System Preferences:

Click on this icon on the Dock or from the Applications folder in the Finder

Don't forget

For more information about the Dock, see Chapter Four, and for the Finder, Chapter Five.

Hot tip

When viewing a specific System Preference, click on this button at the top of the window to go back to all of the available options.

Personal preferences

General. Options for the overall look of buttons, menus, windows and scroll bars.

Desktop & Screen Saver. This can be used to change the Desktop background and the screen saver.

Dock. Options for the way the Dock looks and functions.

Mission Control. This gives you a variety of options for managing all of your open windows and apps.

Language & Region. Options for the language used.

Security & Privacy. This enables you to secure your Home folder with a master password, for added security.

Spotlight. This can be used to specify settings for the OS X search facility, Spotlight.

Notifications. This can be used to set up how you are notified about items such as email, messages and software updates.

Hardware preferences

CDs & DVDs. Options for what action is taken when you insert CDs and DVDs.

Displays. Options for the screen display, such as resolution.

Energy Saver. Options for when the computer is inactive.

Keyboard. Options for how the keyboard functions and also keyboard shortcuts.

Mouse. Options for how an external mouse functions.

Trackpad. Options for when you are using a trackpad.

Printers & Scanners. Options for selecting and installing printers and scanners.

Sound. Options for adding sound effects and playing and recording sound.

Internet & Wireless preferences

iCloud. Options for the online iCloud service.

Internet Accounts. This can be used to set up contacts on your MacBook, using a variety of online services.

Extensions. This detemines how plug-ins and extensions are installed on your MacBook.

Network. This can be used to specify network settings for linking two or more computers together.

Bluetooth. Options for attaching Bluetooth wireless devices.

Sharing. Options for selecting how files are shared on a network.

System preferences

Users & Groups. This can be used to allow different users to create their own accounts for use on the same computer.

Parental Controls. This can be used to limit access to the MacBook and various online functions.

App Store. This can be used to connect to the App Store to access and install available software updates.

Dictation & Speech. Options for using speakable commands to control the computer.

Date & Time. Options for changing the computer's date and time to time zones around the world.

Startup Disk. This can be used to specify the disk from which your computer starts up. This is usually the OS X volume.

Time Machine. This can be used to configure and set up the OS X backup facility.

Accessibility. This can be used to set options for users who have difficulty with viewing text on screen, hearing commands, using the keyboard or using the mouse.

The headings for System Preferences shown here are how they are grouped by default, although the headings themselves do not appear. To change the way System Preferences are organized, click on **View** on the System Preferences Menu bar and select either **Organize by Categories** or **Organize Alphabetically**.

Notifications

The Notification Center option provides a single location to view all of your emails, messages, updates and alerts. It appears at the top right-hand corner of the screen. The items that appear in Notifications are set up within System Preferences. To do this:

1. Open **System Preferences** and click on the **Notifications** button

2. The items that will appear in the Notification Center are listed here. Click on an item to select it and set its notification options

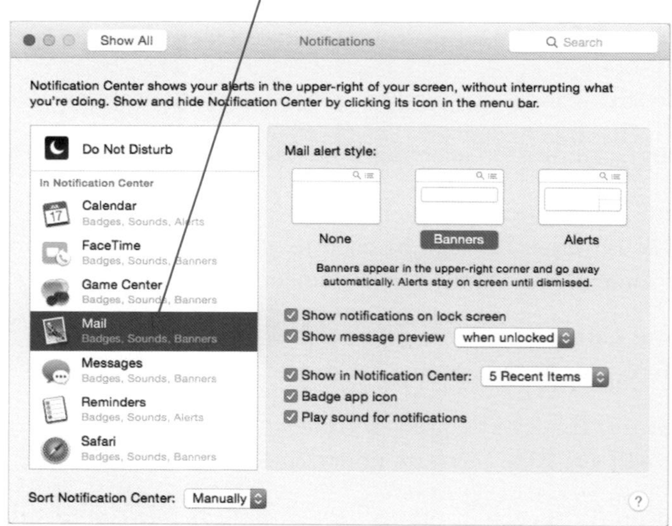

3. To disable an item so that it does not appear in the Notification Center, select it as above and check off the **Show in Notification Center** box

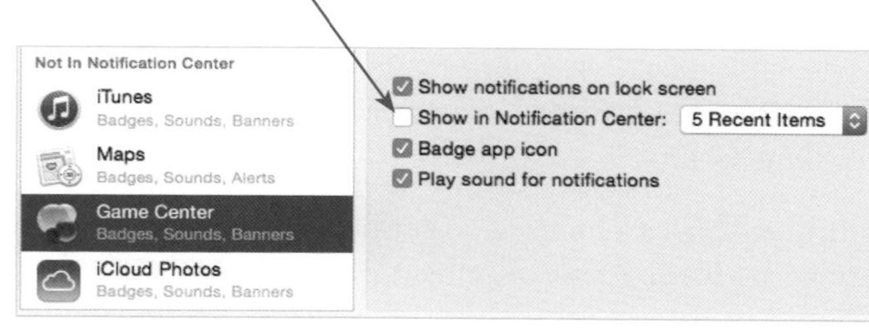

Notifications can be accessed regardless of the app in which you are working, and they can be actioned directly without having to leave the current app.

Twitter and Facebook feeds can also be set up to appear in the Notification Center, if you have accounts with these sites.

Viewing Notifications

Notifications appear in the Notification Center. The way they appear can be determined in the System Preferences:

1. Select an alert style. A banner alert comes up on the screen and then disappears after a few seconds

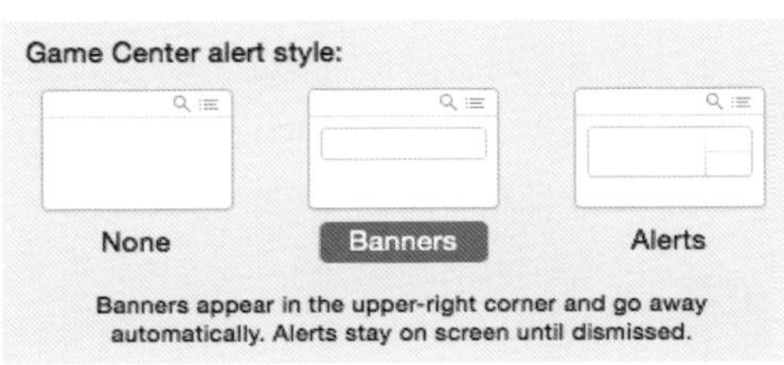

The Notification Center can also be displayed with a Trackpad or Magic Trackpad by dragging with two fingers from right to left, starting from the far right edge.

2. The **Alerts** option shows the notification and it stays on screen until dismissed (such as this one for reminders)

3. Click on this button in the top right-hand corner of the screen to view all of the items in the Notification Center. Click on it again to hide the Notification Center

Software updates also appear in the Notification Center, when they are available.

4. In the Notification Center, click on the **Today** button to view the weather forecast, calendar events and stock market reports for the current day. Click on the **Edit** button to change the items that appear

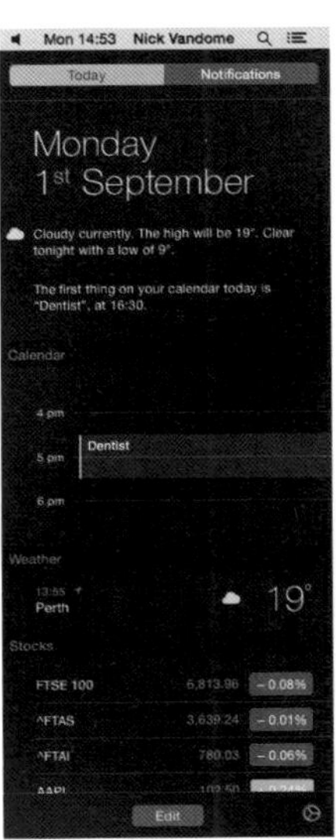

5. Click on the **Notifications** button to view the items that have been selected for here. Items such as emails and iMessages can be replied to directly by clicking on them from within the Notifications section

CDs and DVDs

Although there is no built-in SuperDrive with the latest range of MacBook Air and MacBook Pro versions, CDs and DVDs can still be used with an external USB SuperDrive. As with many of the functions of a MacBook there are settings that can be applied within the System Preferences. To do this:

1. Open **System Preferences** and click on the **CDs & DVDs** button

2. There are various options for what happens when you insert blank CDs/DVDs and also for music, picture and video CDs/DVDs

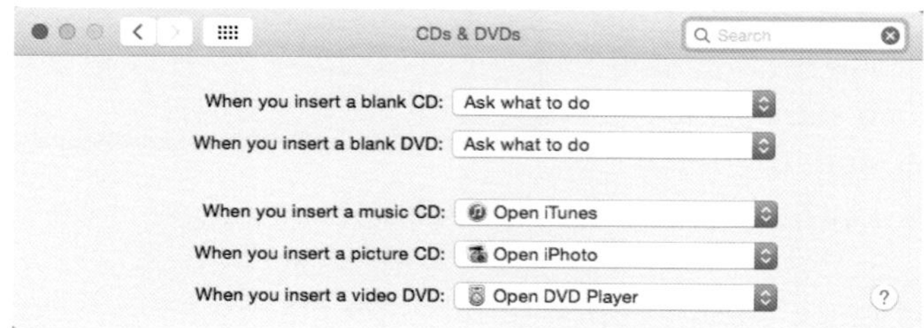

3. If you insert a blank CD or DVD the following window appears automatically. The Action box offers options for what you want to do with the CD or DVD. Click on the **OK** button to select an action or click on the **Ignore** button if you do not want to use any of these actions

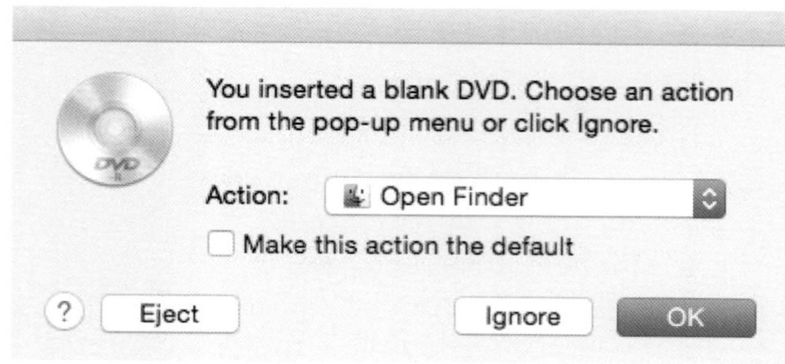

USB pen drives can also be used if you want to copy content from a MacBook.

Connecting a Printer

Using a printer on any computer is essential and MacBooks allow you to quickly add a printer to aid your productivity. To do this:

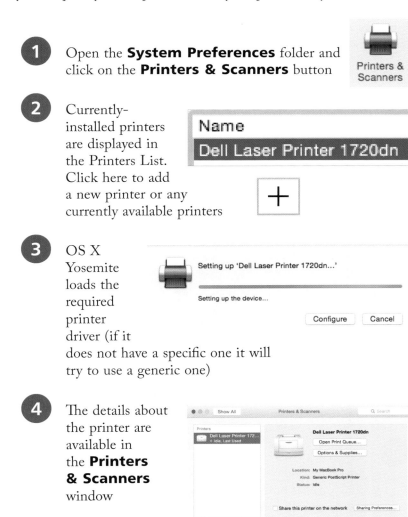

1. Open the **System Preferences** folder and click on the **Printers & Scanners** button

2. Currently-installed printers are displayed in the Printers List. Click here to add a new printer or any currently available printers

3. OS X Yosemite loads the required printer driver (if it does not have a specific one it will try to use a generic one)

4. The details about the printer are available in the **Printers & Scanners** window

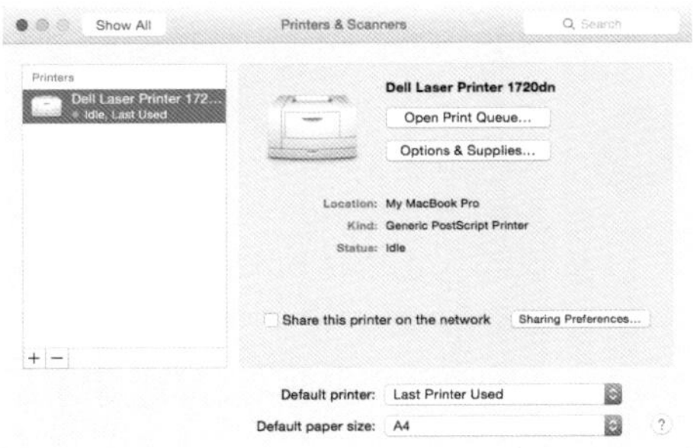

5. Once a printer has been installed, documents can be printed by selecting **File > Print** from the Menu bar. Print settings can be set at this point and they can also be set by selecting **File > Page/Print Setup** from the Menu bar in most apps

Printer drivers are programs that enable the printer to communicate with your computer. Printer drivers are usually provided on a disc when the printer is purchased. In addition, MacBooks will have a number of printer drivers pre-installed. If your MacBook does not recognize your printer, you can load the driver from the disc.

External Drives

Attaching external drives is an essential part of mobile computing; whether it is to back up data as you are traveling or for downloading photos and other items. On MacBooks, external drives are displayed on the Desktop once they have been attached and they can then be used for the required task. To do this:

External drives can be items such as pen drives, digital cameras or external hard disks.

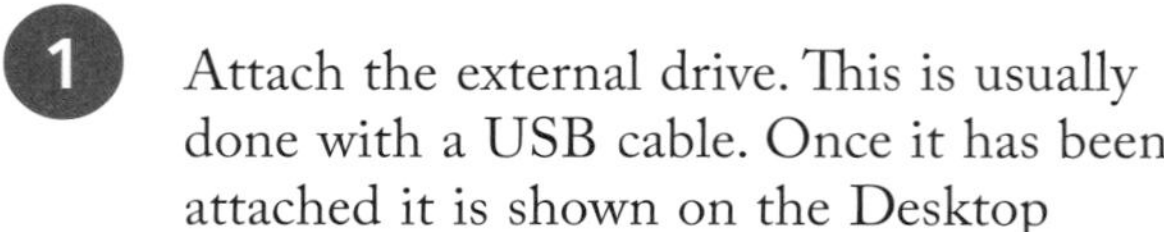

1. Attach the external drive. This is usually done with a USB cable. Once it has been attached it is shown on the Desktop

2. The drive is shown in the Finder

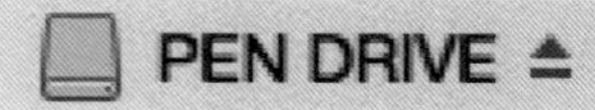

3. Perform the required task for the external drive (such as copying files or folders onto it from the hard drive of your MacBook)

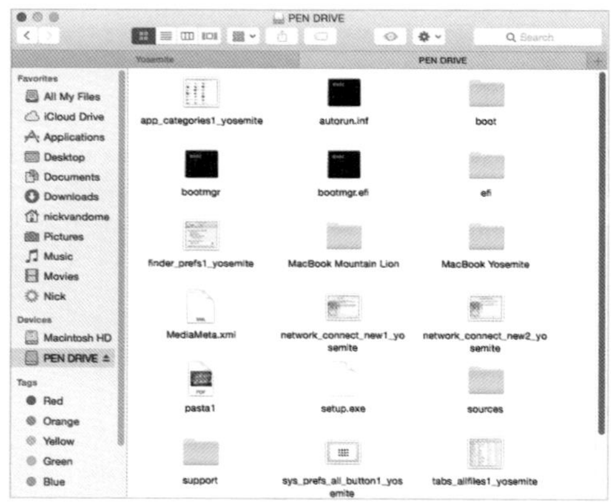

An external drive can be renamed by Ctrl + clicking on its name in the Finder and overtyping it with a new name.

4. External drives have to be ejected properly, not just pulled out or removed. To do this, click on this button next to the drive in the Finder window, or drag its icon on the Desktop over the **Trash** icon on the Dock. This will then change into an **Eject** icon

3 Introducing Yosemite

Yosemite is the latest operating system for MacBooks. Not only is it fun to use, it also has a raft of features that transform a number of traditional ways for using computers.

About OS X Yosemite

OS X Yosemite is the tenth version (10.10) of the operating system for Apple computers; the MacBook, iMac, Mac Mini and Mac Pro. When OS X (pronounced 'ten') was first introduced it was a major breakthrough in terms of ease of use and stability. It is based on the UNIX programming language, which is a very stable and secure operating environment and ensures that OS X is one of the most stable consumer operating systems that has ever been designed. More importantly for the user, it is also one of the most stylish and user-friendly operating systems available.

Don't forget

UNIX is an operating system that has traditionally been used for large commercial mainframe computers. It is renowned for its stability and ability to be used within different computing environments.

Through the previous nine versions of OS X, it has been refined and improved in terms of both performance and functionality. This process continues with OS X Yosemite, which further develops the innovations introduced by its two immediate predecessors, OS X Mountain Lion and OS X Mavericks.

When OS X Mountain Lion was introduced, in 2012, it contained a range of innovative functions that were inspired by Apple's mobile devices: iPhone, iPad and iPod touch. This was continued with the next version of the operating system, OS X Mavericks, and now OS X Yosemite. The two main areas where the functionality of the mobile devices has been transferred to the desktop and laptop operating system are:

- The way apps can be downloaded and installed. Instead of using a disc, OS X Yosemite utilizes the Mac App Store to provide apps, which can be installed in a couple of steps.
- Options for navigating around pages and applications with a trackpad or a Magic Mouse. Instead of having to use a mouse or a traditional laptop trackpad, OS X Yosemite allows Multi-Touch Gestures that provide a range of ways for accessing apps and web pages and navigating around them.

Yosemite has a Power Nap function that updates items from the online iCloud service even when a MacBook is in sleep mode. This can be set up by checking On the **Wake for Network Access** option in the **Energy Saver** section of System Preferences.

OS X Yosemite continues the evolution of the operating system, by adding more features and enhancing the ones that were already there. This includes greater integration with the online iCloud service, so that a wider range of files and documents can be stored and backed up there and also shared across any other Apple devices that you have. This is done with the iCloud Drive and Family Sharing features (covered in Chapter four), which have also bridged the gap between working on a desktop or a laptop computer and a mobile device, such as an iPad or an iPhone.

Installing OS X Yosemite

When it comes to installing OS X Yosemite you do not need to worry about an installation CD or DVD: it can be downloaded and installed directly from the online Mac App Store. New Macs will have Yosemite installed and the following range of Macs are compatible with Yosemite and can be upgraded with it.

- iMac (Mid 2007 or newer)
- MacBook (Late 2008 Aluminum, or Early 2009 or newer)
- MacBook Pro (Mid/Late 2007 or newer)
- MacBook Air (Late 2008 or newer)
- Mac Mini (Early 2009 or newer)
- Mac Pro (Early 2008 or newer)

If you want to install OS X Yosemite on an existing Mac you will need to have minimum requirements of:

- OS X Snow Leopard (version 10.6.8), OS X Lion, OS X Mountain Lion or OS X Mavericks
- Intel Core 2 Duo, Core i3, Core i5, Core i7, or Xeon processor, or above
- 2GB of memory and 8GB of available storage for installation

If your Mac meets these requirements, you can download and install OS X Yosemite, for free, as follows:

1. Click on this icon on the Dock to access the App Store (or select **App Store** from the Apple menu)

2. Locate the **OS X Yosemite** icon (this will be on the **Featured** page or within the **Productivity** category)

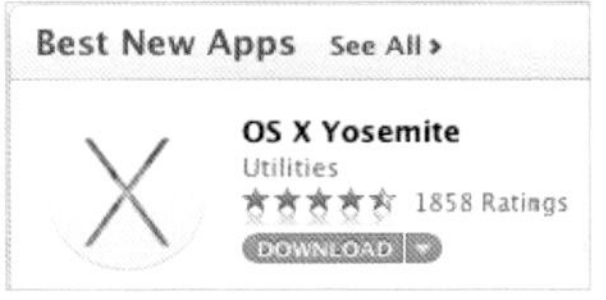

3. Click on the **Download** button and follow the installation instructions

OS X Yosemite is a free upgrade from the App Store if you already have the Snow Leopard, Lion, Mountain Lion or Mavericks versions of OS X.

To check your computer's software version and upgrade options, click on **Apple menu > About This Mac** from the main Menu bar. See pages 40-43 for details.

The OS X Environment

The first most noticeable element about OS X is its elegant user interface. This has been designed to create a user friendly graphic overlay to the UNIX operating system at the heart of OS X and it is a combination of rich colors and sharp, original graphics. The main elements that make up the initial OS X environment are:

The Dock is designed to help make organizing and opening items as quick and easy as possible. For a detailed look at the Dock, see Chapter Four.

The **Apple menu** is standardized throughout OS X, regardless of the app in use

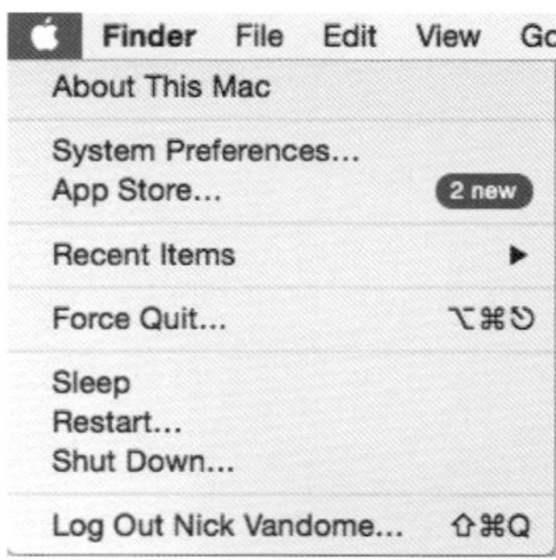

Many of the behind-the-scenes features of OS X Yosemite are aimed at saving power on your MacBook. These include time coalescing technologies for saving processing and battery power, features for saving energy when apps are not being used; power saving features in Safari for ignoring additional content provided by web page plug-ins and memory compression to make your MacBook quicker and more responsive.

Menus

Menus in OS X contain commands for the operating system and any relevant apps. If there is an arrow next to a command it means there are subsequent options for the item. Some menus also incorporate the same transparency as the sidebar so that the background shows through.

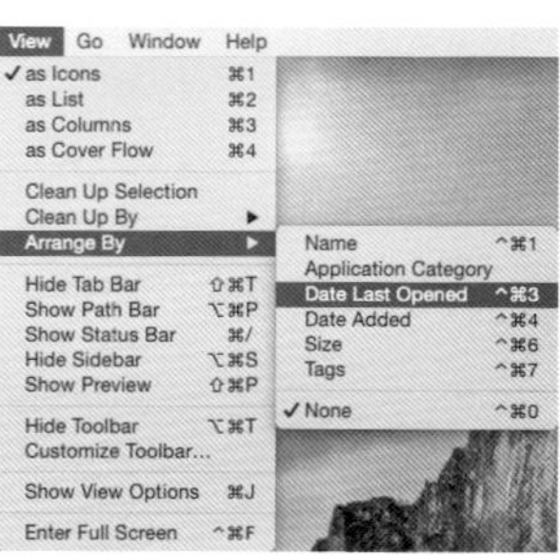

Transparency

One new feature in OS X Yosemite is that the sidebar and toolbars in certain apps are transparent so that you can see some of the screen behind it. This also helps the upper-most window blend in with the background:

1. In certain apps with a sidebar, such as the Finder or the Safari sidebar, the background appears behind the sidebar

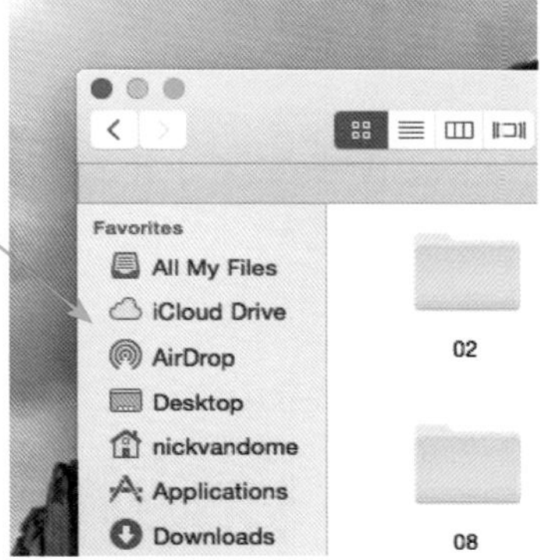

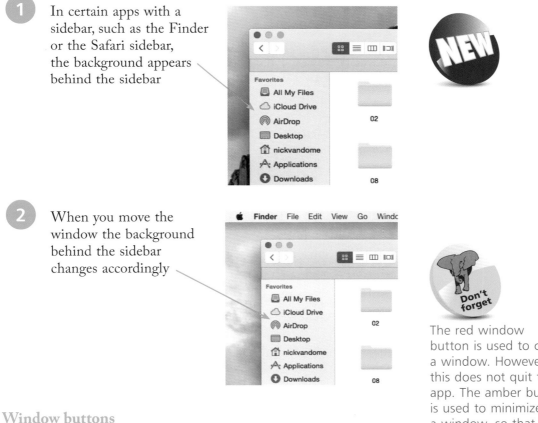

2. When you move the window the background behind the sidebar changes accordingly

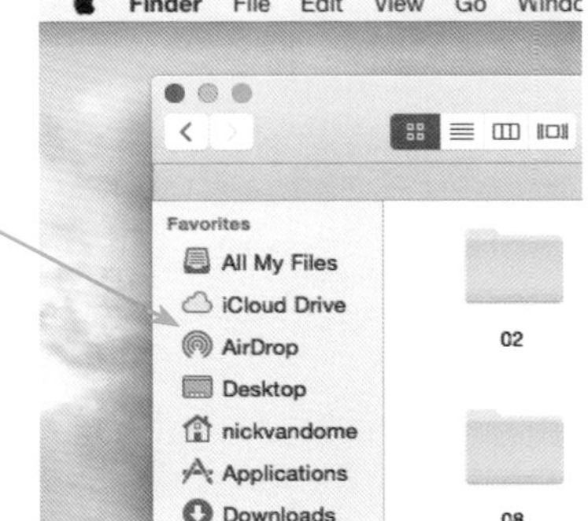

The red window button is used to close a window. However, this does not quit the app. The amber button is used to minimize a window, so that it appears at the right-hand side of the Dock.

Window buttons

These appear in any open OS X window and can be used to manipulate the window. In Yosemite they have been updated to include a full-screen options, which previously had to be accessed separately from within an app. Use the window button to, from left to right, close a window, minimize a window or maximize a window.

If can app has full-screen functionality, this green button is available:

About Your Mac

When you buy a new Mac you will almost certainly check the technical specifications before you make a purchase. Once you have your Mac, there will be times when you will want to view these specifications again, such as the version of OS X in use, the amount of memory and the amount of storage. This can be done through the **About This Mac** option that can be accessed from the Apple Menu. To do this:

1. Click on the **Apple menu** and click on the **About This Mac** link

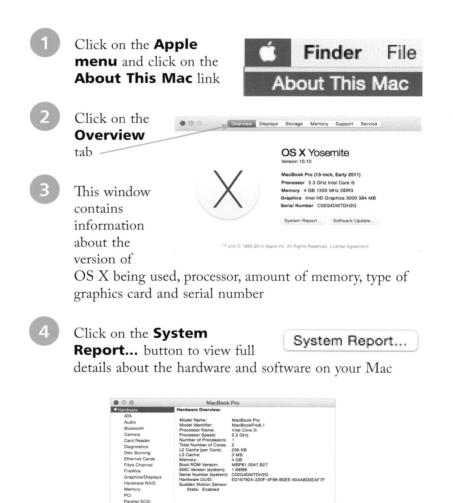

2. Click on the **Overview** tab

3. This window contains information about the version of OS X being used, processor, amount of memory, type of graphics card and serial number

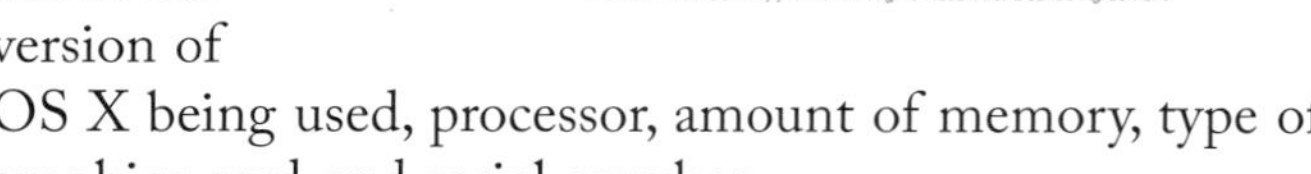

4. Click on the **System Report...** button to view full details about the hardware and software on your Mac

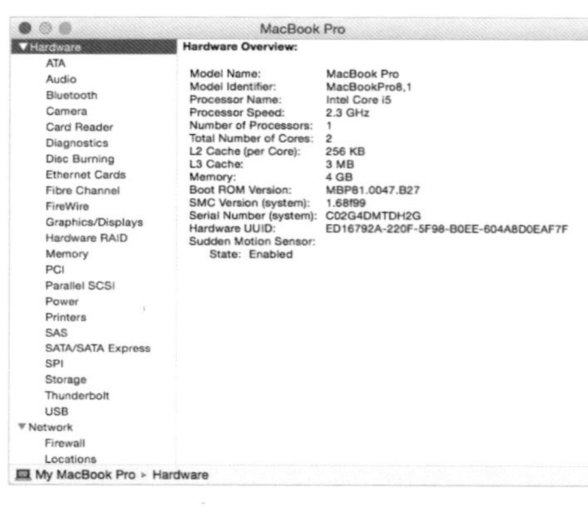

The System Report section is also where you can check whether your Mac is compatible with the Handoff functionality (covered on page 65), which is new to OS X Yosemite, but does not work with most Macs before 2012. Click on the **Bluetooth** section in the **System Report** to see if Handoff is supported.

5. Click on the **Software Update...** button to see available software updates for your Mac

   Software Update...

Display information

This gives information about your Mac's display:

1. Click on the **Displays** tab

   Displays

2. This window contains information about your display including the type, size, resolution and graphics card

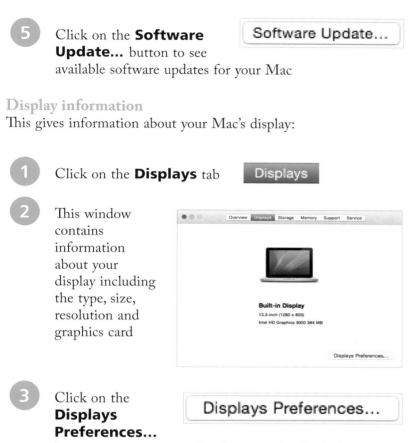

3. Click on the **Displays Preferences...** button to view options for changing the display's resolution, brightness and color

   Displays Preferences...

For more information about Software Updates, see page 205.

...cont'd

Storage information

This contains information about your Mac's physical and removable storage:

1. Click on the **Storage** tab

2. This window contains information about the used and available storage on your hard disk and also options for writing various types of CDs and DVDs

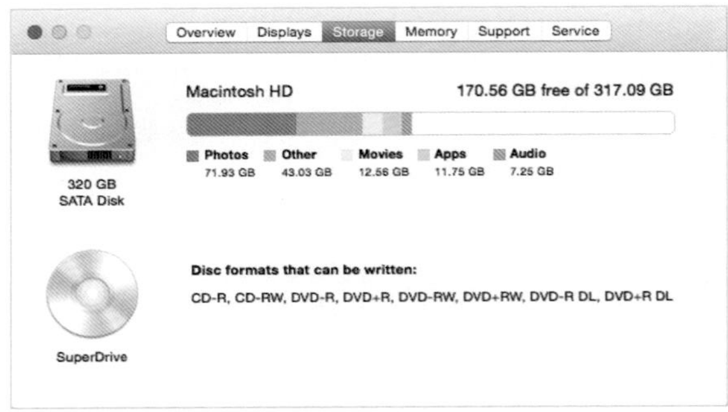

Memory information

This contains information about your Mac's memory, which is used to run OS X and also the applications on your computer:

1. Click on the **Memory** tab

2. This window contains information about the memory chips that are in your Mac

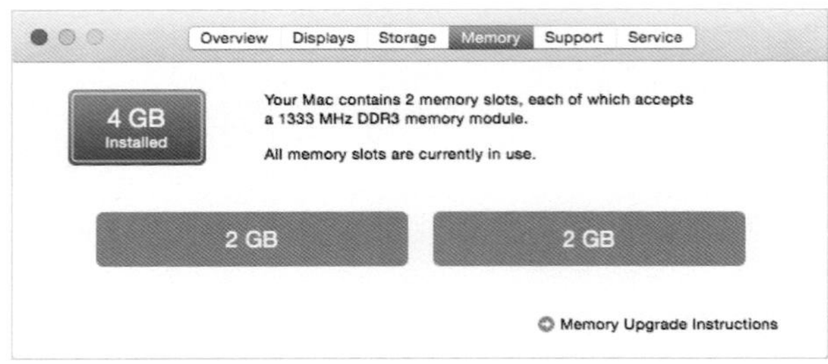

3. Click on the **Memory Upgrade Instructions** if you want to upgrade your memory

Memory Upgrade Instructions

4. A page on the Apple website gives instructions for upgrading memory chips for different makes and models of Macs

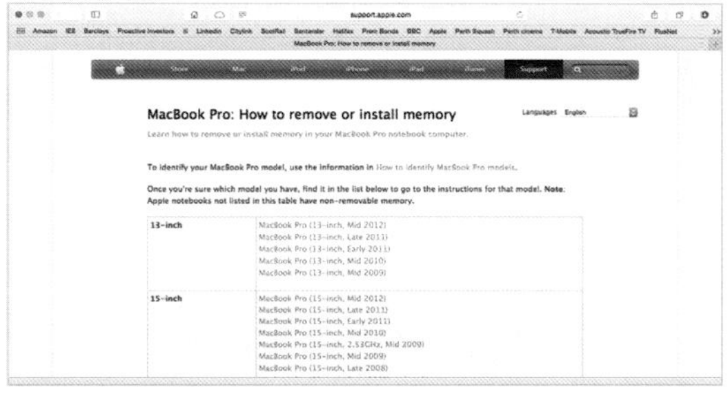

Always wear an anti-static wristband if you are opening your Mac to insert new memory chips, or any other time when you are working on the components of your Mac.

Support

The **Support** tab provides links to a range of help options for your Mac and OS X.

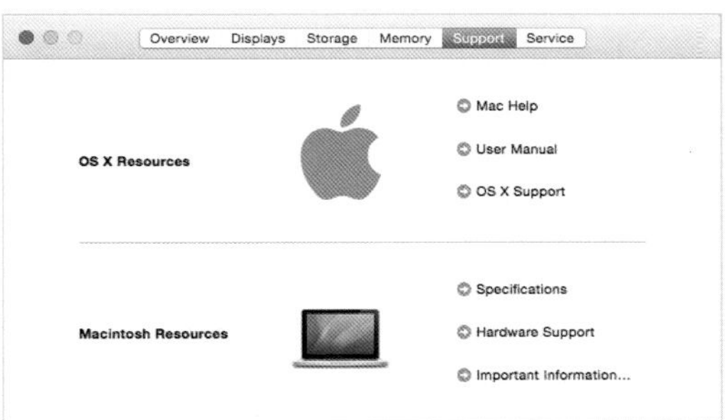

Service

The **Service** tab provides links to service and repair options and also the AppleCare Protection Plan, for extending the initial one-year warranty for your Mac.

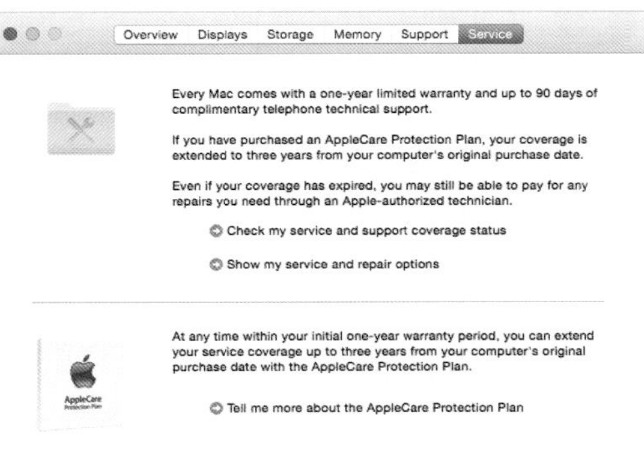

Customizing Your MacBook

Background imagery is an important way to add your own personal touch to your MacBook. (This is the graphical element upon which all other items on your computer sit.) There is a range of background options that can be used. To select your own background:

You can select your own photographs as your Desktop background, once you have loaded them onto your MacBook. To do this, select the iPhoto folder and browse to the photograph you want.

The **General** option within System Preferences can be used to change the default color and appearance of buttons, menus and windows within OS X.

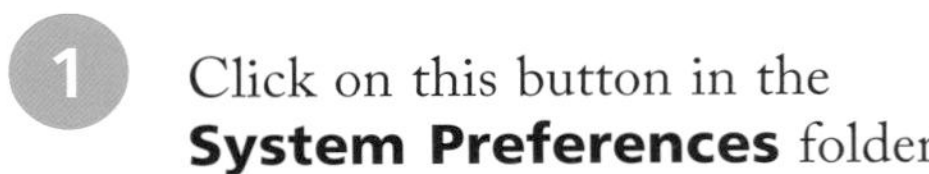

1. Click on this button in the **System Preferences** folder

2. Click on the **Desktop** tab

3. Select a location from where you want to select a background

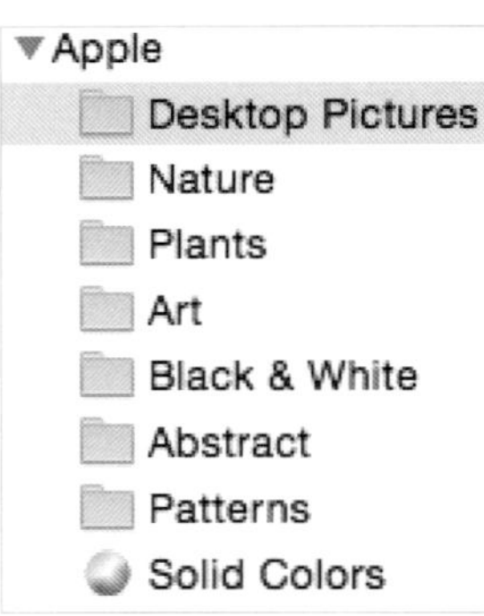

4. Click on one of the available backgrounds

5. The background is applied as the Desktop background imagery

Accessibility

In all areas of computing it is important to give as many people access to the system as possible. This includes users with visual impairments and also people who have problems using the mouse and keyboard. In OS X this is achieved through the functions of the **Accessibility** System Preferences. To use these:

1. Click on the Accessibility button in the **System Preferences** folder

2. Click on the **Display** button for options for changing the display colors, contrast and increasing the cursor size

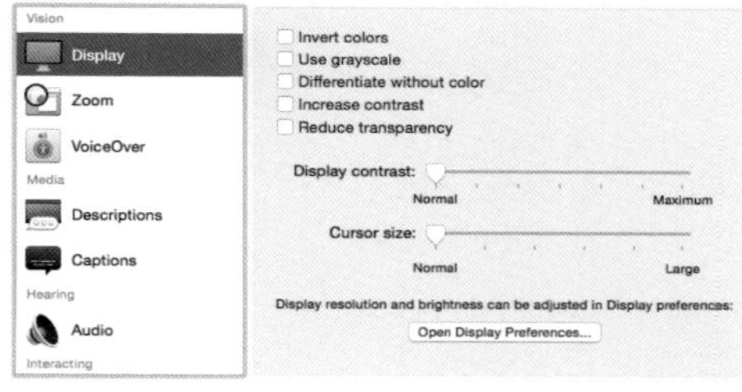

3. Click on the **Zoom** button for options to zoom in on the screen

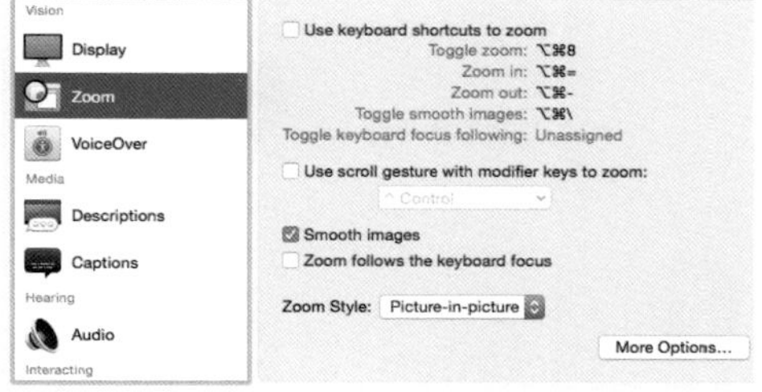

4. Click on the **VoiceOver** button to enable VoiceOver, which provides a spoken description of what is on the screen

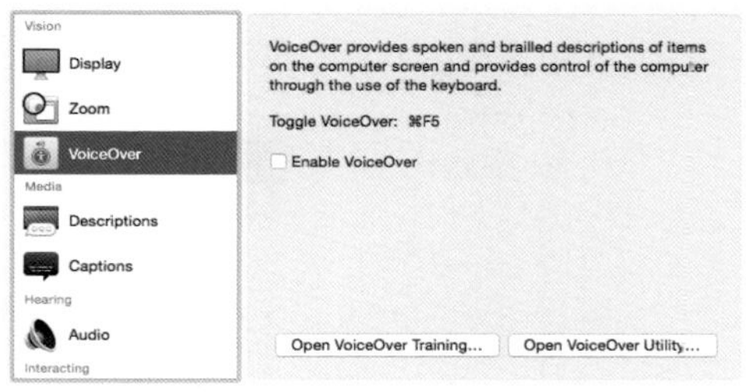

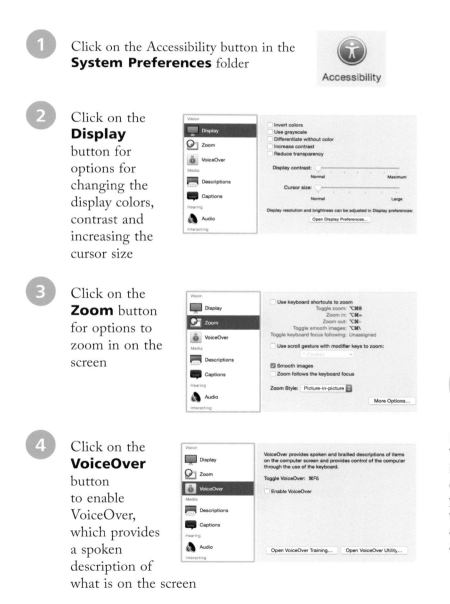

Experiment with the VoiceOver function if only to see how it operates. This will give you a better idea of how visually-impaired users access information on a computer.

...cont'd

5. Click on the **Audio** button to select an on-screen flash for alerts and how sound is played

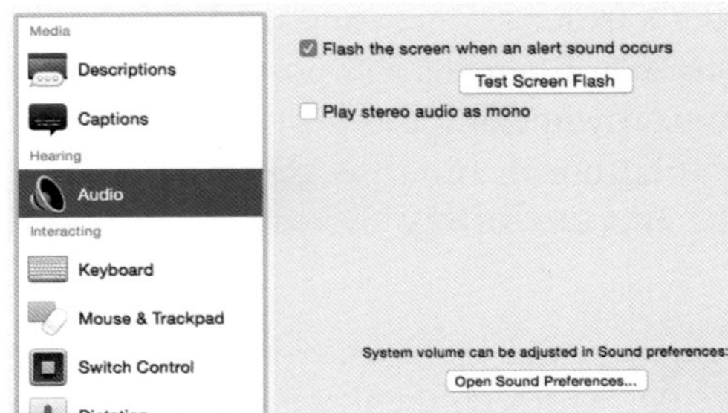

6. Click on the **Keyboard** button to access options for customizing the keyboard

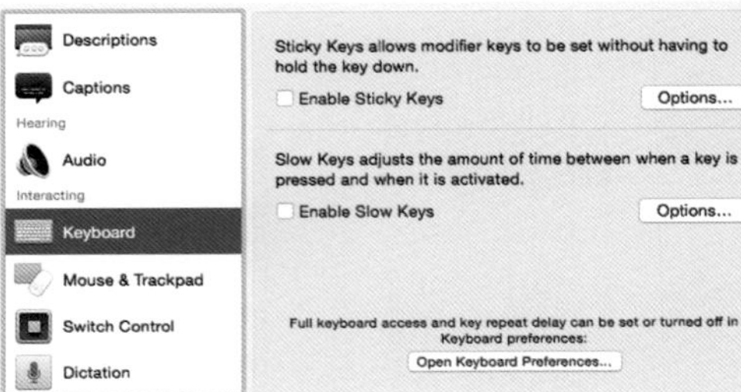

The **Audio**, **Keyboard** and **Mouse & Trackpad** accessibility options have links to additional options within their own System Preferences.

7. Click on the **Mouse & Trackpad** button to access options for customizing these devices

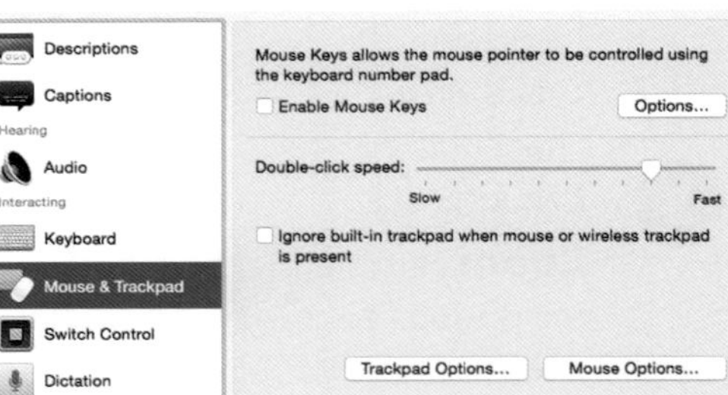

8. Click on the **Dictation** button to select options for using spoken commands

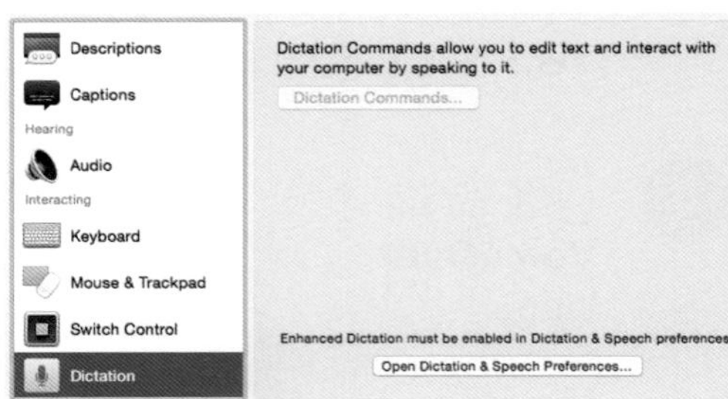

The Spoken Word

OS X Yosemite not only has numerous options for adding text to documents, emails and messages; it also has a dictation function so that you can speak what you want to appear on screen. To set up and use the dictation feature:

1. Click on the **Dictation & Speech** button in the **System Preferences** folder

2. By default, Dictation is **Off**

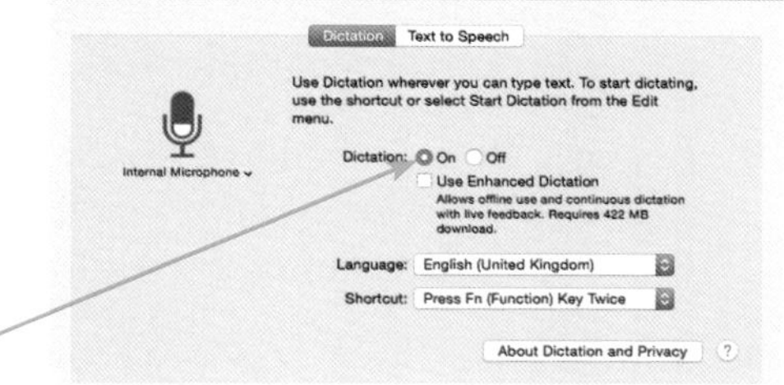

3. Click on the **On** button to enable dictation

4. Click on the **Enable Dictation** button

5. Once Dictation has been turned On, it can be accessed in relevant apps by selecting **Edit > Start Dictation** from the menu bar

Start Dictation

6. Start talking when the microphone icon appears. Click **Done** when you have finished recording your text

7. Click on the **Text to Speech** tab to make selections for dictation

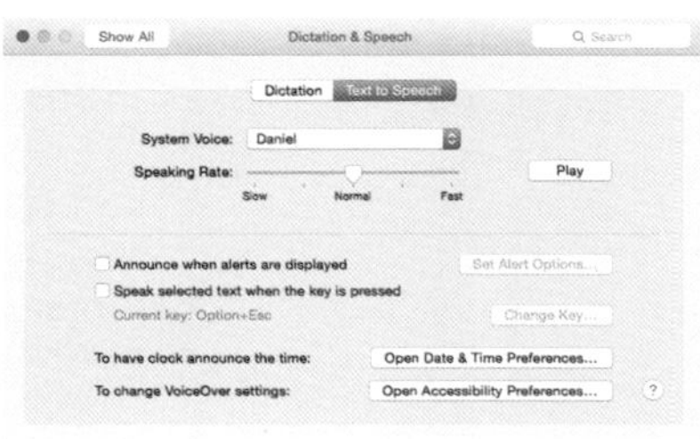

Punctuation can be added with the dictation function, by speaking commands such as 'comma' or 'question mark'. These will then be converted into the appropriate symbols.

Shutting Down

The Apple menu (which can be accessed by clicking on the Apple icon at the top left corner of the Desktop or any subsequent OS X window) has been standardized in OS X. This means that it has the same options regardless of the app in which you are working. This has a number of advantages, not least is the fact that it makes it easier to shut down your MacBook. When shutting down, there are four options that can be selected:

- **Sleep**. This puts the MacBook into hibernation mode, i.e. the screen goes blank and the hard drive becomes inactive. This state is maintained until the mouse is moved or a key is pressed on the keyboard. This then wakes up the MacBook and it is ready to continue work.
- **Restart**. This closes down the MacBook and then restarts it again. This can be useful if you have added new software and your computer requires a restart to make it active.
- **Shut Down**. This closes down the MacBook completely once you have finished working.
- **Log Out**. This logs you out of your current session and closes down your open apps. You can then log back in without turning off your MacBook and return to your previously open apps by using the Resume function, see tip.

Don't forget

When shutting down, make sure you have saved all of your open documents, although OS X will prompt you to do this if you have forgotten.

OS X Yosemite has a Resume function where your MacBook opens up in the same state as when you shut it down. See page 76 for details.

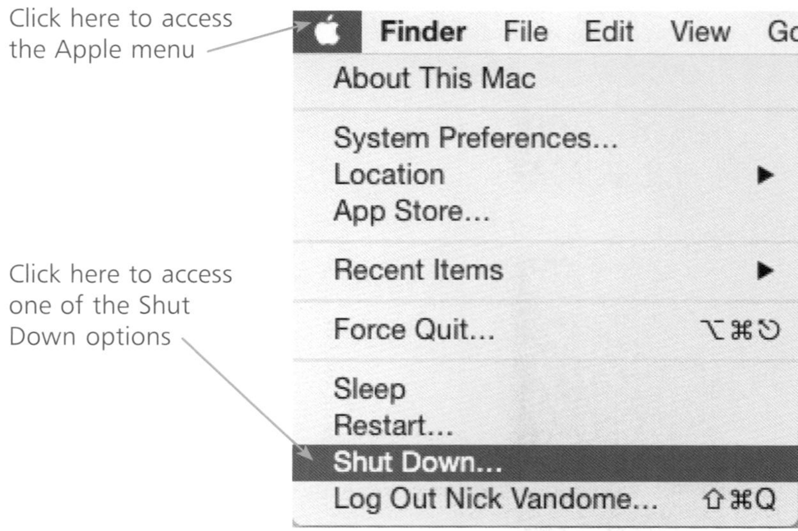

4 Getting Up and Running

This chapter looks at some of the essential features of Yosemite. These include the Dock for organizing and accessing all of the elements of your MacBook and items for arranging folders and files. It also introduces the online sharing service, iCloud, which can be used to back up a variety of content and also share items such as music, books, calendars and apps with up to six other family members.

Introducing the Dock

The Dock is one of the main organizational elements of OS X. Its main function is to help organize and access apps, folders and files. In addition, with its rich translucent colors and elegant graphical icons, it also makes an aesthetically pleasing addition to the Desktop. The main things to remember about the Dock are:

- It is divided into two: apps go on the left of the dividing line; all other items go on the right

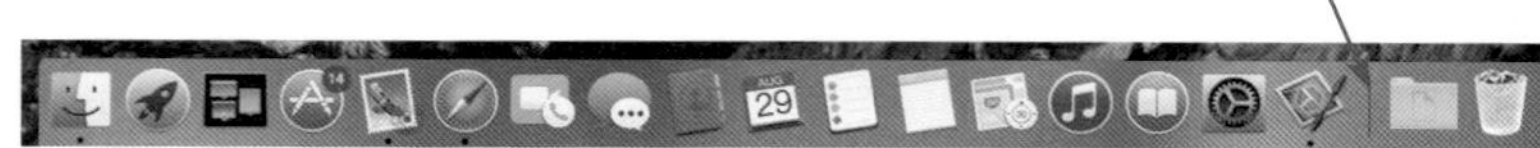

- It can be customized in a number of ways

By default the Dock appears at the bottom of the screen

If an app window is closed, the app remains open and the window is placed within the app icon on the Dock. If an item is minimized it goes on the right of the Dock dividing line.

The Dock is always displayed as a line of icons, but this can be orientated either vertically or horizontally.

Items on the Dock can be opened by clicking on them once, rather than having to double-click on them. Once they have been accessed the icon bobs up and down until the item is available.

Setting Dock Preferences

As with most elements of OS X, the Dock can be modified in numerous ways. This can affect both the appearance of the Dock and the way it operates. To set Dock preferences:

1. Select **Apple menu > System Preferences** from the Menu bar

2. Click on the **Dock** button

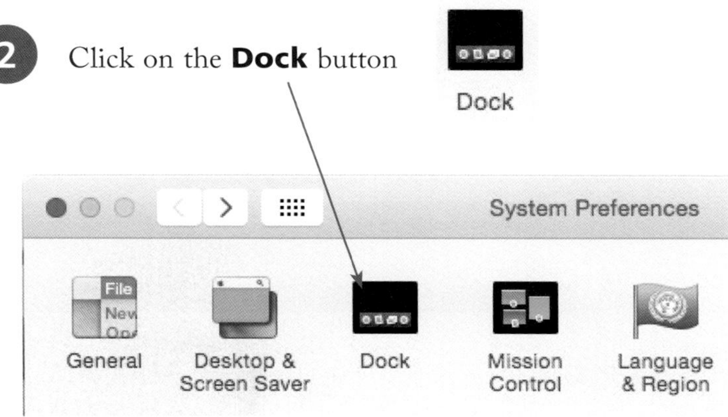

The Apple menu is constantly available in OS X, regardless of the app in which you are working. The menu options are also constant in all apps.

The Dock Preferences allow you to change its size, orientation, the way icons appear and effects for when items are minimized:

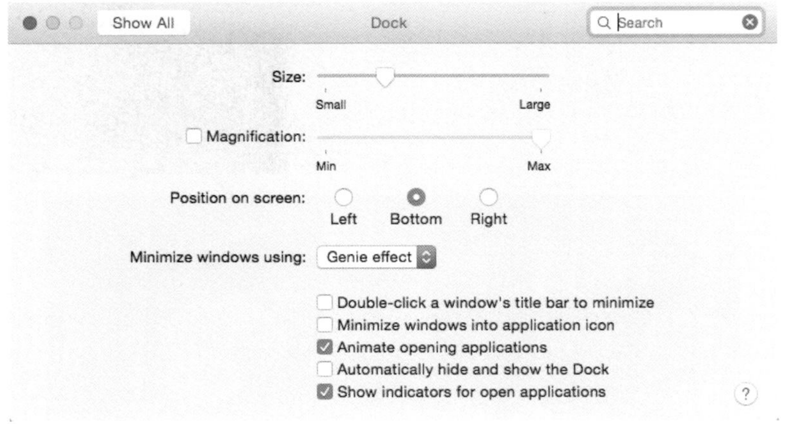

You will not be able to make the Dock size too large so that some of the icons would not be visible on the Desktop. By default, the Dock is resized so that everything is always visible.

...cont'd

The **Position on screen** options enable you to place the Dock on the left, right or bottom of the screen

The Dock cannot be moved by dragging it physically, this can only be done in the Dock Preferences window.

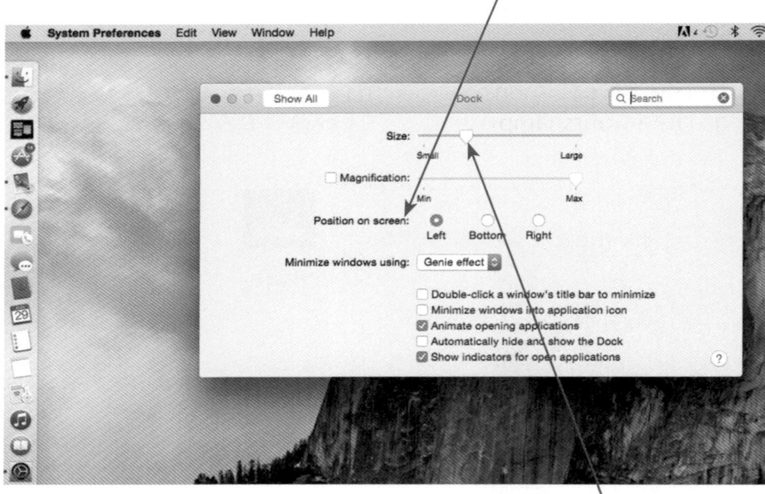

Drag the **Dock Size** slider to increase or decrease the size of the Dock

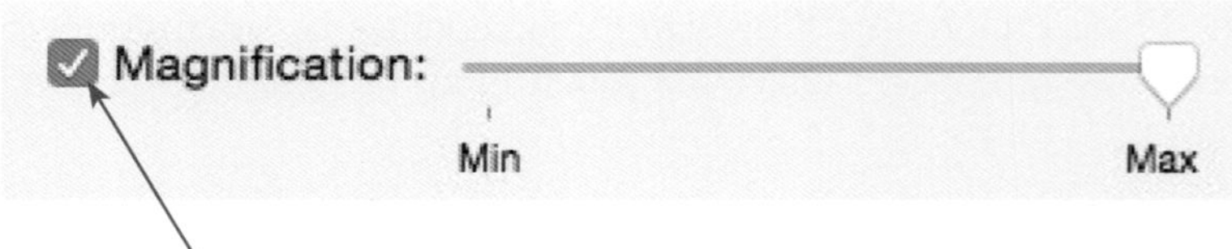

When the cursor is moved over an item in the Dock, the name of that item is displayed above it.

Check on the **Magnification** box and drag the slider to determine the size to which icons are enlarged when the cursor is moved over them

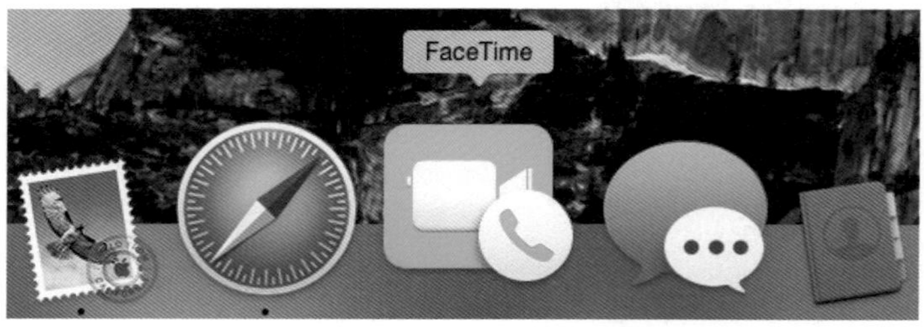

The effects that are applied to items when they are minimized is one of the features of OS X (it is not absolutely necessary but it sums up the Apple ethos of trying to enhance the user experience as much as possible).

The **Genie effect** shrinks the item to be minimized like a genie going back into its lamp

Open windows can also be minimized by double-clicking on their title bar (the thinly lined bar at the top of the window, next to the three window buttons.)

Manual resizing

In addition to changing the size of the Dock by using the Dock Preference dialog box, it can also be resized manually:

Drag vertically on the Dock dividing line to increase or decrease its size

Stacks on the Dock

Stacking items

To save space on the Dock it is possible to add folders to the Dock, from where their contents can be accessed. This is known as Stacks. By default, a stack for downloaded files is created on the Dock. To use Stacks:

1. Stacked items are placed on the right of the Dock dividing line

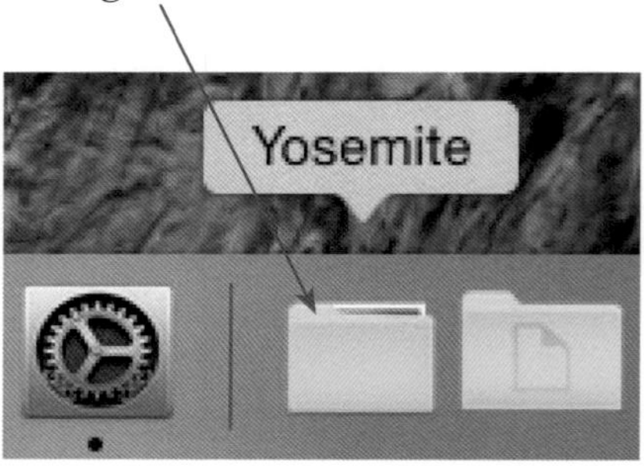

To create a new Stack, drag a folder to the right-hand side of the Dock, i.e. to the right of the dividing line.

2. Click on a Stack to view its contents

3. Stacks can be viewed as a grid, or

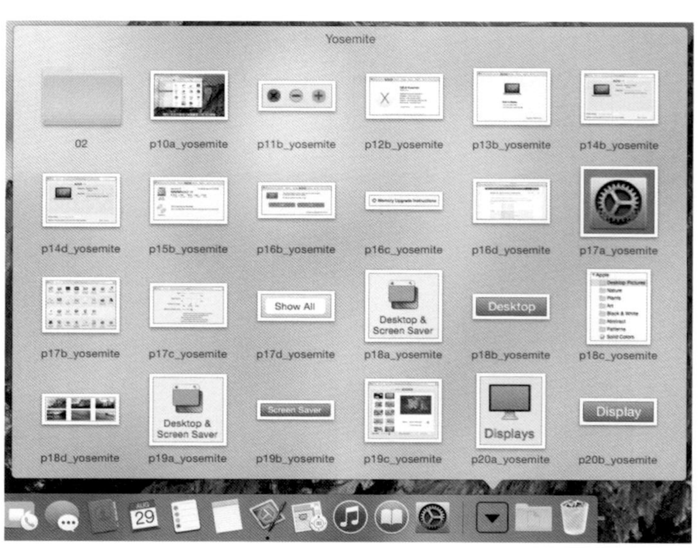

4. As a fan, depending on the number of items it contains, or

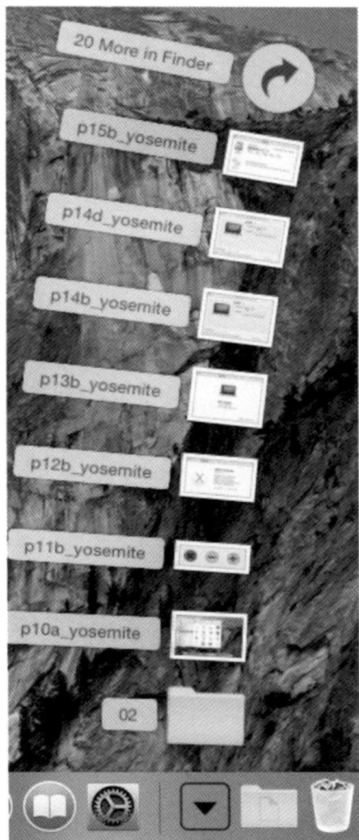

Move the cursor over a Stack and press Ctrl+click to access options for how that Stack is displayed.

5. As a list. Click on a folder to view its contents within a Stack. Click on files to open them in their relevant app

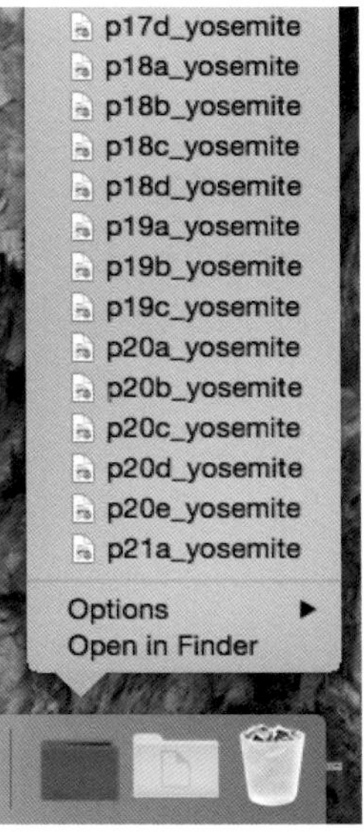

6. To create a new Stack, drag a folder onto the Dock. Any new items that are added to the folder will also be visible through the Stack

Dock Menus

One of the features of the Dock is that it can display contextual menus for selected items. This means that it shows menus with options that are applicable to the item that is being accessed. This can only be done when an item has been opened.

Click on **Quit** on the Dock's contextual menu to close an open app or file, depending on which side of the dividing bar the item is located.

1. Click and hold on the black button below an app's icon to display an item's individual menu

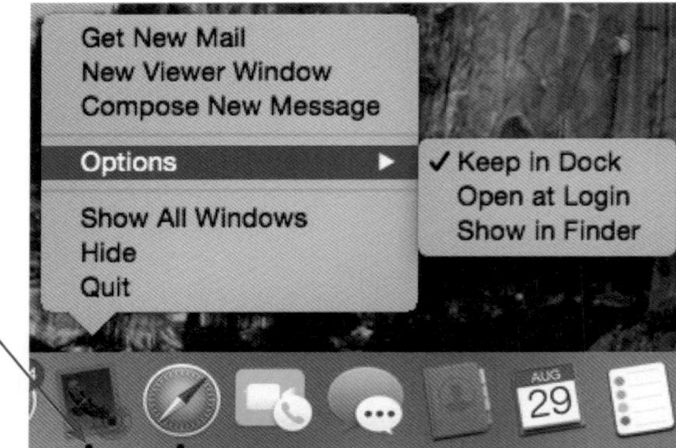

2. Click on **Show in Finder** to see where the item is located on your computer

Working with Dock Items

Adding items

As many items as you like can be added to the Dock; the only restriction is the size of monitor in which to display all of the Dock items (the size of the Dock can be reduced to accommodate more icons but you have to be careful that all of the icons are still legible). To add items to the Dock:

Locate the required item and drag it onto the Dock. All of the other icons move along to make space for the new one

Icons on the Dock are shortcuts to the related item, rather than the item itself, which remains in its original location.

Keep in Dock

Every time you open a new app, its icon will appear in the Dock for the duration that the program is open, even if it has not previously been put in the Dock. If you then decide that you would like to keep it in the Dock, you can do so as follows:

1. Click and hold on the button below an open app
2. Click on **Keep in Dock** to ensure the app remains in the Dock when it is closed

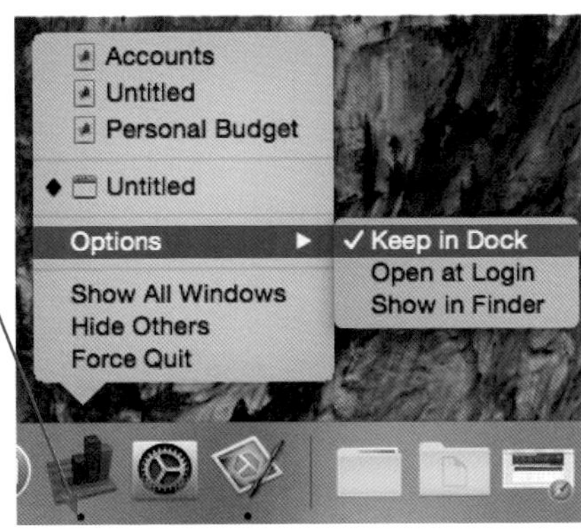

You can add as many items as you like to the Dock, but it will automatically shrink to display all of its items if it becomes too big for the available space.

Removing items

Any item, except the Finder, can be removed from the Dock. However, this does not remove it from your computer, it just removes the shortcut for accessing it. You will still be able to locate it in its folder on your hard drive and, if required, drag it back onto the Dock. To remove items from the Dock:

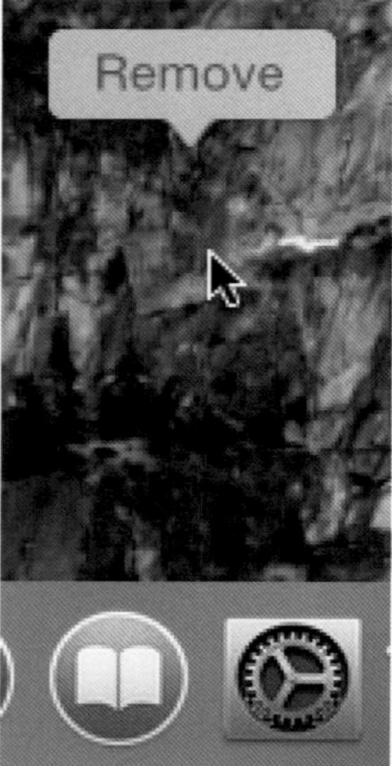

1. Drag it away from the Dock and release. The **Remove** box appears when the app can be removed from the Dock. Release the cursor. All of the other icons then move up to fill in the space on the Dock

Removing open apps

You can remove an app from the Dock, even if it is open and running. To do this:

1. Drag an app off the Dock while it is running. Initially, the icon will remain on the Dock because the app is still open

2. When the app is closed its icon will be removed from the Dock (unless Keep in Dock has been selected from the item's Dock menu)

Trash

The Trash folder is a location for placing items that you do not want to use anymore. However, when items are placed in the Trash, they are not removed from your computer. This requires another command, as the Trash is really a holding area before you decide you want to remove items permanently. The Trash can also be used for ejecting removable disks attached to your MacBook.

Items can also be sent to the Trash by selecting them and then selecting **File > Move to Trash** from the Menu bar.

Sending items to the Trash

Items can be sent to the Trash by dragging them from the location in which they are stored:

1. Drag an item over the **Trash** icon to place it in the Trash folder

2. Click once on the **Trash** icon on the Dock to view its contents

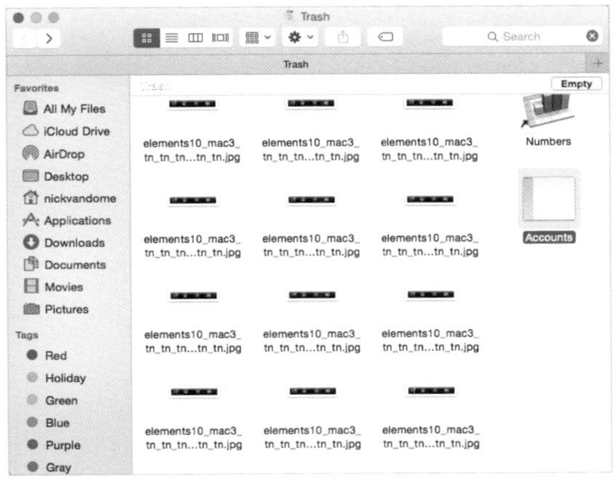

All of the items within the Trash can be removed in a single command: Select **Finder > Empty Trash** from the Menu bar to remove all of the items in the Trash folder.

About iCloud

The standard iCloud service is free and this includes an iCloud email address and 5GB of online storage (*at the time of printing*).

Cloud computing is an attractive proposition and one that has gained greatly in popularity in recent years. As a concept, it consists of storing your content on an external computer server. This not only gives you added security in terms of backing up your information, it also means that the content can then be shared over a variety of mobile devices.

iCloud is Apple's consumer cloud computing product that consists of online services such as email, a calendar, contacts and saving documents. iCloud provides users with a way to save their files and content to the online service and then use them across their Apple devices such as other Mac computers, iPhones, iPads and iPod Touches.

About iCloud

iCloud can be set up from this icon with System Preferences:

There is also a version of iCloud for Windows.

You can use iCloud to save and share the following:

- Music
- Photos
- Documents
- Apps
- Books
- Backups
- Contacts and calendars

When you save an item to the iCloud it automatically pushes it to all of your other compatible devices; you do not have to manually sync anything, iCloud does it all for you.

Setting up iCloud

To use iCloud with Yosemite you need to first have an Apple ID. This is a service you can register for to be able to access a range of Apple facilities, including iCloud. You can register with an email address and a password. When you first start using iCloud you will be prompted for your Apple ID details. If you do not have an Apple ID you can apply for one at this point:

1. Sign in with your Apple ID, or

2. Click on the **Create an Apple ID...** button

Create Apple ID...

Setting up iCloud

To use iCloud

1. Open **System Preferences** and click on the **iCloud** button

2. Check on the items you want included within iCloud. All of these items will be backed up and shared across all of your Apple devices

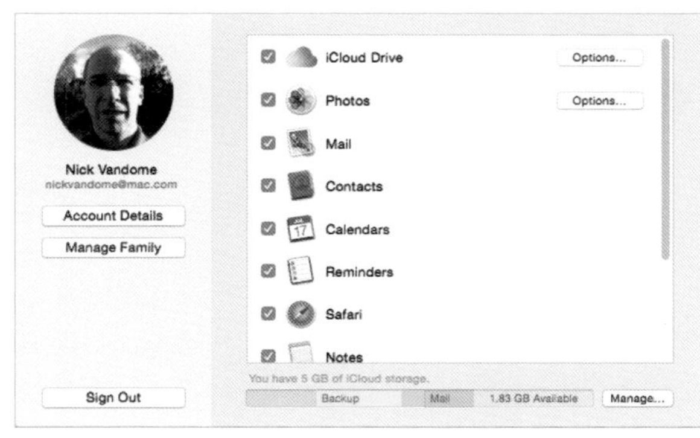

Music and photos are not included in your 5GB storage limit on iCloud. This only includes emails, documents, account information, Camera Roll (for saved or edited photos) and account settings.

About the iCloud Drive

One of the options in the iCloud section is for the Cloud Drive. This can be used to store documents and other content so that you can use them on any other Apple devices that you have, such as an iPhone or an iPad. With iCloud Drive you can start work on a document on one device and continue on another device from where you left off. To setup the iCloud Drive:

1. Click on the **iCloud** button in System Preferences

2. Check On the **iCloud Drive** option and click on the **Options** button

3. Select the apps that you want to use with the iCloud Drive

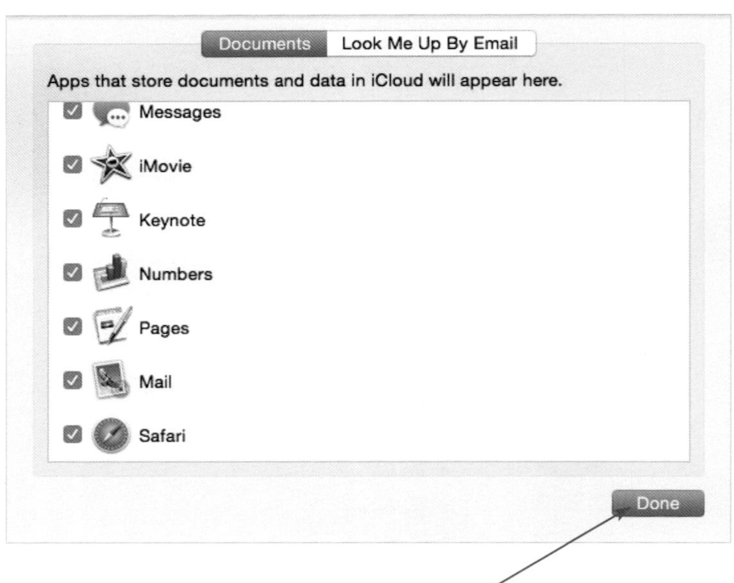

4. Click on the **Done** button

Pages is the Apple app for word processing, Numbers for spreadsheets and Keynote for presentations.

Using the iCloud Drive

To work with files in the iCloud Drive:

1. In the Finder Sidebar click on the **iCloud Drive** button

2. Certain iCloud Drive folders are already created, based on the apps that you have selected on the previous page. These are the default folders into which content from their respective apps will be placed (although others can also be selected, if required). Double-click on a folder to view its contents

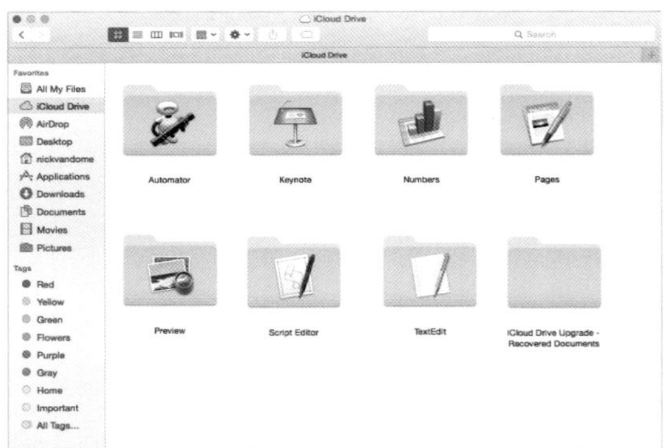

Another useful iCloud function is the iCloud Keychain (see pages 72-75 for details).

3. To save files into an iCloud Drive folder, select **File > Save As** from the Menu bar, click on the **iCloud Drive** button in the Finder Sidebar and navigate to the required folder for the file

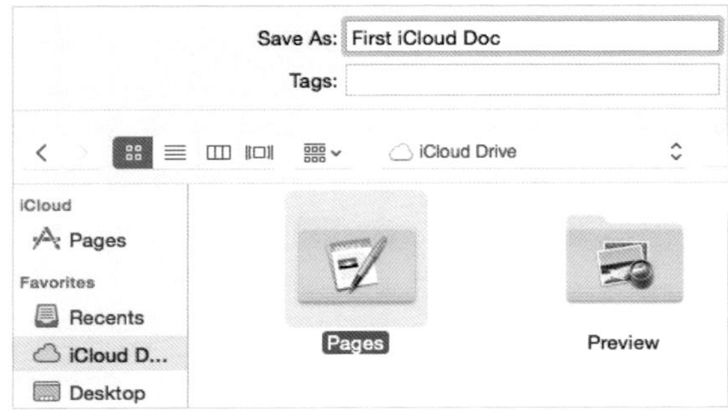

Continuity

One of the main themes of OS X Yosemite, and iOS 8 for mobile devices, is to make all of your content available on all of your Apple devices. This is known as Continuity: when you create something on one device you can then pick it up and finish it on another device. This is done through iCloud. To do this:

1. Ensure the app has iCloud activated, as on page 61
2. Create the content on the app on your MacBook

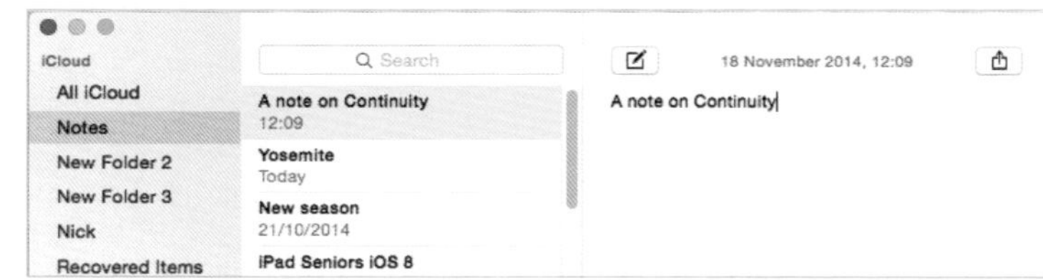

3. Open the same app on another Apple device, e.g. an iPad. The item created on your MacBook should be available to view and edit. Any changes will then show up on the file on your MacBook too

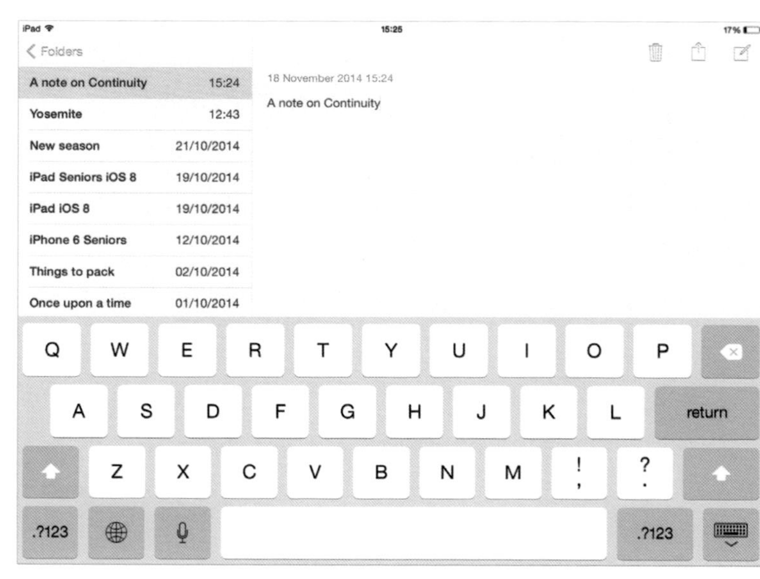

Hot tip

It is also possible to continue an email with the continuity feature. First create it on your Mac and then close it. You will be prompted to save the email as a draft and, if you do this, you will be able to open it from the **Drafts** mailbox on another Apple device.

Handoff

Handoff is one of the key features of Continuity and it displays icons of items that you have opened on another device, such as Safari web pages. Handoff does not work with all devices and it only works if both devices have OS X Yosemite and iOS 8, for mobile devices.

Handoff has had some teething problems and it sometimes takes a bit of trial and error to make it work properly. To use Handoff you will need to do the following:

- Your Mac must be running OS X Yosemite and your mobile device (iPhone 5 and later, iPad 4th generation and later, all models of iPad mini and the 5th generation iPod Touch) must have iOS 8.
- Your Mac has to support Bluetooth 4.0, which means that most pre-2012 Macs are not compatible with Handoff.
- To check if your Mac supports Handoff, select **Apple Menu > About This Mac > System Report**. Click on **Bluetooth** to see if Handoff is supported.

The apps that work with Handoff are Mail, Safari, Maps, Messages, Reminders, Calendar, Contacts, Notes, Pages, Numbers and Keynote.

Bluetooth Low Energy Supported:	Yes
Handoff Supported:	Yes
Instant Hotspot Supported:	Yes

- Turn on Bluetooth on your Mac (System Preferences) and on your mobile device (Settings).
- Turn on Handoff on your Mac (**System Preferences > General** and check on **Allow Handoff Between this Mac and your iCloud Devices**) and on your mobile device (**Settings > General > Handoff & Suggested Apps**).
- When Handoff is activated, compatible apps will be displayed at the left-hand side of the Dock when then have been opened on another device.

Handoff does not always work perfectly, even between compatible devices. If it is not working, try turning both devices off and on and do the same with Bluetooth. Also, try logging out, and then back in, of your iCloud account on both devices.

About Family Sharing

As everyone gets more and more digital devices it is becoming increasingly important to be able to share content with other people, particularly family members. In OS X Yosemite, and iCloud, the Family Sharing function enables you to share items that you have downloaded from the App Store, such as music and movies, with up to six other family members, as long as they have an Apple Account. Once this has been set up it is also possible to share items such as family calendars, photos and even see where family members' devices are located. To set up Family Sharing:

To use Family Sharing, other family members must have an Apple device using either iOS 8 for a mobile device (iPad, iPhone or iPod Touch) or OS X Yosemite for a desktop or laptop Mac computer.

1. Click on the **iCloud** button in System Preferences

2. Click on the **Set Up Family Sharing** (or the **Manage Family** button if Family Sharing has already been set up)

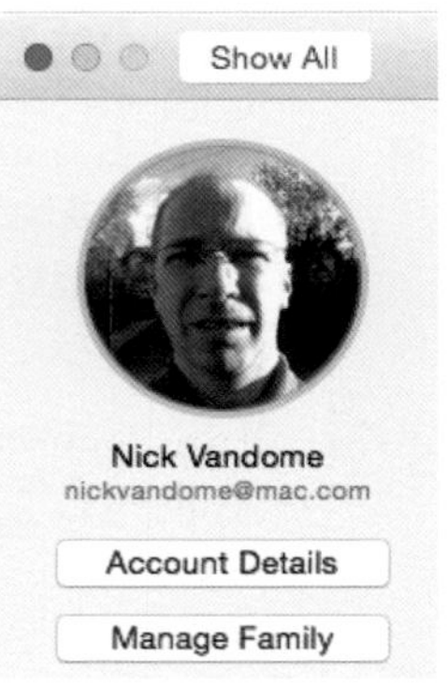

3. One person will be the organizer of Family Sharing, i.e. in charge of it, and if you set it up then it will be you. Click on the **+** button to add other family members

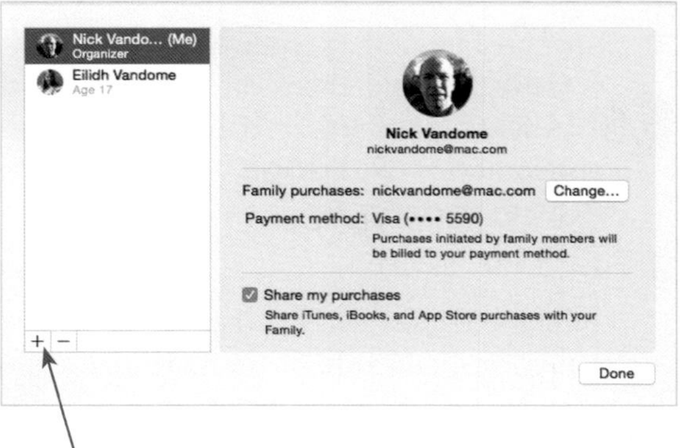

4. Enter the name or email address of a family member and click on the **Continue** button

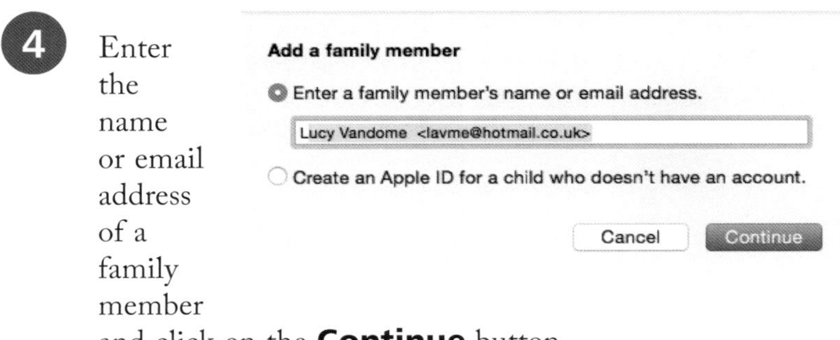

5. Verify your debit or credit card information for your iCloud account as this will be used by the family member for making purchases. Click on the **Continue** button

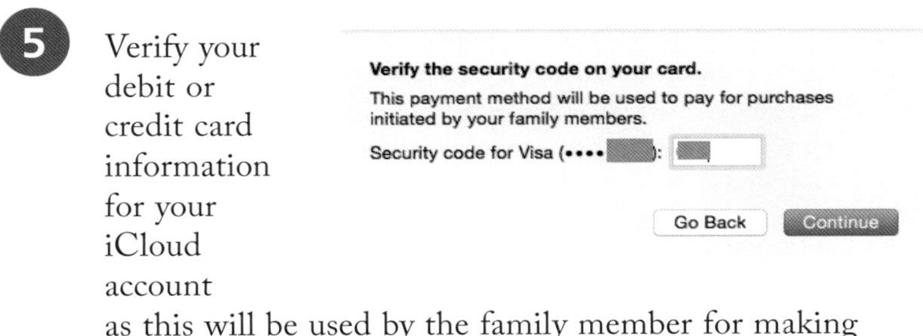

Verify the security code on your card.
This payment method will be used to pay for purchases initiated by your family members.
Security code for Visa (••••
Go Back
Continue

6. Enter your Apple ID password and click on the **Continue** button

7. An invitation is sent to the selected person. They have to accept this before they can participate in Family Sharing

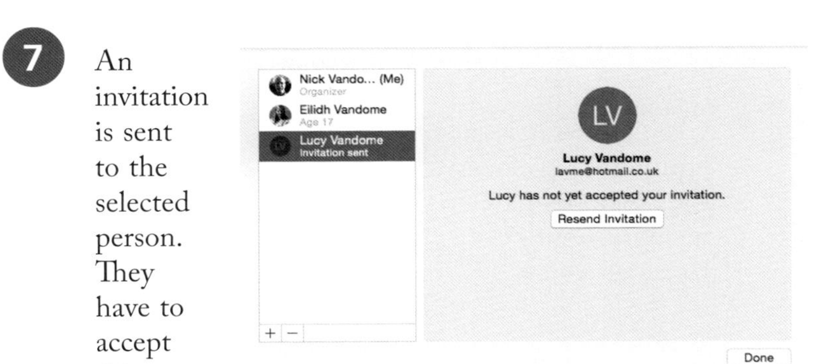

If children are part of the Family Sharing group you can specify that they need your permission before downloading any items from the iTunes Store, the App Store or the iBooks Store. To do this, click on **iCloud** in **System Preferences** and click on the **Manage Family** button. Select a family member and check **On** the **Ask to Buy** button. You will then receive a notification whenever they want to buy something and you can either allow or deny their request.

Using Family Sharing

Once Family Sharing has been set up it can be used by members of the groups to share music, apps, movies and books. There is also a shared Family calendar that can be used and it is also possible to view the location of the devices of the family members.

Sharing music

To share music, and other content from the iTunes Store such as movies and TV shows:

1. Click on the **iTunes** app on the Dock

2. Click on the **Purchased** link

MUSIC QUICK LINKS
Redeem | Account
Send iTunes Gifts | Support
Purchased

3. By default, your own purchases are displayed. Click on the **Purchased** button to view other members of Family Sharing

Purchased Nick

4. Click on another family member to view their purchases (they will be able to do this for your purchases too)

5. Click on the iCloud button to download the other family member's music tracks or albums

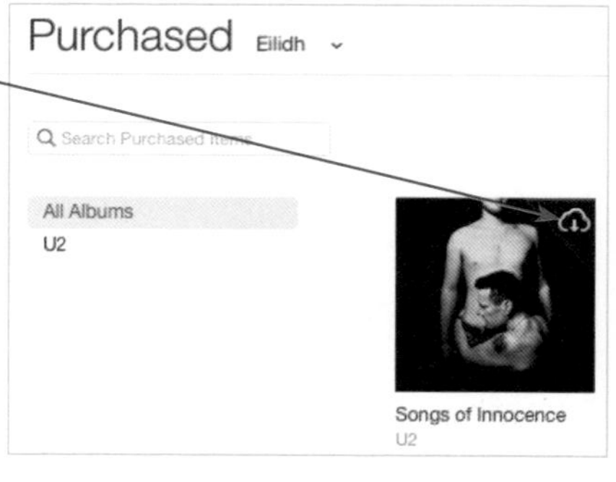

You have to be connected to the Internet and online to access the iTunes Store and view purchases from other family members. When you do this, you can play their songs without having to download them. However, if you want to be able to use them when you are offline then you will have to download them first, as in Step 5.

Sharing apps

Apps can also be shared from the App Store. To do this:

1. Click on the **App Store** app on the Dock

2. Click on the **Purchases** button

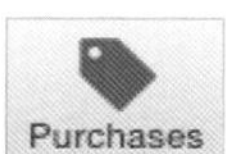

3. By default, your own purchases are displayed. Click on the **My Purchases** button to view other members of Family Sharing

Purchases My Purchases

4. Click on another family member to view and download their purchased apps (they will be able to do this for your apps too)

More than one family member can use content in the Family Sharing group at the same time.

Sharing books

Books can also be shared in a similar way to items from the iTunes Store and the App Store. To do this:

1. Click on the **iBooks** app on the Dock

2. Click on the **iBooks Store** button

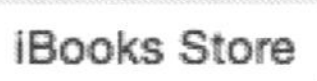

3. Click on the **Purchased** link

QUICK LINKS
Account
Purchased

4. By default, your own purchases are displayed. Click on the **Purchased** button to view other members of Family Sharing and any books they have downloaded

...cont'd

Sharing calendars

Family Sharing also generates a Family calendar that can be used by all Family Sharing members:

1. Open the **Calendar** app 

2. Click and hold on a date to create a **New Event**. The current calendar (shown in the top right-hand corner) will probably not be the Family one. Click on this button to change the calendar

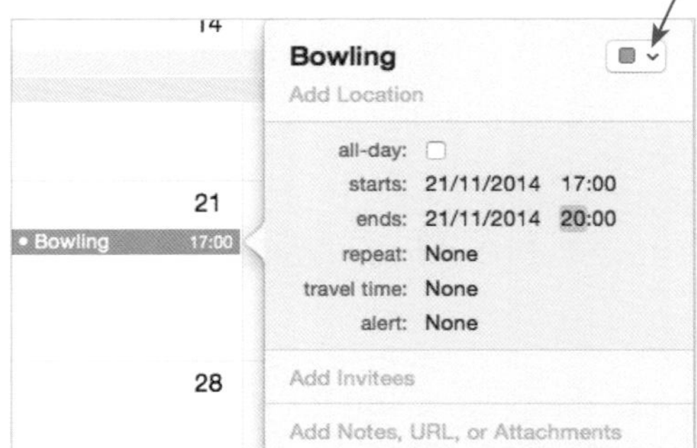

3. Click on the **Family** calendar

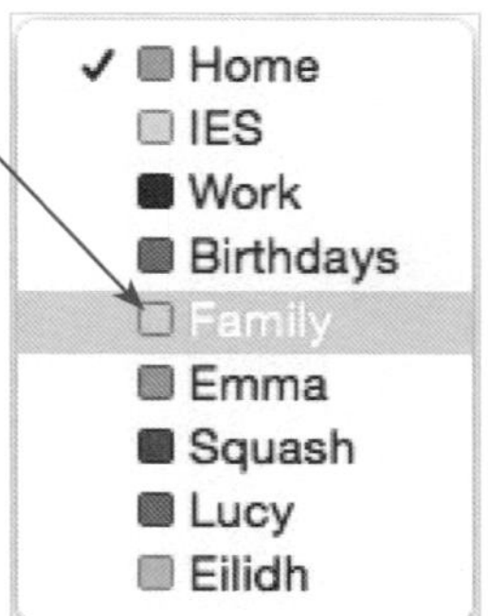

4. Complete the details for the event. It will be added to your calendar, with the Family color tag. Other people in your Family Sharing circle will have this event added to their Family calendar too and they will be sent a notification

Other members of the Family Sharing group can add items to the Family calendar and, when they do, you will be sent a notification that appears on your Mac.

Finding lost family devices

Family Sharing also makes it possible to see where everyone's devices are, which can be useful for locating people, but particularly if a device belonging to a Family Sharing member is lost or stolen. To do this:

1. Ensure that the **Find My Mac** function is turned on in the **iCloud** System Preferences and log in to your online iCloud account at **www.icloud.com**

2. Click on the **Find My iPhone** button (this works for other Apple devices too)

3. Devices that are turned on, online and with iCloud activated are shown by green dots

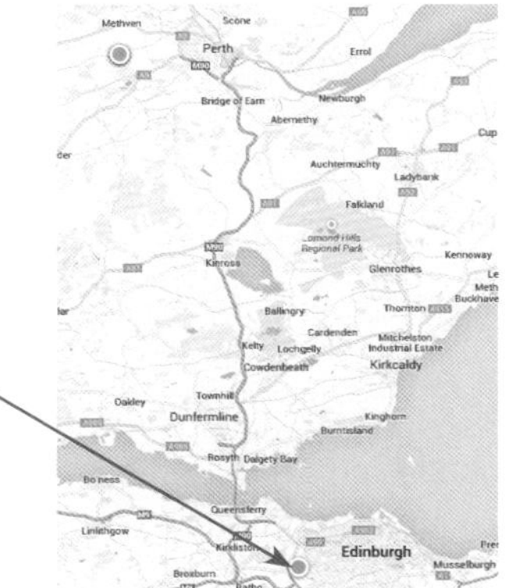

4. Click on a green dot to display information about the device. Click on the **i** symbol to access options for managing the device remotely

5. There are options to send an alert sound to the device, lock it remotely or erase its contents (if you are concerned about it having fallen into the wrong hands)

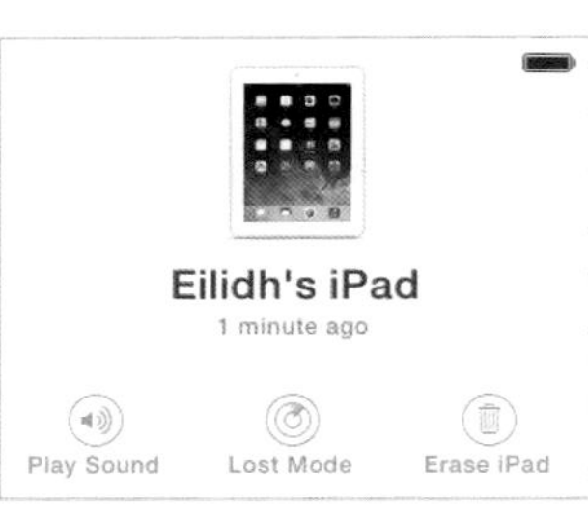
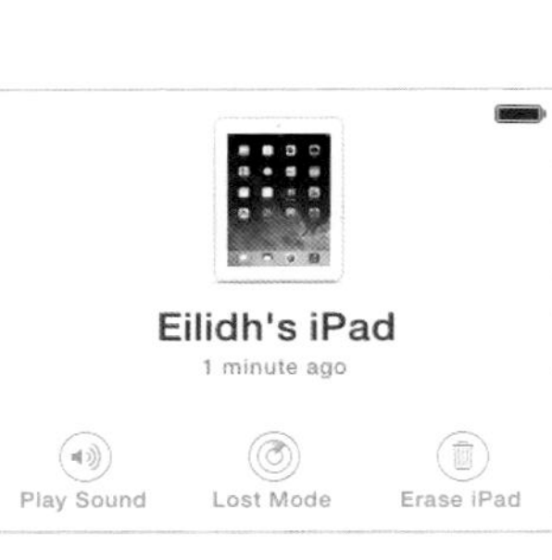

The locations of devices are shown on a map and you can zoom in on the map to see their locations more exactly.

iCloud Keychain

One of the big issues of online activity is remembering passwords on websites and also ensuring that they are as secure as possible. This is made all the more significant if you are using different devices to access websites.

On Mac computers and iOS 8 mobile devices, password management and security is handled through the iCloud Keychain function, using Safari as your web browser. This can be used to save passwords and credit card information when you enter them into websites and also generate new, secure, passwords, if required. This information is stored in the iCloud and so is available on all of the compatible Apple devices on which you are accessing the Web with Safari. To set up iCloud Keychain:

1. Click on the **iCloud** button in System Preferences

2. In the iCloud window, click on the **Keychain** checkbox

3. Enter your **Apple ID** to set up iCloud Keychain. Click on the **OK** button

You have to have an Apple ID and have iCloud turned on in order to use the iCloud Keychain functionality.

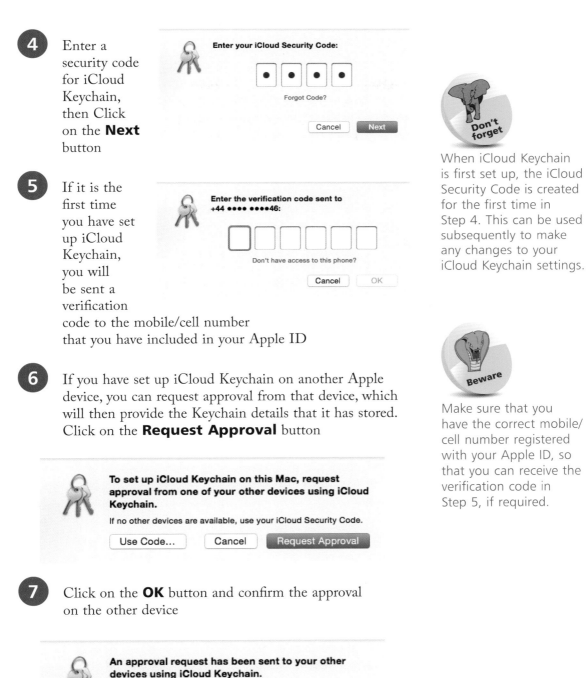

4. Enter a security code for iCloud Keychain, then Click on the **Next** button

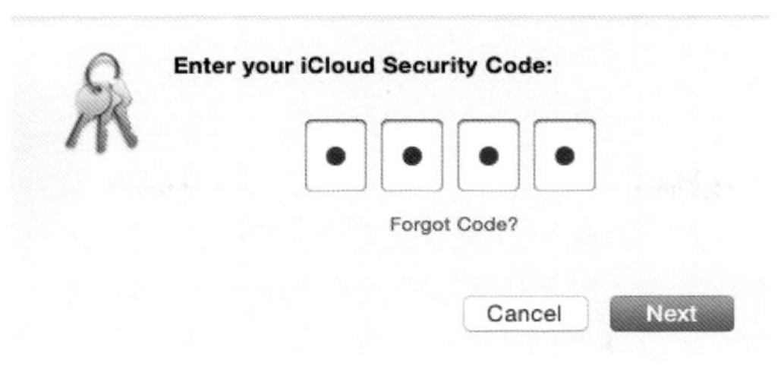

5. If it is the first time you have set up iCloud Keychain, you will be sent a verification code to the mobile/cell number that you have included in your Apple ID

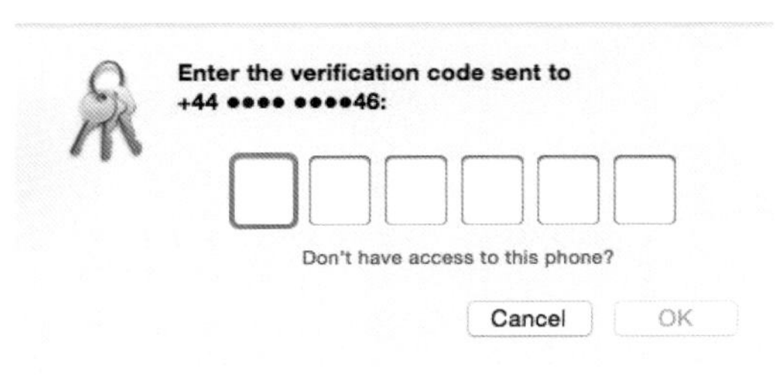

6. If you have set up iCloud Keychain on another Apple device, you can request approval from that device, which will then provide the Keychain details that it has stored. Click on the **Request Approval** button

7. Click on the **OK** button and confirm the approval on the other device

An approval request has been sent to your other devices using iCloud Keychain.

You can approve this Mac at any time from one of these devices.

OK

When iCloud Keychain is first set up, the iCloud Security Code is created for the first time in Step 4. This can be used subsequently to make any changes to your iCloud Keychain settings.

Make sure that you have the correct mobile/cell number registered with your Apple ID, so that you can receive the verification code in Step 5, if required.

Using iCloud Keychain

Once iCloud Keychain has been set up, it can be used to remember passwords and credit card information on websites and ensure this information is available across all of your compatible Apple devices. Passwords can also be autofilled so that you do not have to enter them each time. This can be set up within the Preferences of the Safari browser app. To do this:

1. Open Safari and select **Safari > Preferences** from the Menu bar

2. Click on the **Passwords** tab and check On the **AutoFill user names and passwords** checkbox

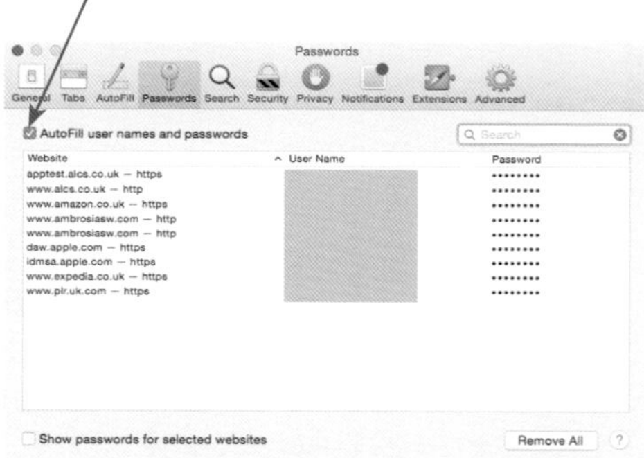

3. Click on the **AutoFill** tab and select the items that you want to be included for AutoFill

4. When you first enter an existing password into a website you will be prompted to save it in iCloud Keychain. Click on the **Save Password** button to do this

If AutoFill is turned On, and iCloud Keychain is being used, Safari will remember usernames and passwords and pre-insert them whenever you visit a website that has been set up for this.

5. Once AutoFill has been activated, when you start to fill in the username and password on a website that has been used before, you will be prompted to fill the fields from the AutoFill information

6. For a website on which you have not created a password, you will be prompted by iCloud Keychain to use the Safari suggested one

Although the passwords created by iCloud Keychain are generally more secure than the ones created by individuals, they are not always considered the most secure in terms of Internet security. However, for most purposes they will provide a good level of online security.

Keychain settings

Some of the Keychain settings can be changed within the iCloud System Preferences:

1. Click on the Keychain **Options** button

2. Make any changes to the options, as required. These include allowing approval for your iCloud security code to be used to set up Keychain on other devices and also the phone number needed for verification purposes

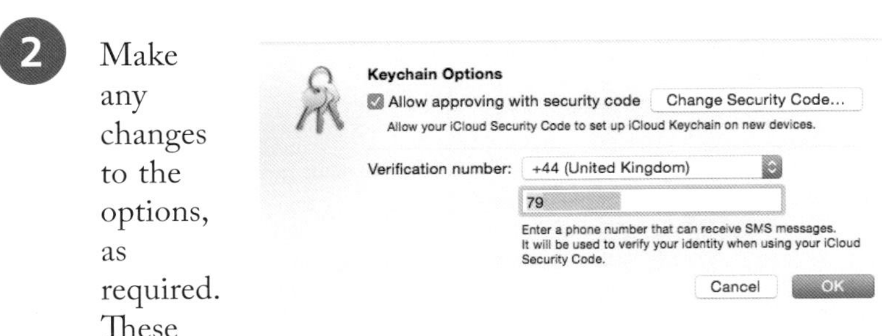

Keychain Options
Allow approving with security code
Change Security Code...
Allow your iCloud Security Code to set up iCloud Keychain on new devices.
Verification number:
+44 (United Kingdom)
79
Enter a phone number that can receive SMS messages.
It will be used to verify your identity when using your iCloud Security Code.
Cancel
OK

Resuming

One of the chores of computing is that when you close down your computer you have to first close down all of your open documents and apps and then open them all again when you turn your machine back on again. However, OS X has an innovative feature that allows you to continue working exactly where you left off, even if you turn off your computer. To do this:

1. Before you close down, all of your open documents and apps will be available as shown

2. Select the **Shut Down** or **Restart** option from the Apple menu

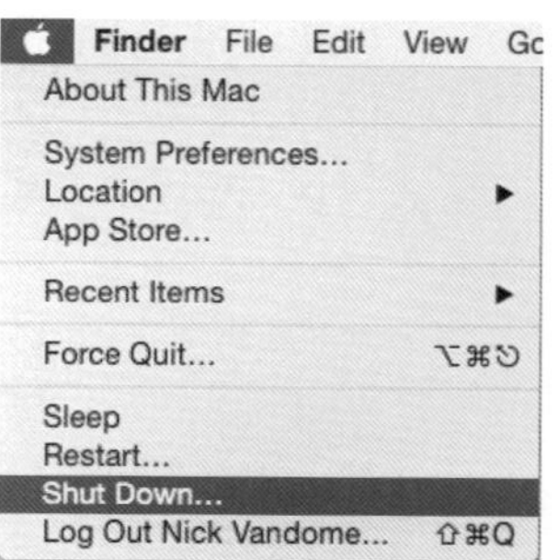

3. Make sure this box is checked on (this will ensure that all of your items will appear as before once the MacBook is closed down and then opened again)

Reopen windows when logging back in

4. Confirm the **Shut Down** or **Restart** command

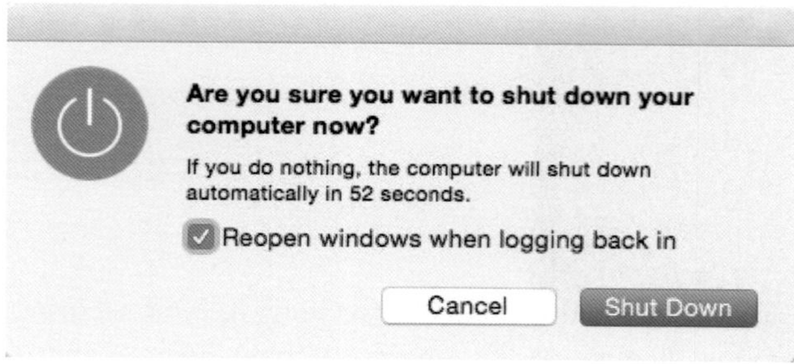

5 Finder

The principal way of moving around Yosemite is the Finder. This enables you to access items and organize your apps, folders and files. This chapter looks at how to use the Finder and get the most out of this powerful tool for navigating around Yosemite. It covers how to customize the interface and numerous options for working with folders and files and also sharing items with other apps, directly from the Finder.

Working with the Finder

If you were only able to use one item on the Dock it would be the Finder. This is the gateway to all of the elements of your computer. It is possible to get to selected items through other routes, but the Finder is the only location where you can gain access to everything on your system. If you ever feel that you are getting lost within OS X, click on the Finder and then you should begin to feel more at home. To access the Finder:

Click once on this icon on the Dock

The Finder Sidebar is transparent so shows through the background window behind it.

Overview

The Finder has its own toolbar, a Sidebar from which items can be accessed and a main window where the contents of selected items can be viewed:

Forward and back

View options

Actions button

Search

View all files

Folders are displayed here

Sidebar

Main windows

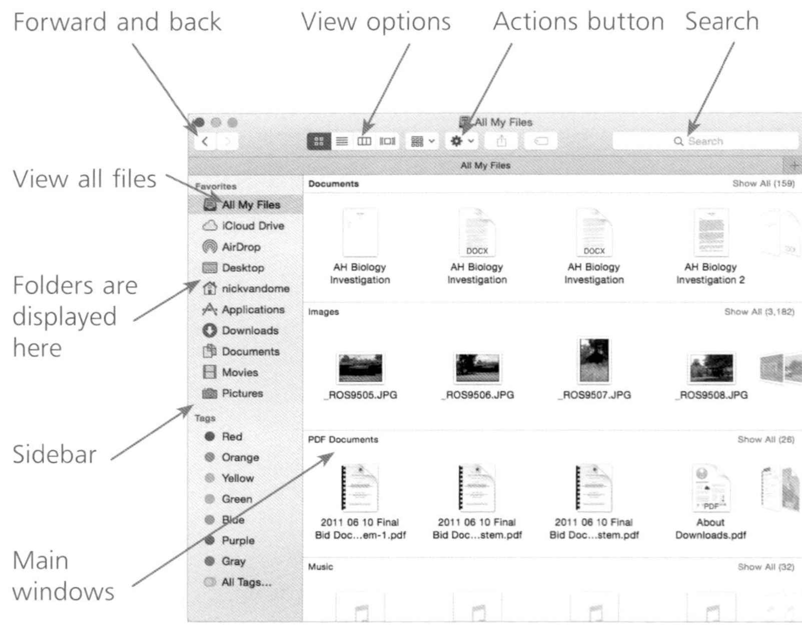

The **Actions** button has options for displaying information about a selected item and also options for how it is displayed within the Finder.

Finder Folders

All My Files

This contains all of the latest files on which you have been working. They are sorted into categories according to file type so that you can search through them quickly. This is an excellent way to locate items without having to look through a lot of folders. To access this:

1. Click on this link in the Finder Sidebar to access the contents of your **All My Files** folder

2. All of your files are displayed in individual categories. Click on the headings at the top of each category to view all of the items in the category

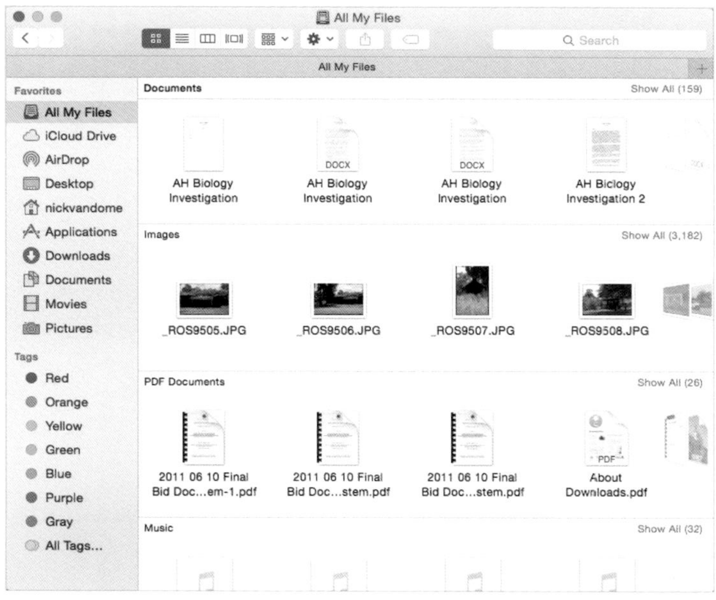

The Finder is always open (as denoted by the graphic underneath its icon on the Dock) and it cannot readily be closed down or removed.

...cont'd

Home folder

This contains the contents of your own home directory, containing your personal folders and files. OS X inserts some pre-named folders which it thinks will be useful, but it is possible to rename, rearrange or delete these as you please. It is also possible to add as many more folders as you want.

1. Click on this link to access the contents of your **Home** folder

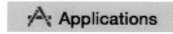

2. The **Home** folder contains the Public folder that can be used to share files with other users if the computer is part of a network

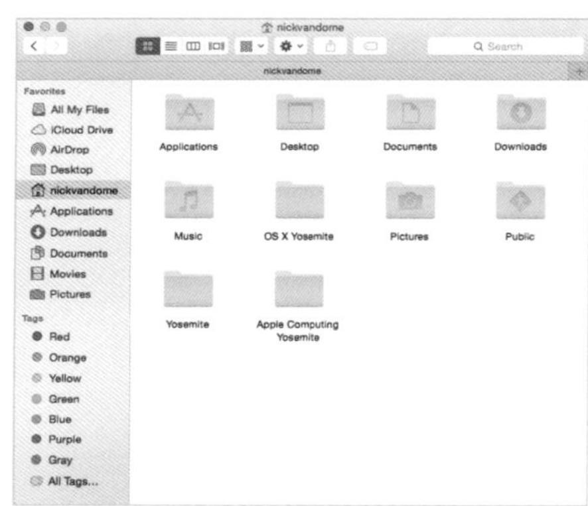

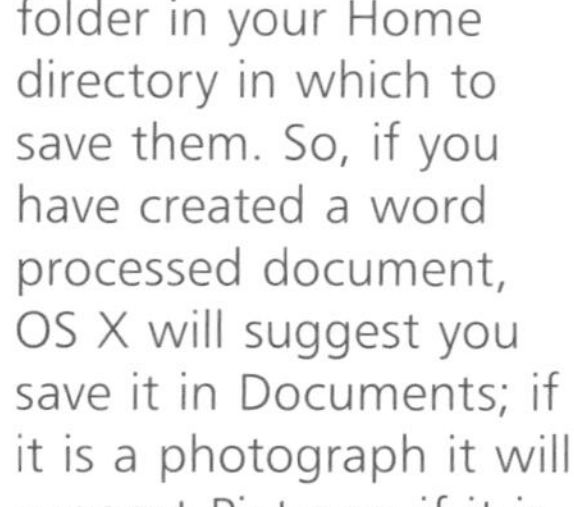

When you are creating documents OS X, by default, recognizes their type and then, when you save them, suggests the most applicable folder in your Home directory in which to save them. So, if you have created a word processed document, OS X will suggest you save it in Documents; if it is a photograph it will suggest Pictures; if it is a video it will suggest Movies, and so on.

Applications

This folder contains all of the applications on your MacBook. They can also be accessed from the Launchpad as shown on pages 114-115.

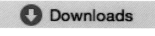

Downloads

This is the default folder for any files or apps that you download (other than those from the Apple App Store).

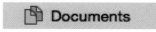

Documents

This is part of your Home folder but is put on the Finder Sidebar for ease of access. New folders can be created for different types of documents.

Finder Views

The way in which items are displayed within the Finder can be amended in a variety of ways, depending on how you want to view the contents of a folder. Different folders can have their own viewing options applied to them and these will stay in place until a new option is specified.

Icon view

One of the viewing options for displaying items within the Finder is as icons. This provides a graphical representation of the items in the Finder. It is also possible to customize Icon view:

1. Click here on the Finder toolbar to access **Icon** view

2. Select **View** from the Menu bar, check on **as Icons** and select **Show View Options** to access the options for customizing Icon view

View | Go | Window | Help
✓ as Icons ⌘1
as List ⌘2
as Columns ⌘3
as Cover Flow ⌘4
Clean Up Selection
Clean Up By ▸
Sort By ▸
Hide Tab Bar ⇧⌘T
Show Path Bar ⌥⌘P
Show Status Bar ⌘/
Hide Sidebar ⌥⌘S
Show Preview ⇧⌘P
Hide Toolbar ⌥⌘T
Customize Toolbar...
Show View Options ⌘J
Enter Full Screen ^⌘F

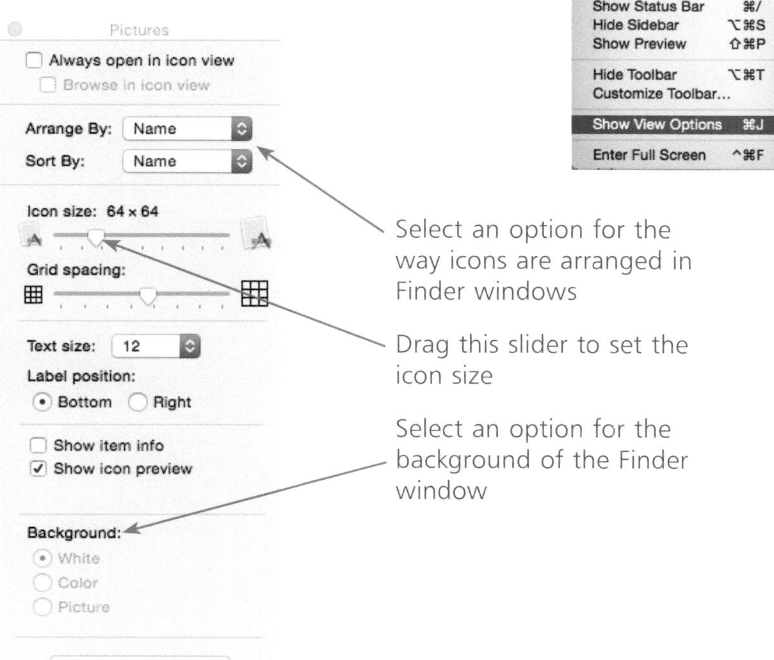

Use the Back and Forward buttons at the top of the Finder to move between windows that you have previously visited.

The **Arrange By** options can be used to arrange icons into specific groups, e.g. by name or type, or to snap them to an invisible grid so that they have an ordered appearance.

A very large icon size can be useful for people with poor eyesight, but it does take up a lot more space in a window.

...cont'd

List view

List view can be used to show the items within a Finder window as a list, with additional information shown next to them. This can be a more efficient method than Icon view if there are a lot of items within a folder: List view enables you to see more items at one time and also view the additional information.

Don't forget

List view can be customized to include a variety of information such as file size and date last modified.

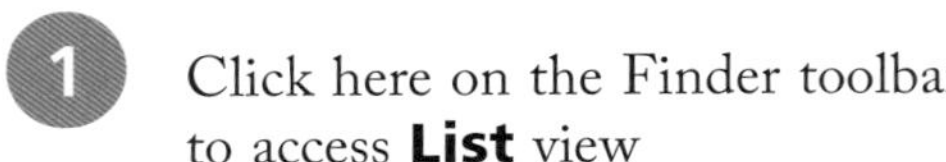

1. Click here on the Finder toolbar to access **List** view

2. The name of each folder or file is displayed here. If any item has additional elements within it, this is represented by a small triangle next to it. Additional information in List view, such as file size and last modified date, is included in columns to the right

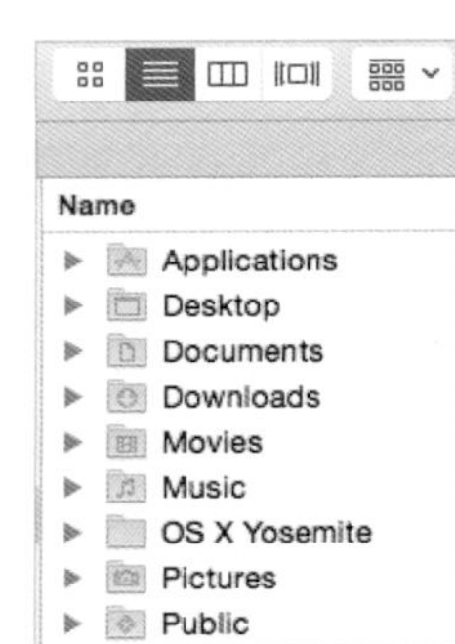

Column view

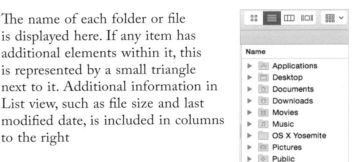

Column view is a useful option if you want to trace the location of a particular item, i.e. see the full path of its location, starting from the hard drive.

1. Click here on the Finder toolbar to access **Column** view

2. Click on an item to see everything within that folder. If an arrow follows an item it means that there are further items to view

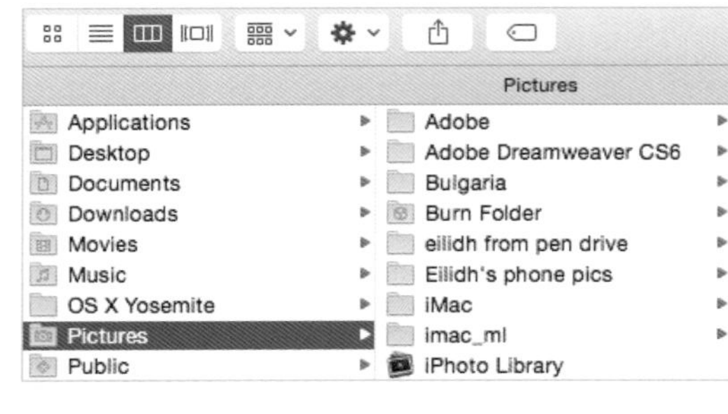

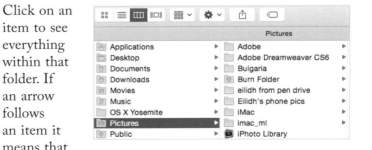

Covers and Quick Look

Covers

Covers is feature on the MacBook that enables you to view items as large icons. To use Covers:

1. Select a folder and at the top of the Finder window click on this button

2. The items within the folder are displayed in their cover state

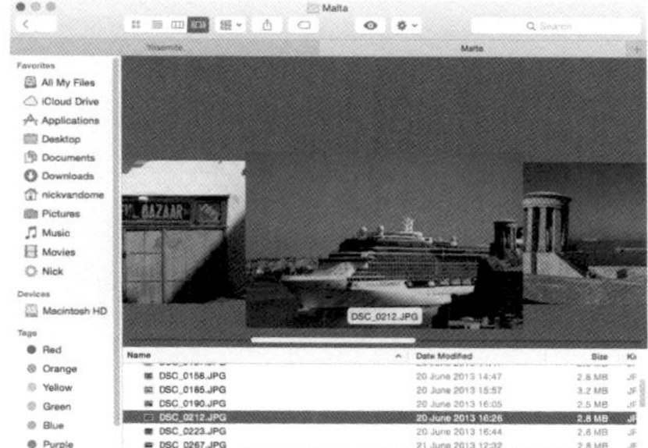

3. Drag each item to view the next one, or click on the slider at the bottom of the window. You can also move between items by swiping left or right on a trackpad

Quick Look

Through a Finder option called Quick Look, it is possible to view the content of a file without having to first open it. To do this:

1. Select a file within the Finder

2. Press the **Space bar**

3. The contents of the file are displayed without it opening in its default app

4. Click on the cross to close Quick Look

In Quick Look it is even possible to preview videos or presentations without having to first open them in their default app.

Finder Toolbar

Customizing the toolbar

As with most elements of OS X, it is possible to customize the Finder toolbar:

1. Select **View > Customize Toolbar** from the Menu bar

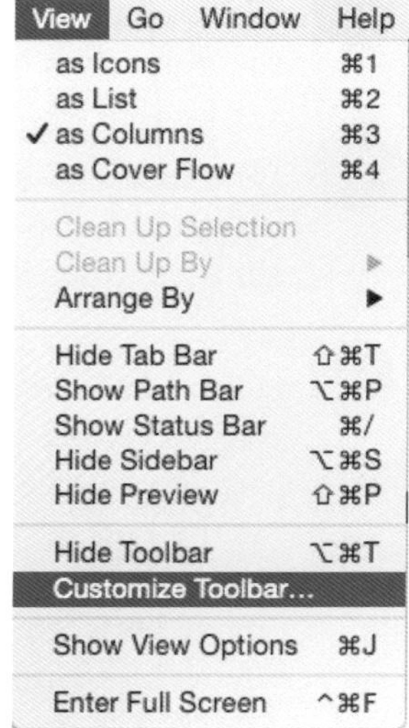

Do not put too many items on the Finder toolbar, because you may not be able to see them all in the Finder window. If there are additional toolbar items, there will be a directional arrow indicating this. Click on the arrow to view the available items.

2. Drag items from the window into the toolbar, or

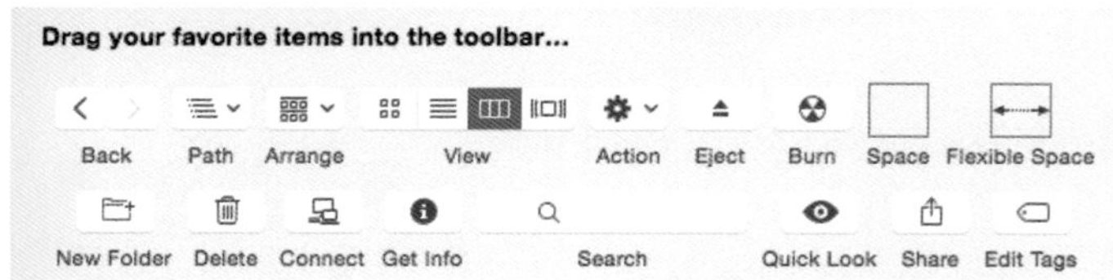

3. Drag the default set of icons into the toolbar

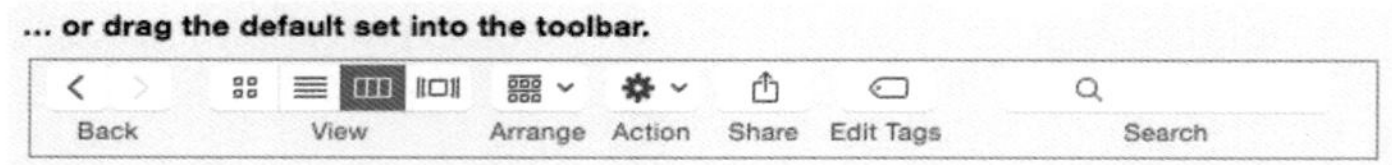

4. Click **Done** at the bottom of the window

Finder Sidebar

Using the Sidebar

The Sidebar is the left-hand panel of the Finder which can be used to access items on your MacBook:

1. Click on a button on the Sidebar

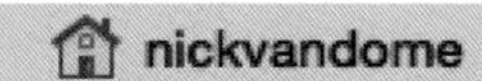

2. Its contents are displayed in the main Finder window

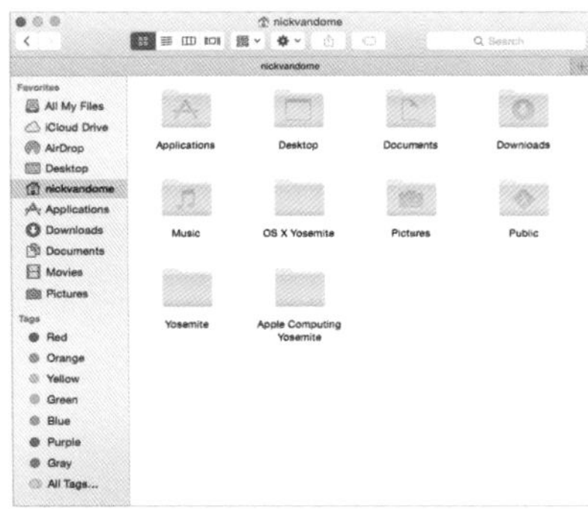

Adding to the Sidebar

Items that you access most frequently can be added to the Sidebar. To do this:

1. Drag an item from the main Finder window onto the Sidebar

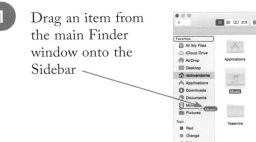

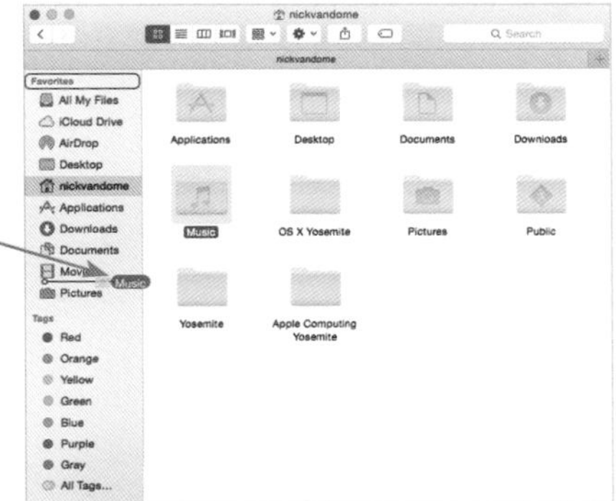

2. The item is added to the Sidebar. You can do this with apps, folders and files

When you click on an item in the Sidebar, its contents are shown in the main Finder window to its right.

When items are added to the Finder Sidebar a shortcut, or alias, is inserted into the Sidebar, not the actual item.

Items can be removed from the Sidebar by Ctrl+clicking on them and selecting Remove from Sidebar from the contextual menu.

Finder Tabs

Tabs in web browsers are now well established, where you can have several pages open within the same browser window. This technology is utilized in the Finder in OS X Yosemite with the use of Finder Tabs. This enables different folders to be open in different tabs within the Finder so that you can organize your content exactly how you want. To do this:

1. Select **View > Show Tab Bar** from the Finder menu bar

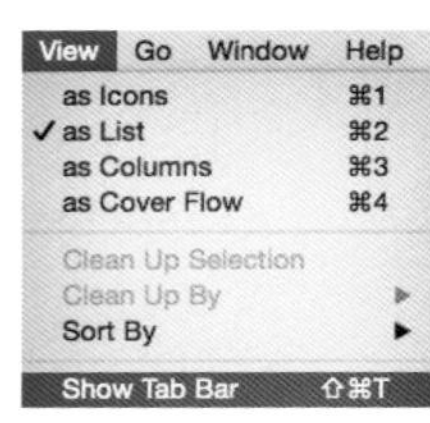

2. A new tab is opened at the right-hand side of the Finder

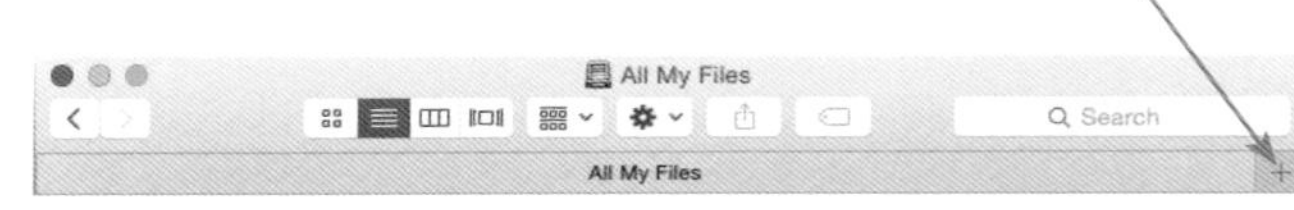

3. Click on this button to view the new tab

4. At this point the content in the new tab is displayed for the window (see tip)

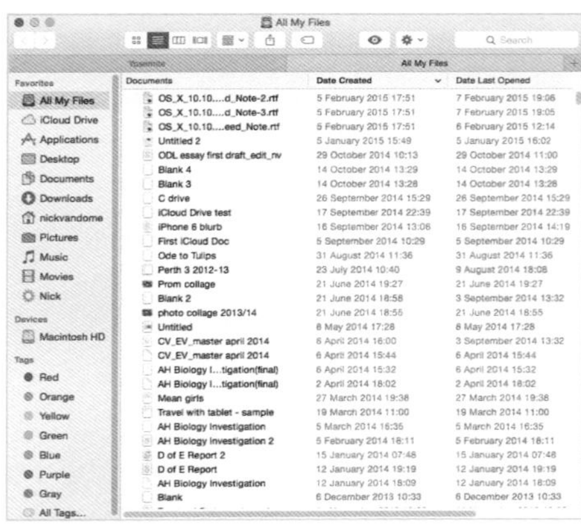

5. Each tab view can be customized and this is independent of the other tabs

To specify an option for what appears as the default for a new Finder window, click on the **Finder** menu and click on **Preferences** and the **General** tab. Under **New Finder windows show**, select the default window to be used.

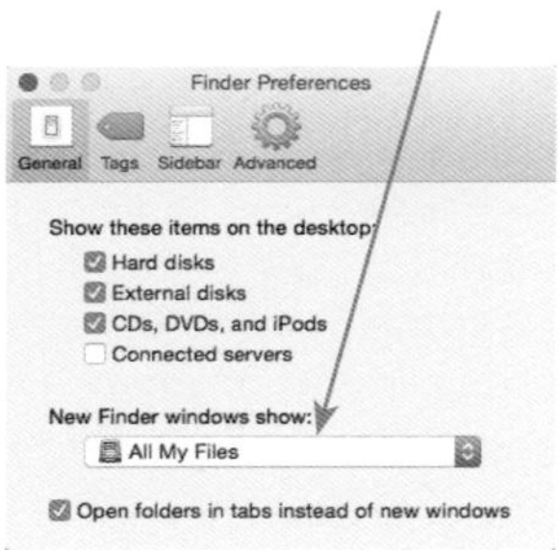

Finder Tags

When creating content in OS X Yosemite you may find that you have documents of different types that cover the same topic. For instance, you may have work-related documents in Pages for reports, Keynote for presentations and Numbers for spreadsheets. With the Finder Tags function it is possible to link related content items through the use of colored tags. These can be added to items in the Finder and also in apps when content is created.

Tags can also be added to items by Ctrl+clicking on them and selecting the required tag from the menu that appears. Also, they can be added from this button on the main Finder toolbar.

1. The tags are listed in the Finder Sidebar

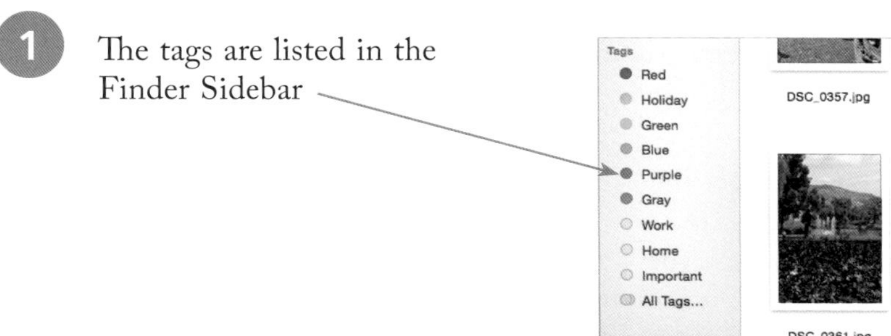

2. To give tags specific names, Ctrl+click on one and click on the **Rename** link

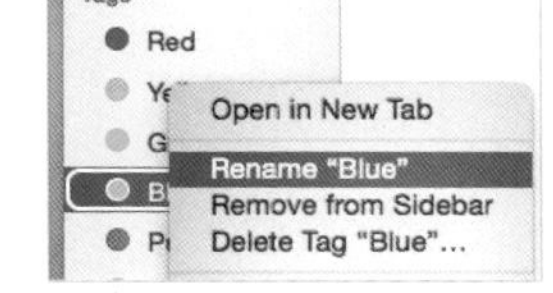

3. To add tags, select the required items in the Finder window

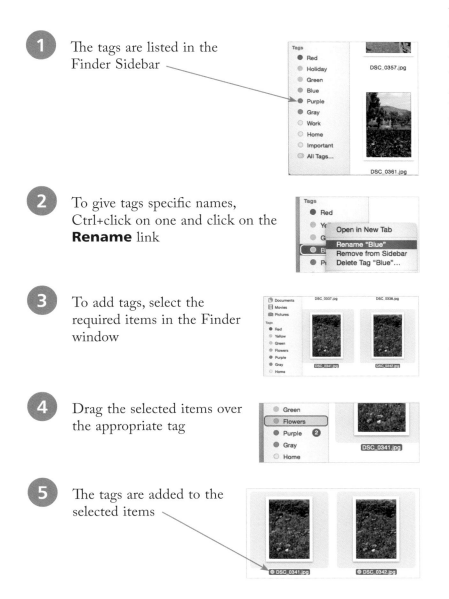

4. Drag the selected items over the appropriate tag

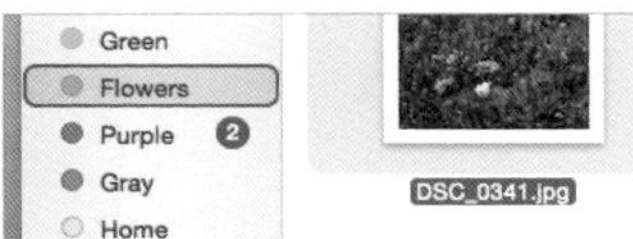

5. The tags are added to the selected items

Tags can also be added when documents are created in certain apps, such as Pages, Keynote and Numbers: Select **File > Save**, click in the **Tags** box and select the required tag. Click on the **Save** button.

Searching for Items

On MacBooks it is also possible to search your folders and files, using the built-in search facilities. This can be done either through the Finder or with the Spotlight search app.

Using Finder

1. In the Finder window, enter the search keyword(s) in this box and select the search criteria. The results are shown in the Finder

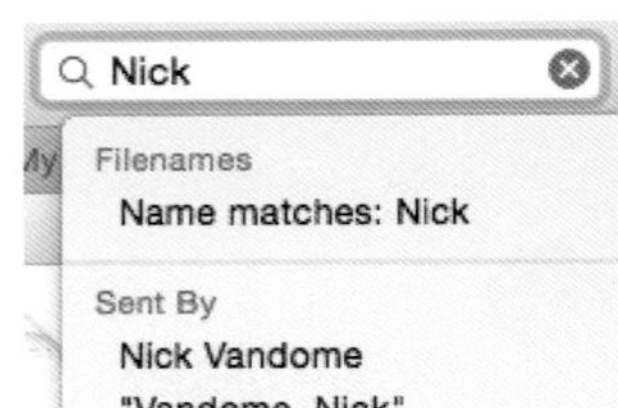

2. Select the areas over which you want the search performed, e.g. Home folder or Documents

3. Double-click on a folder to see its contents or double-click on a file to open it

Using Spotlight

The Spotlight search option can also search over your MacBook:

1. Click on this button in the right corner of the screen on the top toolbar

2. Enter a search word or phrase. Click on an item to view it, including items from the Web and Wikipedia

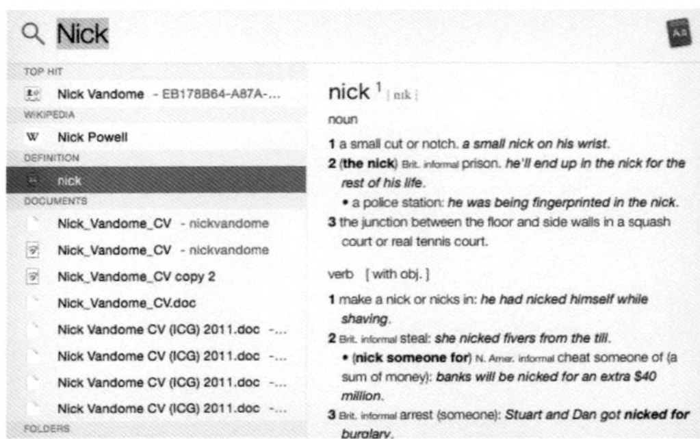

When entering search keywords try to be as specific as possible. This will cut down on the number of unwanted results.

Both folders and files will be displayed in the Finder as part of the search results.

Spotlight search can show results from your Mac, the Internet, iTunes, the App Store and also items such as movies nearby and local restaurants.

Copying and Moving Items

Items can be copied and moved within OS X by using the copy and paste method or by dragging:

Copy and paste

When an item is copied, it is placed on the Clipboard and remains there until another item is copied.

1. Select an item and select **Edit > Copy** from the Menu bar

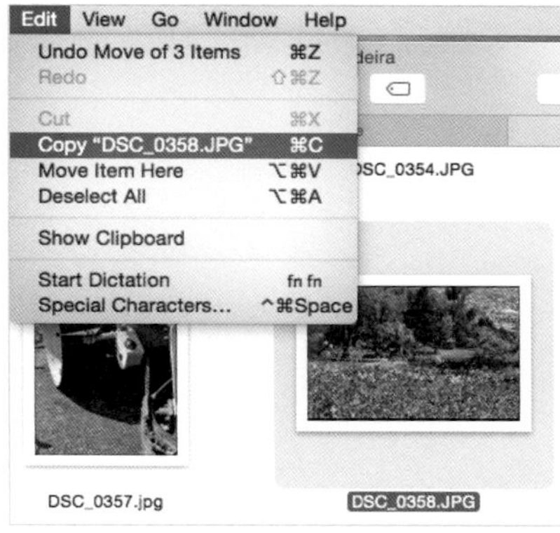

2. Move to the target location and select **Edit > Paste Item** from the Menu bar. The item is then pasted into the new location

Dragging

Drag a file from one location into another to move it to that location

Hold down the Option key while dragging to copy an item rather than moving it.

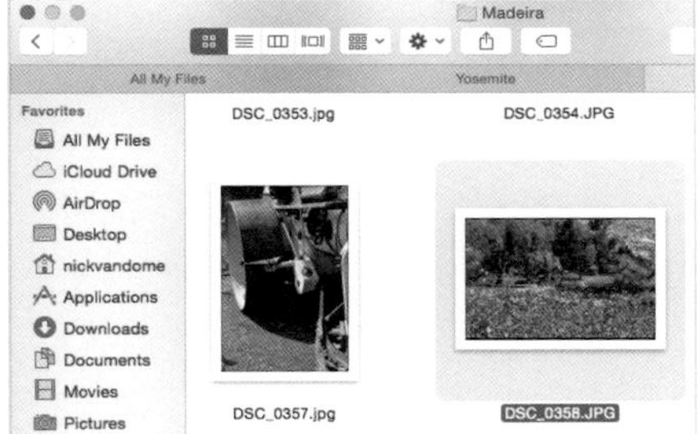

Working with Folders

When OS X is installed, there are various folders that have already been created to hold apps and files. Some of these are essential (i.e. those containing apps) while others are created as an aid for where you might want to store the files that you create (such as the Pictures and Movies folders). Once you start working with OS X you will probably want to create your own folders in which to store and organize your documents. This can be done on the Desktop or within any level of your existing folder structure. To create a new folder:

Don't forget

Folders are always denoted by a folder icon. This is the same regardless of the Finder view which is selected. The only difference is that the icon is larger in Icon view than in List or Column views.

1. Access the location in which you want to create the new folder (e.g. your Home folder) and select **File > New Folder** from the Menu bar

2. A new, empty, folder is inserted at the selected location (named "untitled folder")

You can create as many "nested" folders (i.e. folders within other folders) as you want. However, this makes your folder structure more complicated and, after time, you may forget where all your folders are and what they contain.

3. Overtype the file name with a new one. Press **Enter** on the keyboard

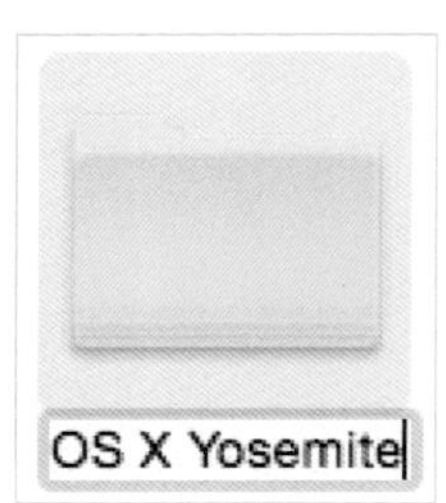

4. Double-click on a folder to view its contents (at this point it should be empty)

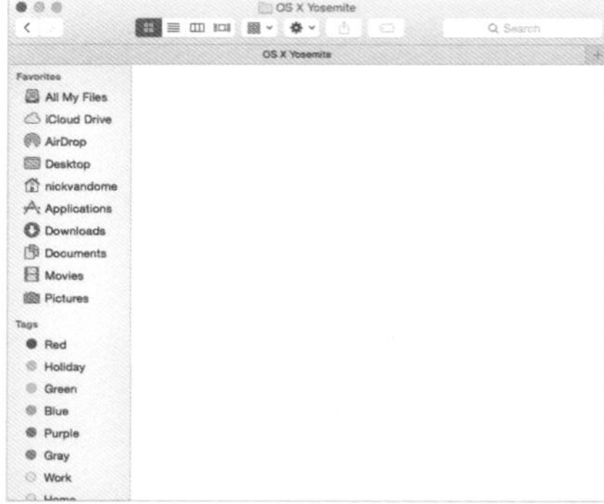

Content can be added to an empty folder by dragging it from another folder and dropping it into the new one.

Spring-loaded Folders

Another method for moving items with the Finder is to use the spring-loaded folder option. This enables you to drag items into a folder and then view the contents of the folder before you drop the item into it. This means that you can drag items into nested folders in a single operation. To do this:

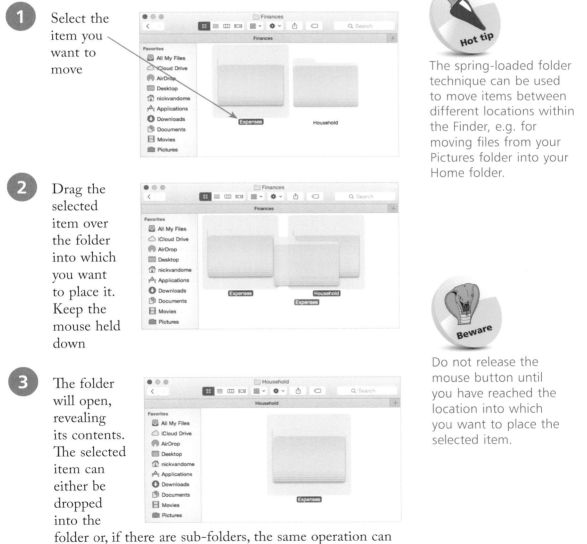

1. Select the item you want to move

2. Drag the selected item over the folder into which you want to place it. Keep the mouse held down

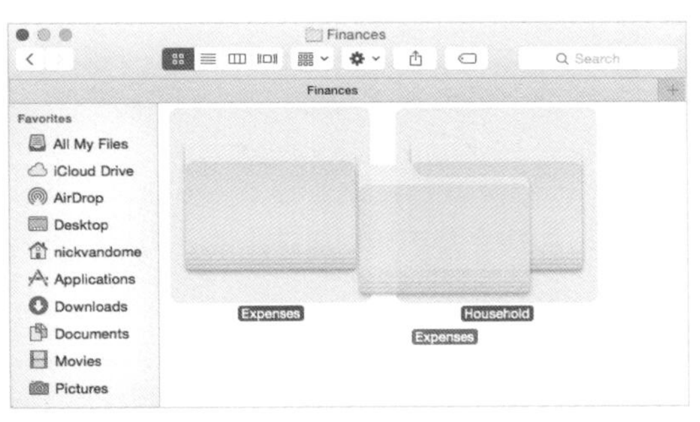

3. The folder will open, revealing its contents. The selected item can either be dropped into the folder or, if there are sub-folders, the same operation can be repeated until you find the folder into which you want to place the selected item

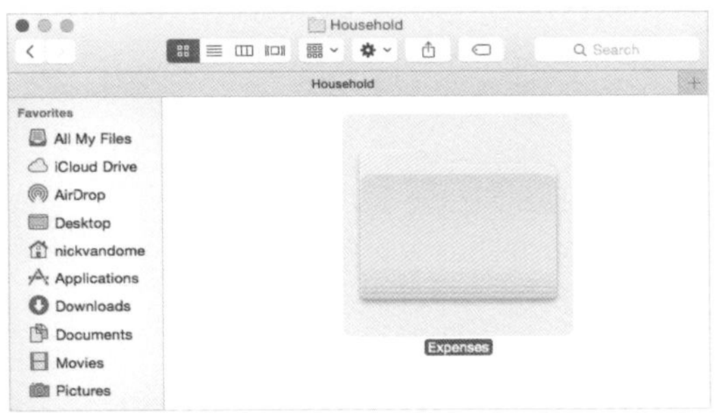

The spring-loaded folder technique can be used to move items between different locations within the Finder, e.g. for moving files from your Pictures folder into your Home folder.

Do not release the mouse button until you have reached the location into which you want to place the selected item.

Smart Folders

When working on any computer it is inevitable that you will soon have a number of related files in different locations. This could be because you save your images in one folder, your word processing documents in another, web pages in another and so on. This can cause difficulties when you are trying to keep track of a lot of related documents. OS X overcomes this problem through the use of Smart Folders. These are folders that you set up using Finder search results as the foundation. Then, when new items are created that meet the original criteria, they are automatically included within the Smart Folder. To create a Smart Folder:

Numerous different Smart Folders can be created, for different types of files and information.

If you set very precise criteria for a Smart Folder this will result in a smaller number of items being included within it.

1. Conduct a search with the Finder search box

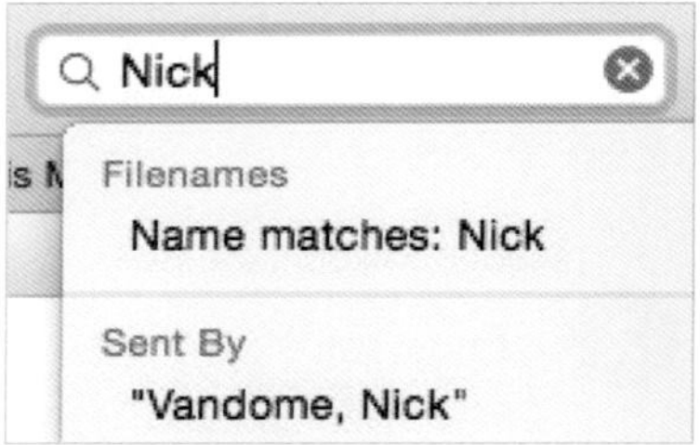

2. Once the search is completed, click the **Save** button to create a Smart Folder

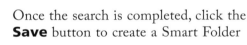

3. Enter a name for the new Smart Folder and click **Save**

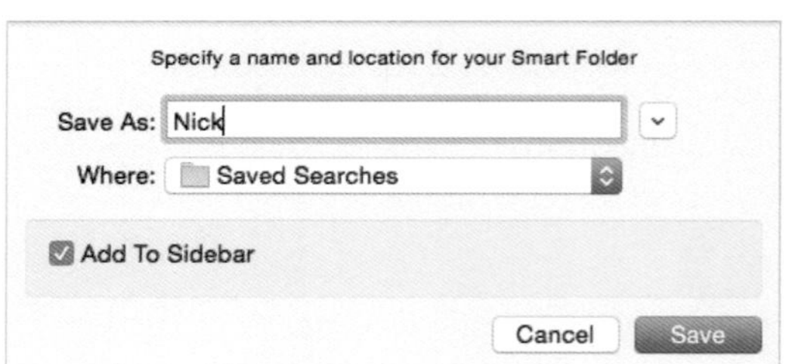

4. The Smart Folder is added to the Finder Sidebar. Click the Smart Folder to view its contents

Selecting Items

Apps and files within OS X folders can be selected by a variety of different methods:

Selecting by dragging

Drag the cursor to encompass the items to be selected. The selected items will become highlighted.

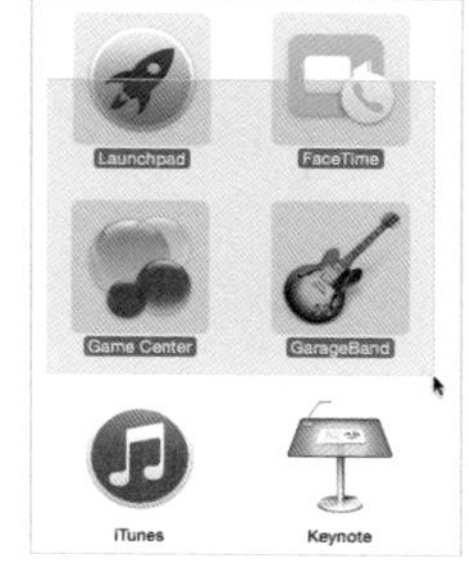

Don't forget

Once items have been selected, a single command can be applied to all of them. For instance, you can copy a group of items by selecting them and then applying the Copy command from the Menu bar.

Selecting by clicking

Click once on an item to select it, hold down Shift and then click on another item in a list to select a consecutive group of items.

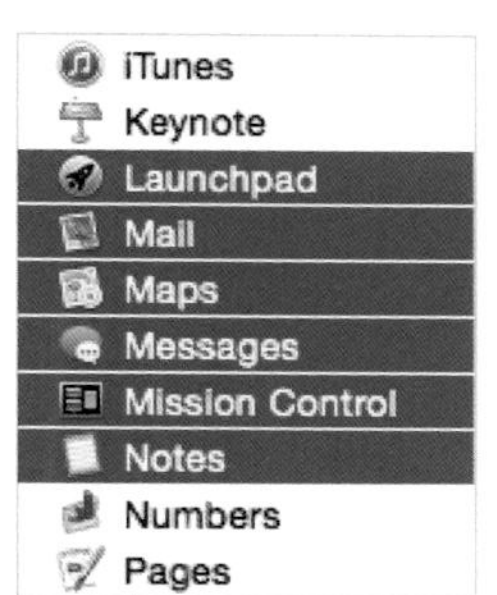

To select a non-consecutive group, select the first item by clicking on it once, then hold down the Command key and select the other required items. The selected items will appear highlighted.

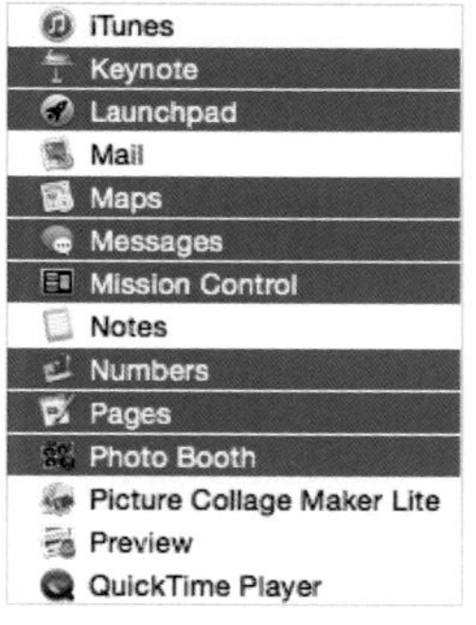

Don't forget

The Select All command selects all of the elements within the active item. For instance, if the active item is a word processing document, the Select All command will select all of the items within the document; if it is a folder it will select all of the items within that folder.

Select All

To select all of the items in a folder, select **Edit > Select All** from the Menu bar:

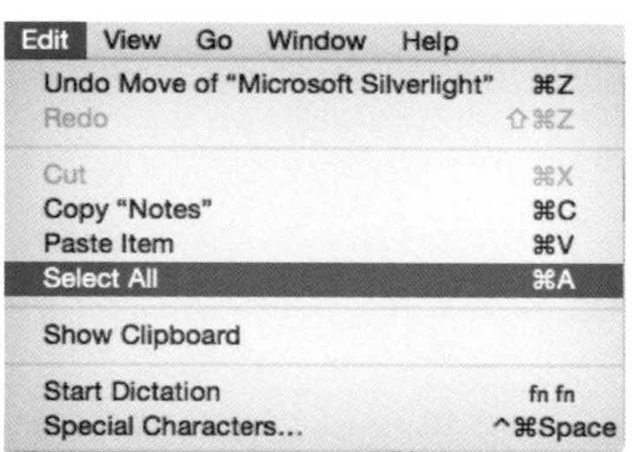

Actions Button

The Finder Actions button provides a variety of options for any item, or items, selected in the Finder. To use this:

1. Select an item, or group of items, about which you want to find out additional information

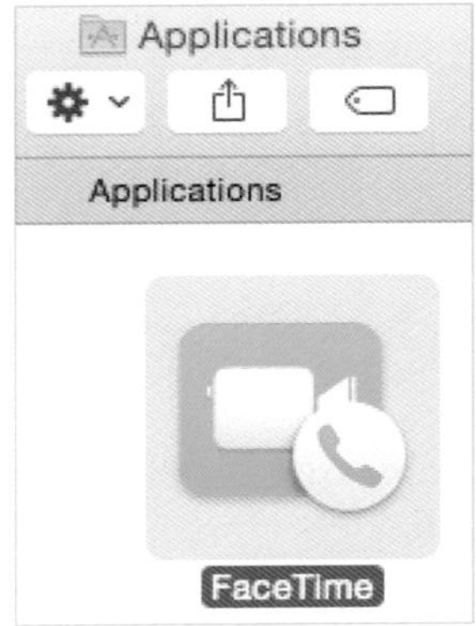

2. Click on the **Actions** button on the Finder toolbar

3. The available options for the selected item, or items, are displayed. These include **Get Info**, which displays additional information about an item, such as file type, file size, creation and modification dates and the default app for opening the item

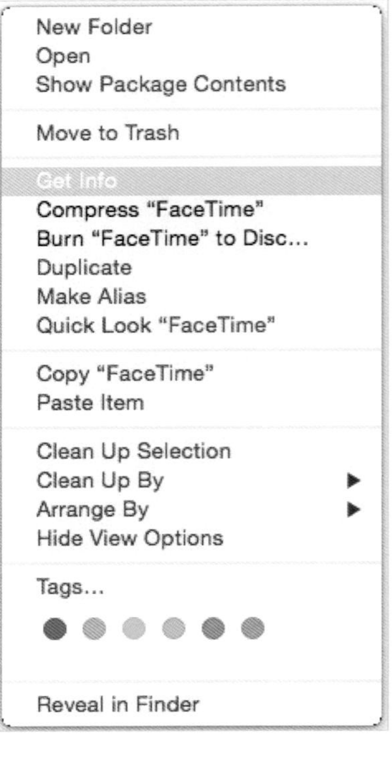

If an image has been selected, the Actions button can be used to set it as the Desktop Picture, by selecting this option at the bottom of the Actions menu.

The **Actions** button can also be used for labeling items. To do this, select the required items in the Finder and click on the colored buttons at the bottom of the Actions button menu. The selected color will be applied to the item names in the Finder.

Sharing from the Finder

Next but one to the Actions button on the Finder is the Share button. This can be used to share a selected item, or items, in a variety of ways appropriate to the type of file that has been selected. For instance, a photo will have options including the photo-sharing site Flickr while a text document will have fewer options. To share items directly from the Finder:

Hot tip

The Share button is available from many apps throughout Yosemite. This means that there is increased functionality for sharing items. For instance, you can share web pages from Safari or share photos from iPhoto.

1. Locate and select the item(s) that you want to share

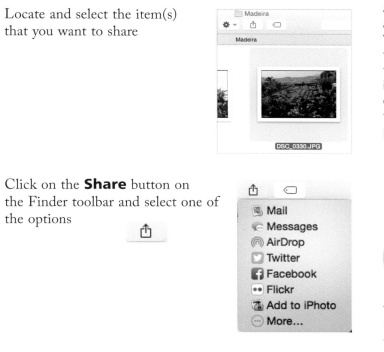

2. Click on the **Share** button on the Finder toolbar and select one of the options

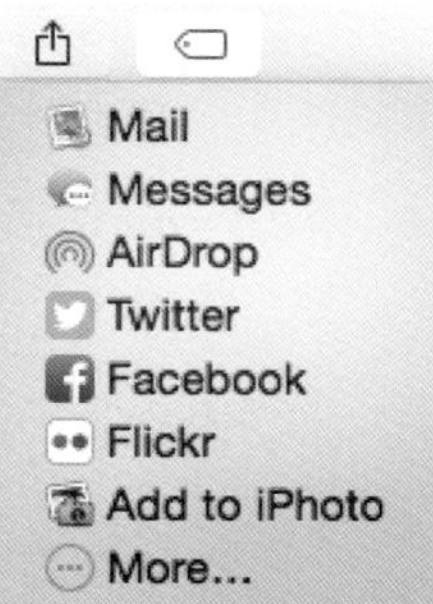

3. For some of the options, such as Twitter and Flickr, you will be asked to add an account. If you already have an account with these services you can enter the details or, if not, you can create a new account

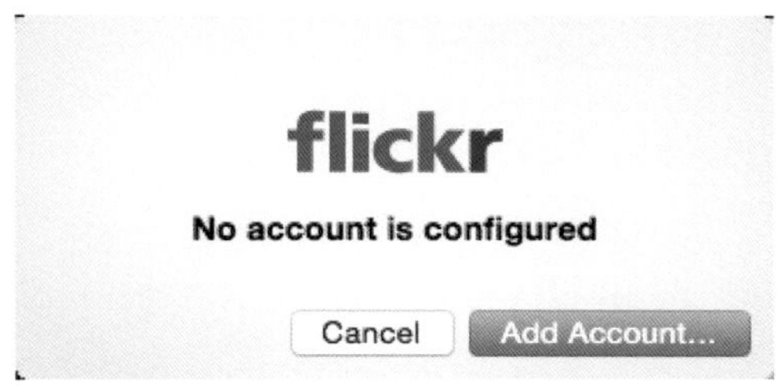

Don't forget

To the left of the Share button on the Finder toolbar is a button for changing the arrangement of items within the Finder. Click on this button to access arrangement options such as Name, Kind, Date and Size.

Menus

The main Apple menu bar in OS X Yosemite contains a variety of menus, which are accessed when the Finder is the active window. When individual apps are open they have their own menu bars, although in a lot of cases these are similar to the standard menu bar, particularly for the built-in OS X Yosemite apps such as the Calendar, Contacts and Notes.

- **Apple menu**. This is denoted by a translucent gray apple and contains general information about the computer, a preferences option for changing the functionality and appearance of your MacBook and options for closing down the computer.
- **Finder menu**. This contains preferences options for amending the functionality and appearance of the Finder and also options for emptying the Trash and accessing other apps (under the Services option).
- **File menu**. This contains common commands for working with open documents, such as opening and closing files, creating aliases, moving to the Trash, ejecting external devices and burning discs.
- **Edit menu**. This contains common commands that apply to the majority of apps used on the Mac. These include undo, cut, copy, paste, select all and show the contents of the clipboard, i.e. items that have been cut or copied.
- **View**. This contains options for how windows and folders are displayed within the Finder and for customizing the Finder toolbar. This includes showing or hiding the Finder Sidebar and selecting view options for the size at which icons are displayed within Finder windows.
- **Go**. This can be used to navigate around your computer. This includes moving to your All My Files folder, your Home folder, your Applications folder and recently accessed folders.
- **Window**. This contains commands to organize the currently open apps and files on your Desktop.
- **Help**. This contains the Mac Help files which contain information about all aspects of OS X Yosemite.

6 Navigating in Yosemite

OS X Yosemite uses multi-touch gestures for navigating your apps and documents. This chapter looks at how to use these to get around your MacBook.

Navigating with MacBooks

One of the most revolutionary features of OS X is the way in which you can navigate around your applications, web pages and documents. This involves a much greater reliance on swiping on a trackpad or adapted mouse; techniques that have been imported from the iPhone and the iPad. These are known as multi-touch gestures and work most effectively with the trackpad on MacBooks. Other devices can also be used to perform multi-touch gestures:

- **A Magic Trackpad**. This is an external trackpad that works wirelessly via Bluetooth, but there should not really be any need for one with a MacBook.
- **A Magic Mouse**. This is an external mouse that works wirelessly via Bluetooth.

These devices, and the trackpad, work using a swiping technique with fingers moving over their surface. This should be done with a light touch; it is a gentle swipe, rather than any pressure being applied to the device.

The trackpads and Magic Mouse do not have any buttons in the same way as traditional devices. Instead, specific areas are clickable so that you can still perform left- and right-click operations:

The new MacBook and MacBook Pro Retina display 13-inch both have Force Touch technology on the trackpad. This still allows for the usual range of multi-touch gestures but can also be used for other functions, depending on the amount of pressure that is applied to the trackpad. Settings for this can be applied in the **Trackpad** section within **System Preferences**.

1. Click on the bottom left corner for traditional left-click operations

2. Ctrl+click on the bottom right corner for traditional right-click operations

Pointing and Clicking

A trackpad or Magic Mouse can be used to perform a variety of pointing and clicking tasks.

1. Tap with one finger in the middle of the trackpad or Magic Mouse to perform a single click operation, e.g. to click on a button or click on an open window

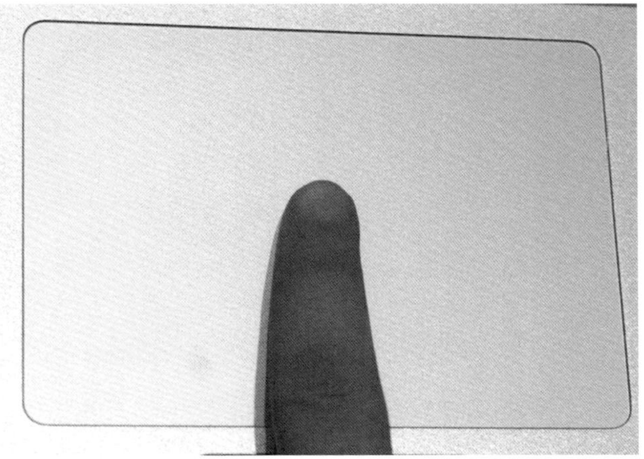

2. Tap with two fingers in the middle of the trackpad or Magic Mouse to access any contextual menus associated with an item (this is the equivalent of the traditional right-click with a mouse)

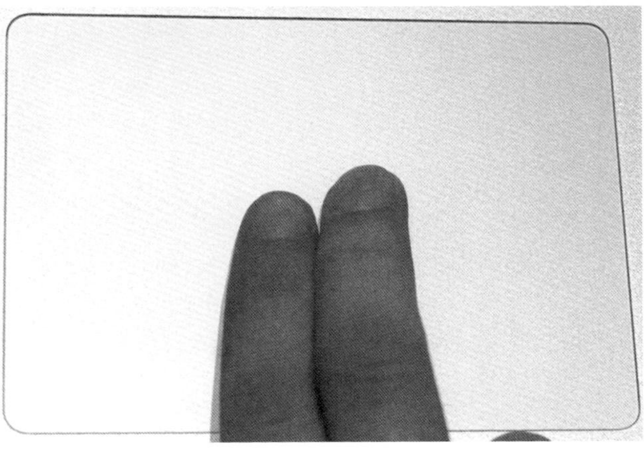

...cont'd

3. Highlight a word or phrase and double-tap with three fingers to see look-up information for the selected item. This is frequently a dictionary definition but it can also be a Wikipedia entry

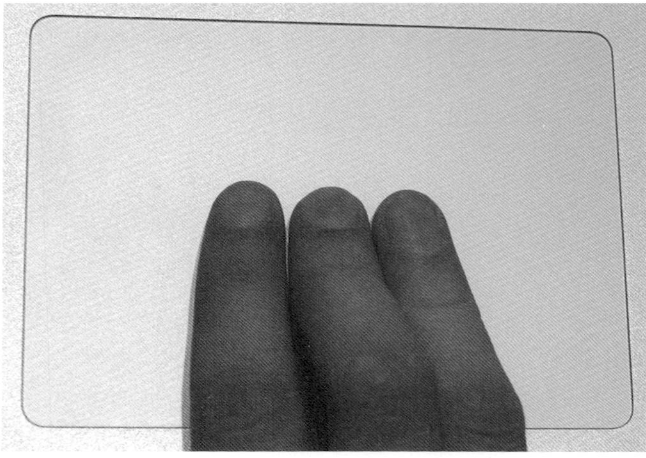

If you have too many functions set using the same number of fingers, some of them many not work. See pages 110–111 for details about setting preferences for multi-touch gestures.

4. Move over an item and drag with three fingers to move the item around the screen

No More Scroll Bars

Another innovation in OS X is the removal of scroll bars that are constantly visible on a web page or document. Instead, there are scroll bars that only appear when you are moving around a page or document. When you stop, the scroll bars melt away. Scrolling is done by multi-touch gestures on a trackpad or Magic Mouse and these gestures are looked at on the following pages. To perform scrolling with OS X Yosemite:

1. Scroll around a web page or document using the two finger multi-touch technique (see pages 102-103). As you move up or down a page the scroll bar appears

Web pages and document windows can also be navigated around by dragging on the scroll bars using a mouse or a trackpad.

2. When you stop scrolling the bar disappears, to allow optimum viewing area for your web page or document

Scrolling and Zooming

One of the common operations on a computer is scrolling on a page, whether it is a web page or a document. Traditionally this has been done with a mouse and a cursor. However, using a trackpad or Magic Mouse you can now do all of your scrolling with your fingers. There are a number of options for doing this:

Scrolling up and down

To move up and down web pages or documents, use two fingers on the trackpad and swipe up or down. The page moves in the opposite direction to the one in which you are swiping, i.e. if you swipe up, the page moves down and vice versa:

Don't forget

Don't worry if you cannot immediately get the hang of multi-touch gestures. It takes a bit of practice to get the correct touch and pressure on the trackpad or Magic Mouse.

1. Open a web page

2. Position two fingers in the middle of the trackpad

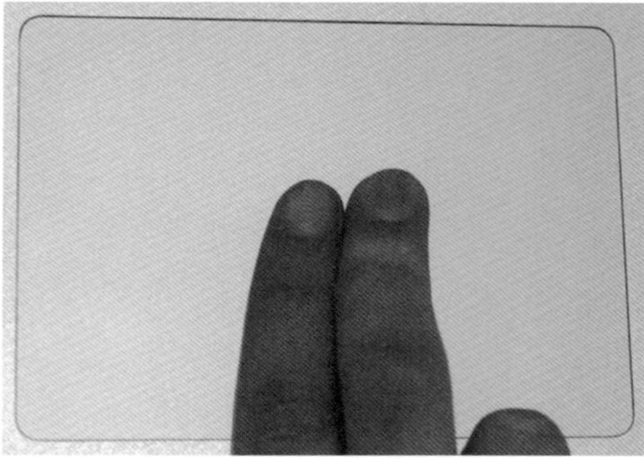

3. Swipe them up to move down the page

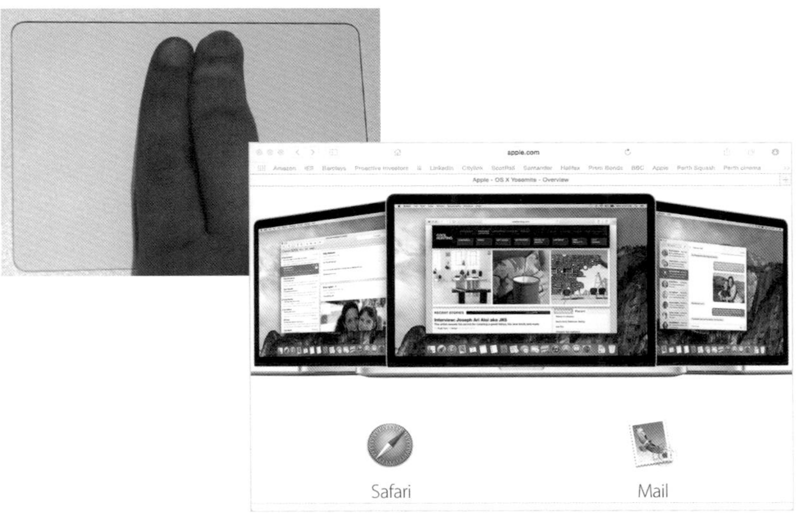

When scrolling up and down pages, the gesture moves the page the opposite way, i.e. swipe down to move up the page and vice versa.

4. Swipe them down to move up a page

...cont'd

Zooming in and out

To zoom in or out on web pages or documents:

1. To zoom in, position your thumb and forefinger in the middle of the trackpad

2. Spread them outwards to zoom in on a web page or document

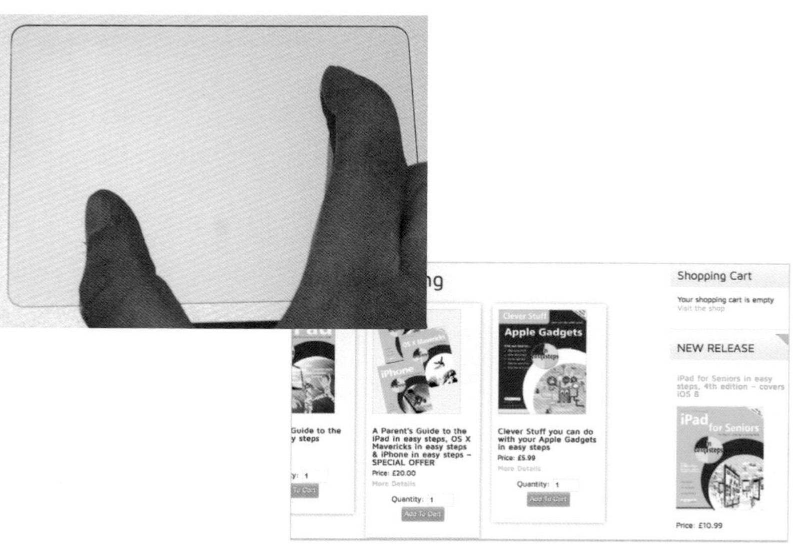

Pages can also be zoomed in on by double-clicking with two fingers.

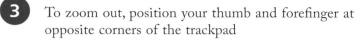

...cont'd

3. To zoom out, position your thumb and forefinger at opposite corners of the trackpad

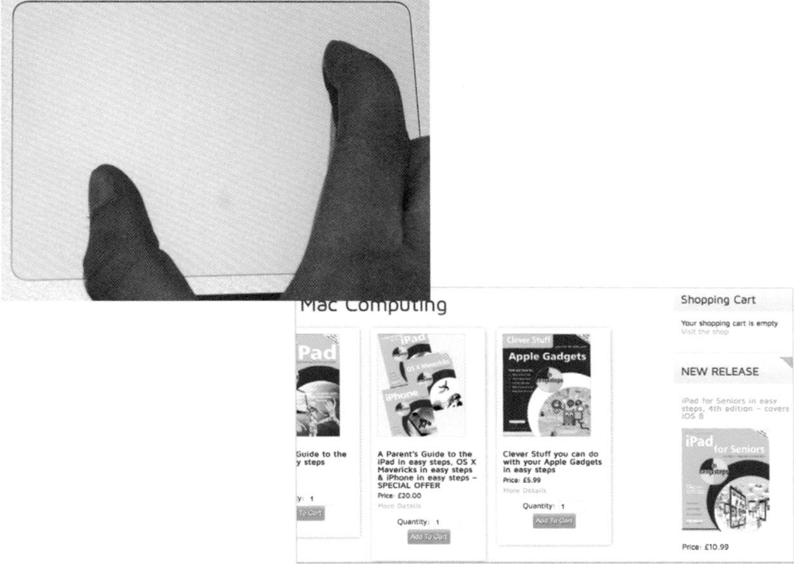

There is a limit on how far you can zoom in or out on a web page or document, to ensure that it does not distort the content too much.

4. Swipe them into the center of the trackpad to zoom out

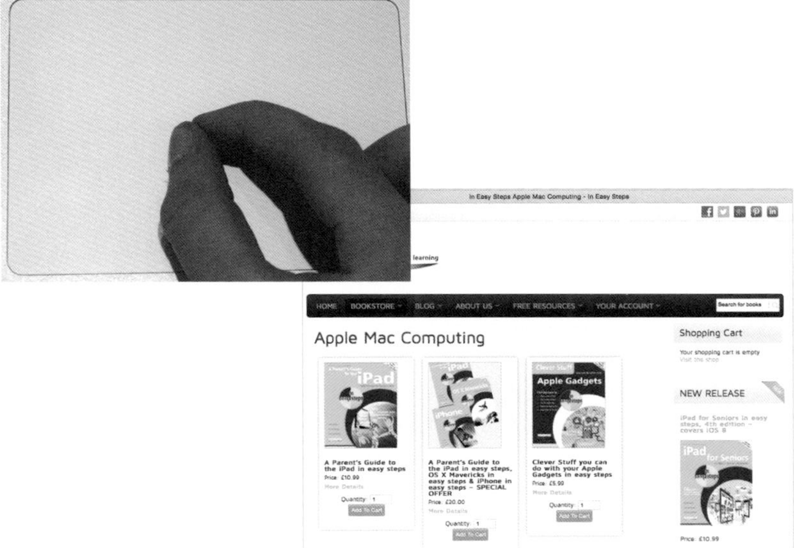

...cont'd

Moving between pages

With multi-touch gestures it is possible to swipe between pages within a document. To do this:

1. Position two fingers to the left or right of the trackpad

2. Swipe to the opposite side of the trackpad to move through the document

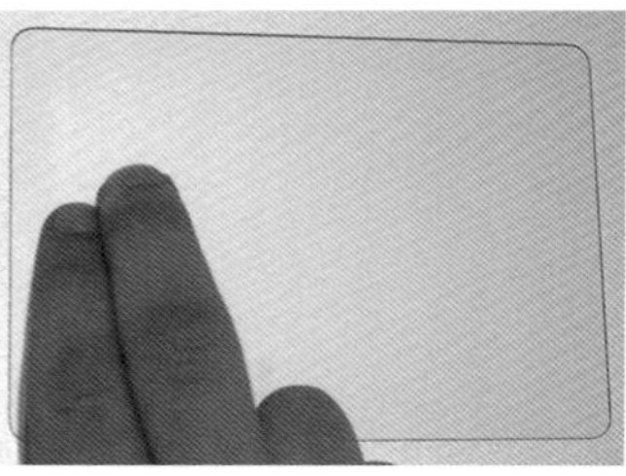

See Chapter Seven for details about using full-screen apps.

Moving between full-screen apps

In addition to moving between pages by swiping, it is also possible to move between different apps, when they are in full-screen mode. To do this:

1. Position three fingers to the left or right of the trackpad

2. Swipe to the opposite side of the trackpad to move through the available full-screen apps

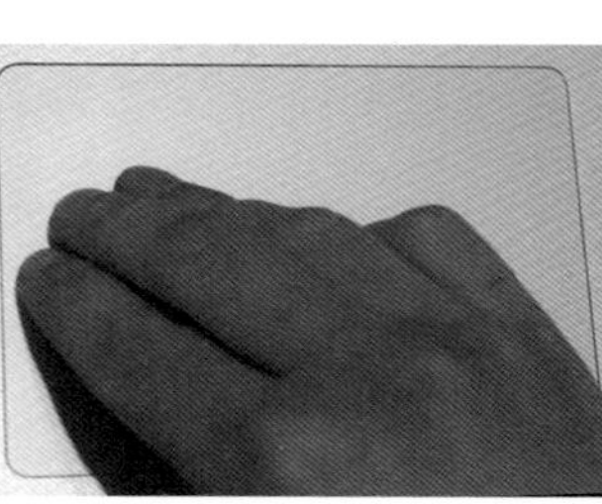

Showing the Desktop

To show the whole Desktop, regardless of how many files or apps are open:

1. Position your thumb and three fingers in the middle of the trackpad

2. Swipe to the opposite corners of the trackpad to display the Desktop

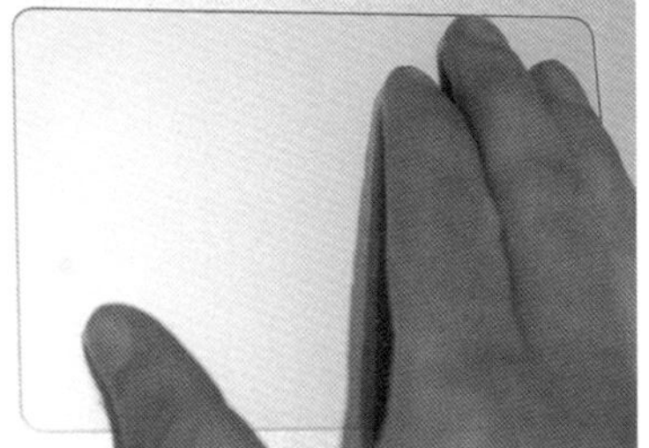

3. The Desktop is displayed, with all items minimized around the side of the screen

Mission Control

Mission Control is a function in OS X Yosemite that helps you organize all of your open apps, full-screen apps and documents. It also enables you to quickly view the Dashboard and Desktop. Within Mission Control there are also Spaces, where you can group together similar types of documents. To use Mission Control:

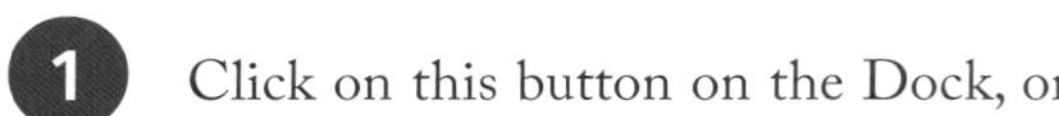

1. Click on this button on the Dock, or

Click on a window in Mission Control to access it and exit the Mission Control window.

2. Swipe upwards with three fingers on the trackpad or Magic Mouse (or press Fn+F9 on the keyboard)

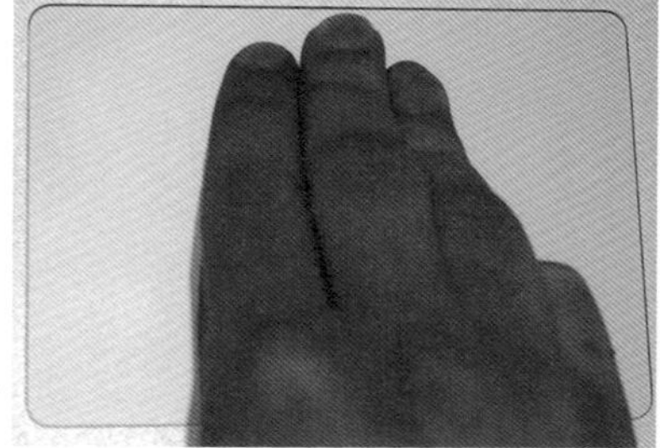

3. All open files and apps are visible via Mission Control

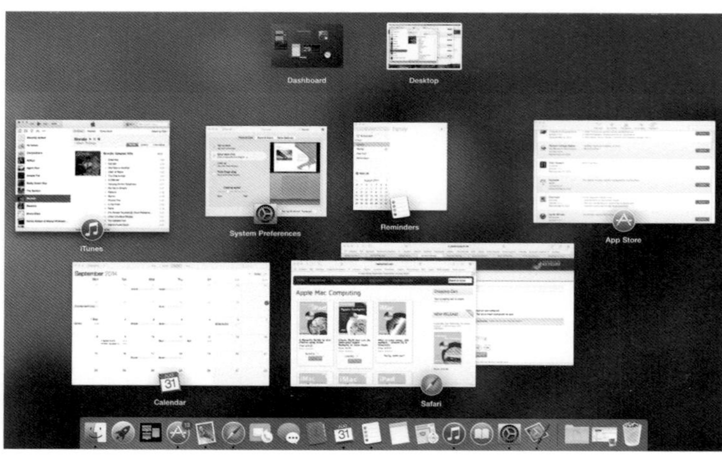

The top row of Mission Control contains the Dashboard, the Desktop and any full-screen apps.

4. If there is more than one window open for an app they will be grouped together by Mission Control

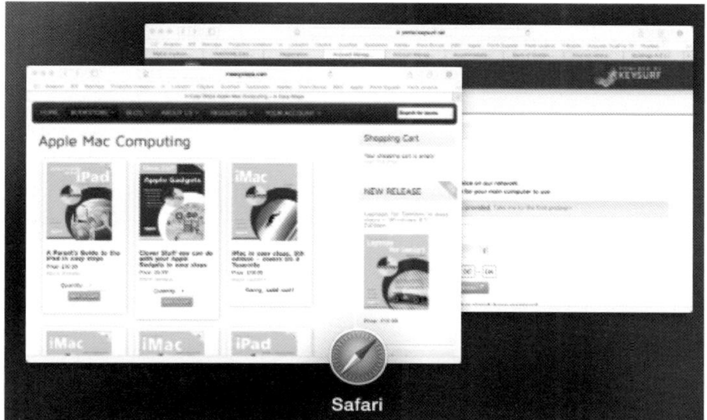

5. If an app is made full-screen it automatically appears along the top row

6. Desktop items are grouped together on the top row within Mission Control within an area called a Space

Any apps or files that have been minimized or closed do not appear within the main Mission Control window. Instead they are located to the right of the dividing line on the Dock.

Multi-Touch Preferences

Some multi-touch gestures only have a single action, which cannot be changed. However, others have options for changing the action for a specific gesture. This is done within the Trackpad preferences, where a full list of multi-touch gestures is shown:

Point & Click Preferences

1. Access the System Preferences and click on the **Trackpad** button

2. Click on the **Point & Click** tab

3. The actions are described on the left, with a graphic explanation on the right

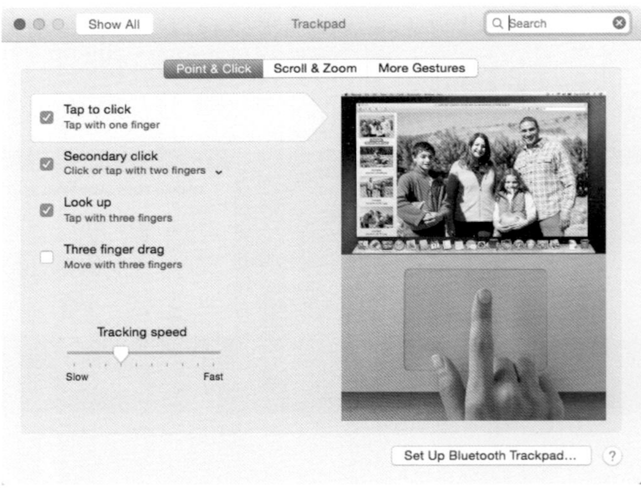

4. If there is a down arrow next to an option, click on it to change the way an action is activated

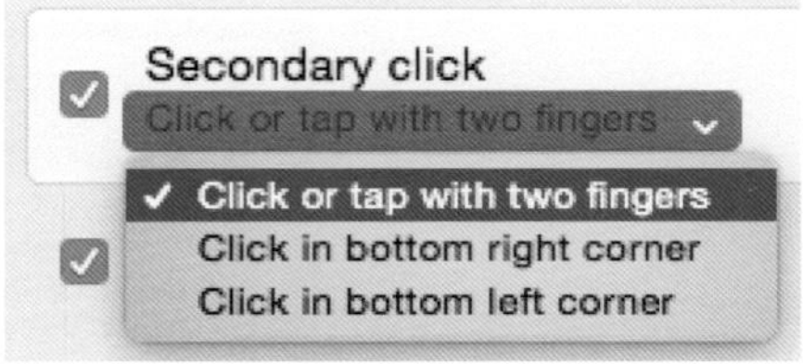

When setting multi-touch preferences try to avoid having too many gestures using the same number of fingers, in case some of them over-ride the others.

Scroll & Zoom Preferences

1. Click on the **Scroll & Zoom** tab

2. The actions are described on the left, with a graphic explanation on the right

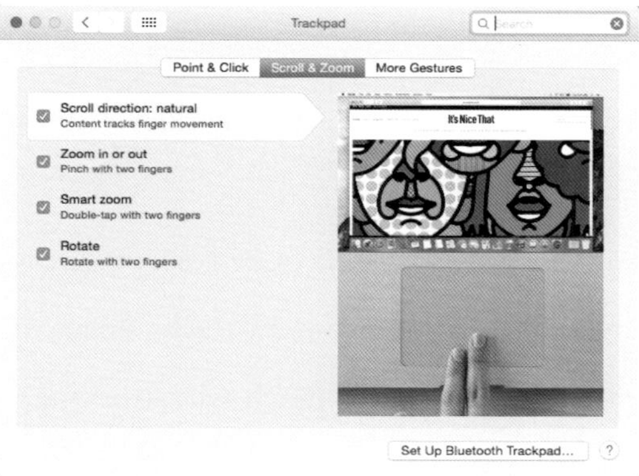

More Gestures Preferences

1. Click on the **More Gestures** tab

2. The actions are described on the left, with a graphic explanation on the right

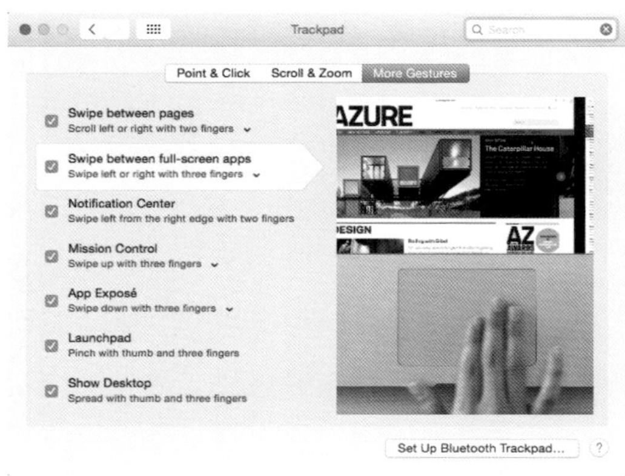

...cont'd

Multi-Touch Gestures

The full list of multi-touch gestures, with their default actions are:

Point & Click

- Tap to click – tap with one finger
- Secondary click – click or tap with two fingers
- Look up – double-tap with three fingers
- Three finger drag – move with three fingers

Scroll & Zoom

- Scroll direction: natural – content tracks finger movement
- Zoom in or out – spread or pinch with two fingers
- Smart zoom – double-tap with two fingers
- Rotate – rotate with two fingers

More Gestures

- Swipe between pages – scroll left or right with two fingers
- Swipe between full-screen apps – swipe left or right with three fingers
- Access Mission Control – swipe up with three fingers
- Access the Notification Center – swipe left from the right-hand edge of the trackpad or Magic Trackpad
- App Exposé – swipe down with three fingers. This displays the open windows for a specific app
- Access Launchpad – pinch with thumb and three fingers
- Show Desktop – spread with thumb and three fingers

7 Yosemite Apps

Apps, or applications, are the programs with which you start putting Yosemite to use. This chapter looks at accessing your apps and obtaining more via the online Mac App Store.

Launchpad

Even though the Dock can be used to store shortcuts to your applications, it is limited in terms of space. The full set of applications on your MacBook can be found in the Finder (in the Applications folder) but OS X Yosemite has a feature that allows you to quickly access and manage all of your applications. These include the ones that are pre-installed on your MacBook and also any that you install yourself or download from the Apple App Store. This feature is called Launchpad. To use it:

If the apps take up more than one screen, swipe from right to left with two fingers to view the additional pages. (For more information on multi-touch gestures, see Chapter Six.)

1. Click once on this button on the Dock

2. All of the apps are displayed

To launch an app from within Launchpad, click on it once.

3. Similar types of apps can be grouped together in individual folders. By default, the Utilities are grouped in this way

4. To create a group of similar apps, drag the icon for one over another

5. The apps are grouped together in a folder and Launchpad gives it a name, based on the types of apps within the folder

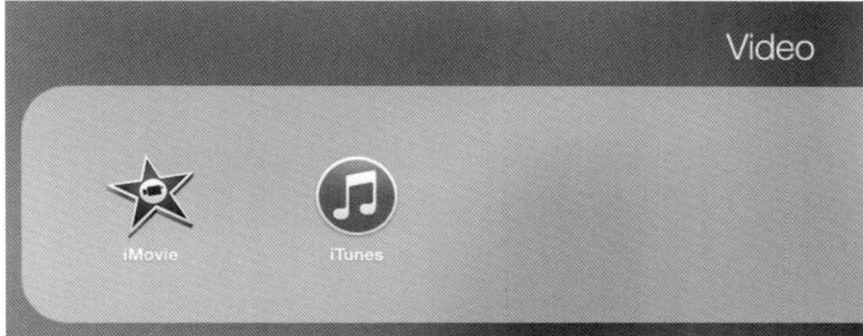

6. To change the name, click on it once and overtype it with the new name

7. The folder appears within the Launchpad window

8. To remove an app, click and hold on it until it starts to jiggle and a cross appears. Click on the cross to remove it

System apps, i.e. the ones that already come with your MacBook, cannot be removed in the Launchpad, only ones you have downloaded.

Full-Screen Apps

When working with apps we all like to be able to see as much of a window as possible. With OS X Yosemite this is possible with the full-screen app. This allows you to expand an app with this functionality so that it takes up the whole of your monitor or screen with a minimum of toolbars visible. Some apps have this functionality but some do not. To use full-screen apps:

1. By default an app appears on the Desktop with other windows behind it

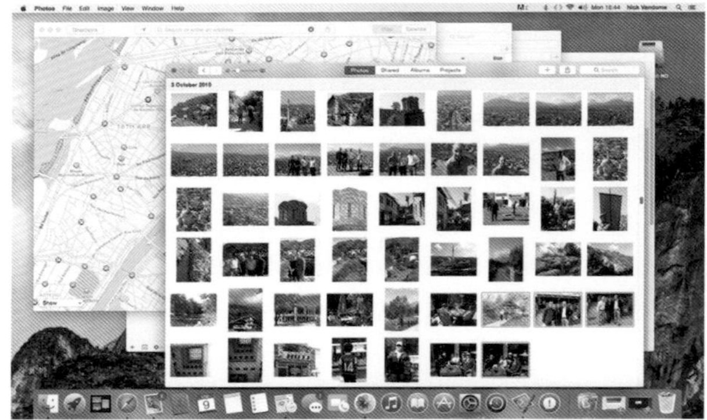

If the button in Step 2 is not visible then the app does not have the full-screen functionality.

2. Click on this button at the top left-hand corner of the app's window

3. The app is expanded to take up the whole window. The main Apple Menu bar and the Dock are hidden

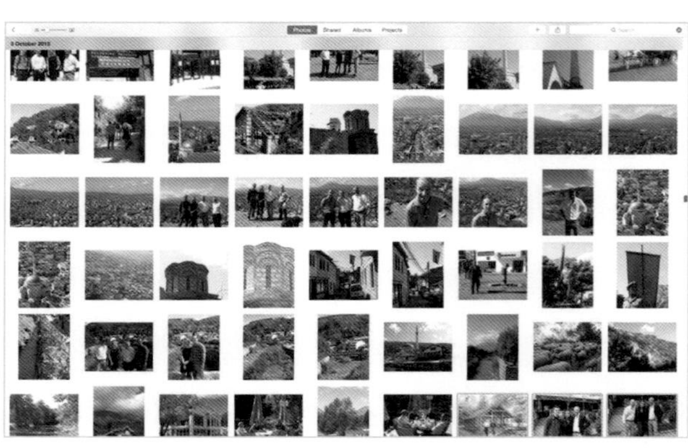

4. To view the main Menu bar, move the cursor over the top of the screen

5. You can move between all full-screen apps by swiping with three fingers left or right on the trackpad

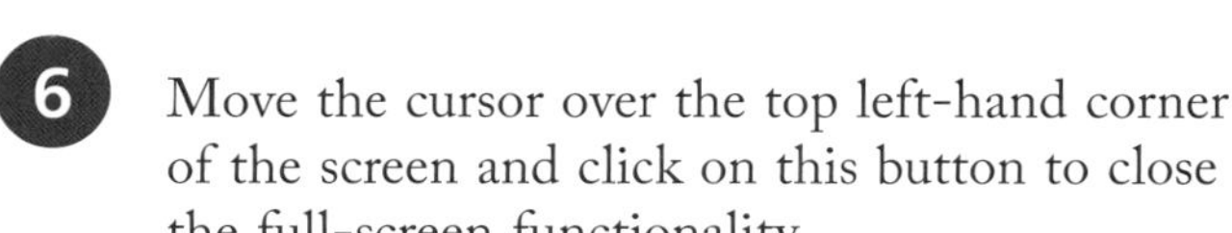

6. Move the cursor over the top left-hand corner of the screen and click on this button to close the full-screen functionality

7. In Mission Control all of the open full-screen apps are shown in the top row

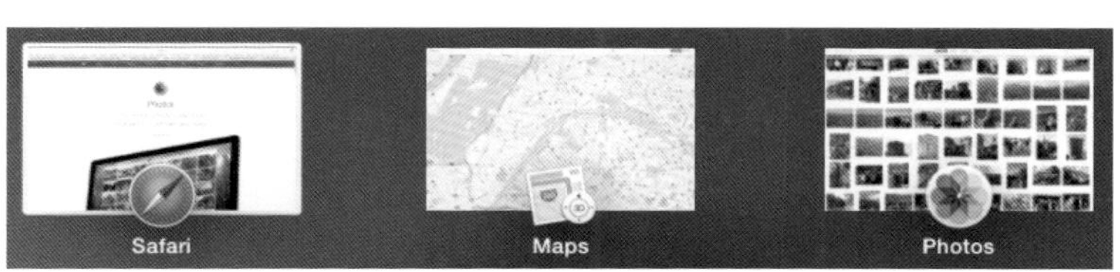

For more information about navigating with multi-touch gestures see Chapter Six.

OS X Apps

OS X Yosemite apps include:

- **Automator**. An app for creating automated processes
- **Calculator.** A basic calculator
- **Calendar**. The Yosemite calendar app
- **Contacts**. An app for storing contact information
- **Dashboard**. A set of useful widgets, accessed from the Dock, the Launchpad or the F12 key
- **Dictionary**. A digital dictionary
- **DVD Player.** Used to play and view DVDs
- **FaceTime.** Can be used for video calls, see page 142
- **Font Book.** Use this to add and change fonts
- **Image Capture**. For downloading digital images from a camera or a scanner
- **Photos, iTunes, iMovie,** and **GarageBand**, see Chapter Nine
- **Mail**. The default email app
- **Mission Control.** The function for organizing your Desktop
- **Notes**. An app for creating and sharing notes
- **Pages**, **Numbers** and **Keynote**. This suite of productivity apps (word processing, spreadsheets and presentation, respectively) are now included with OS X Yosemite
- **Photo Booth.** An app for creating photo effects
- **Preview.** Can be used to view a variety of different file types
- **QuickTime Player**. The default application for viewing video
- **Reminders**. App for setting reminders
- **Safari**. The OS X specific web browser
- **TextEdit**. An app for editing text files
- **Time Machine**. OS X's backup facility

Apps such as Notes and Reminders can be shared via the online iCloud facility. Ensure they are checked on within the iCloud System Preference. They can also be set to appear in the Notification Center via the Notifications System Preference.

Accessing the App Store

The App Store is another OS X app. This is an online facility where you can download and buy new apps. These cover a range of categories such as productivity, business and entertainment. When you select or buy an app from the App Store, it is downloaded automatically by Launchpad and appears here next to the rest of the apps.

To buy apps from the App Store you need to have an Apple ID and account. If you have not already set this up, it can be done when you first access the App Store. To use the App Store:

The App Store is an online function so you will need an Internet connection to access it.

1. Click on this icon on the Dock or within the Launchpad

2. The homepage of the App Store contains the current top featured apps

You can set up an Apple ID when you first set up your MacBook or you can do it when you register for the App Store or the iTunes Store.

3. Your account information and quick link categories are listed at the right-hand side of the page

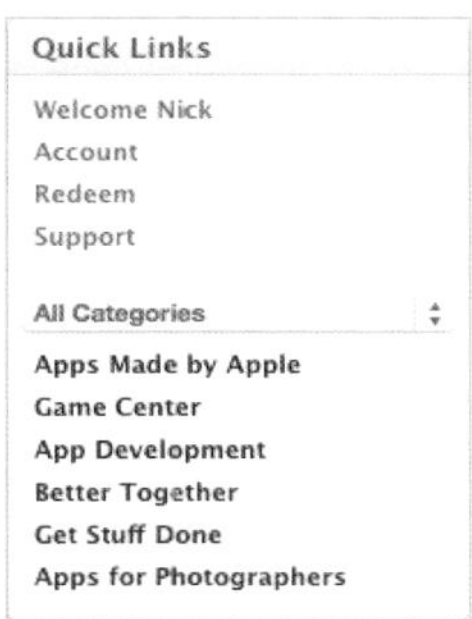

Downloading Apps

The App Store contains a wide range of apps: from small, fun apps, to powerful productivity ones. However, downloading them from the App Store is the same regardless of the type of app. The only differences are whether they need to be paid for or not and the length of time they take to download. To download an app from the App Store:

1. Browse through the App Store until you find the required app

2. Click on the app to view a detailed description about it

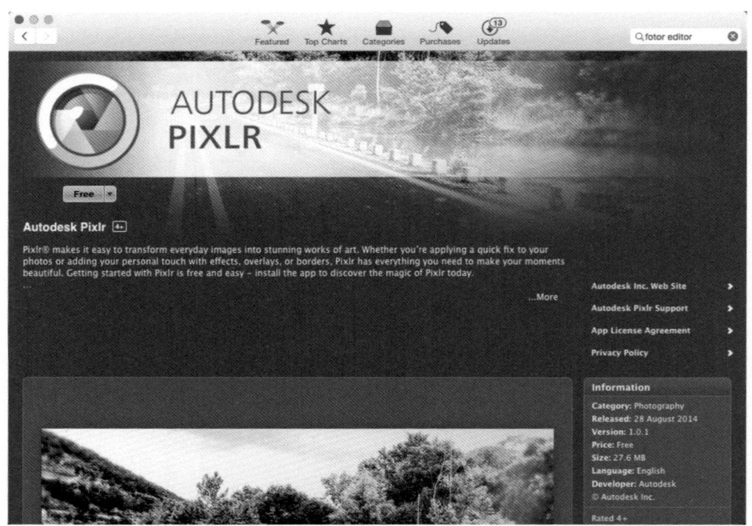

3. Click on the button underneath the app icon to download it. If there is no charge for the app the button will say Free

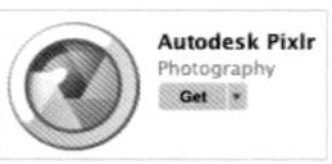

When downloading apps, start with a free one first so that you can get used to the process before you download paid-for apps.

4. If there is a charge for the app, the button will say **Buy App**

Buy App

5. Click on the **Install App** button

Install App

6. Enter your Apple ID account details to continue downloading the app

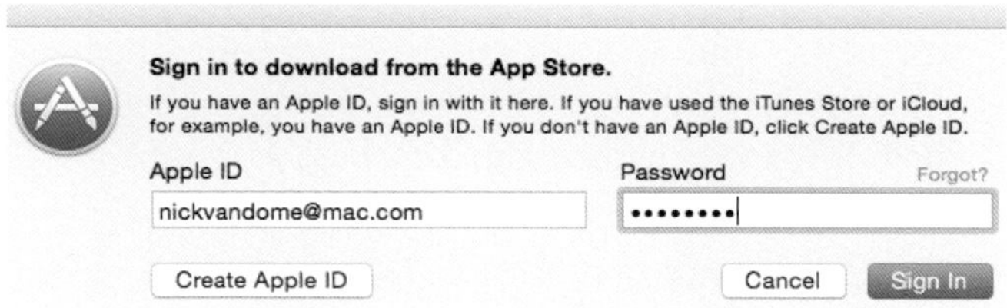

7. The progress of the download is displayed in a progress bar underneath the Launchpad icon on the Dock

8. Once it has been downloaded, the app is available within Launchpad

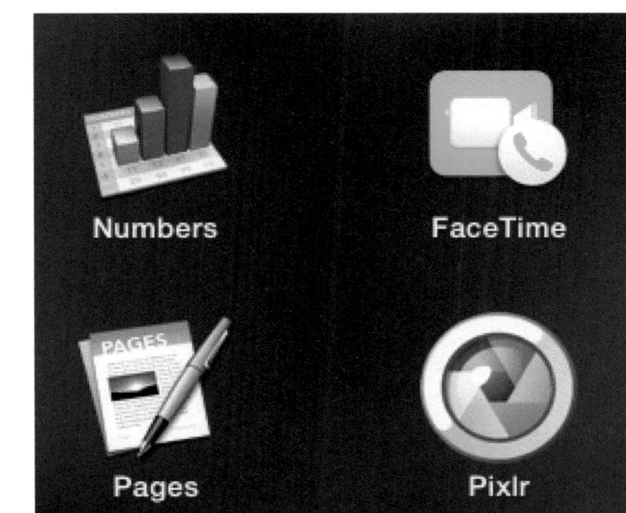

Don't forget

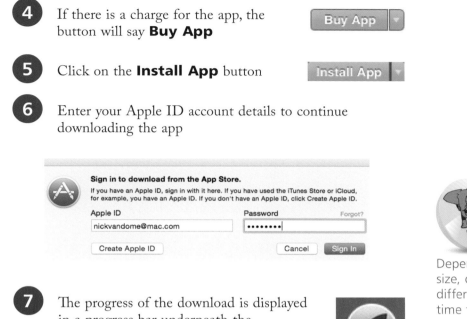

Depending on their size, different apps take differing amounts of time to be downloaded.

As you download more apps, additional pages will be created within the Launchpad to accommodate them.

Finding Apps

There are thousands of apps in the App Store and sometimes the hardest task is locating the ones you want. However, there are a number of ways in which finding apps is made as easy as possible.

1. Click on the **Featured** button

2. The main window has a range of categories such as New, What's Hot and Staff Favorites. At the right-hand side there is a panel with a Top Ten Paid For apps

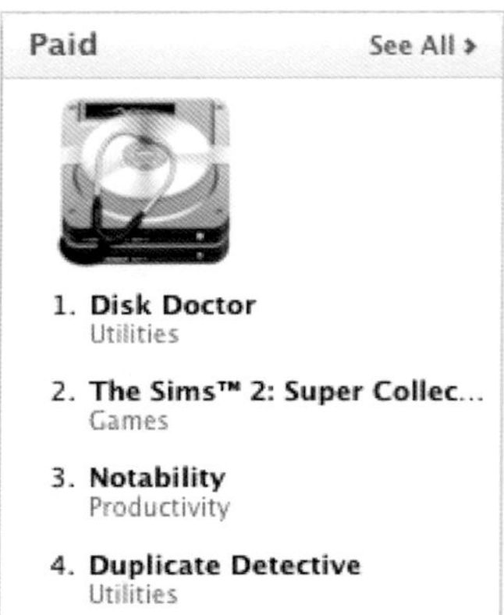

3. Underneath this is a list of the Top Ten Free apps

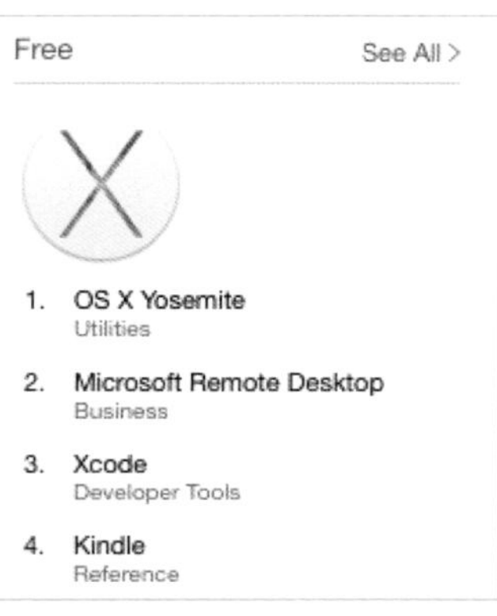

Another way to find apps is to type a keyword into the Search box at the top right-hand corner of the App Store window.

4. Click on the **Top Charts** button

5. The top apps for different categories are displayed

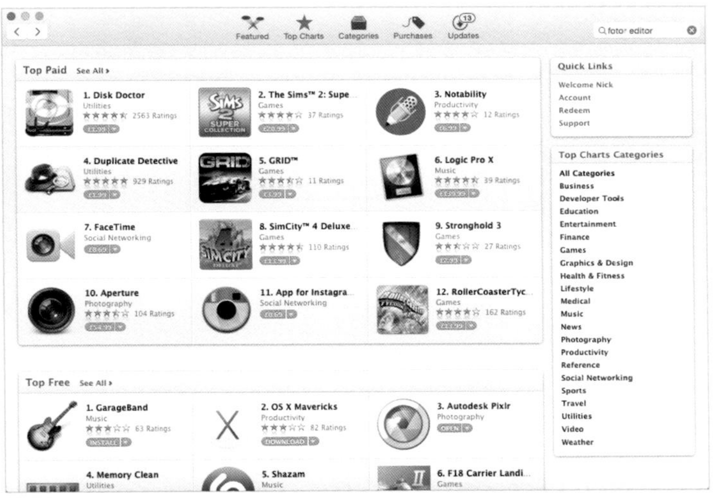

6. Click on the **Categories** button

7. Browse through the apps by specific categories, such as Business, Entertainment and Finance

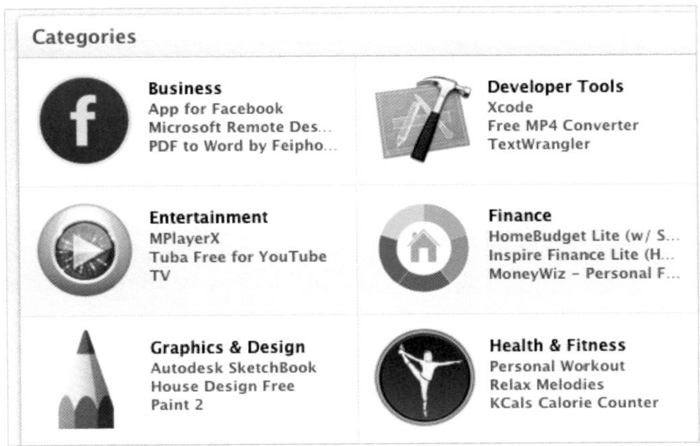

Managing Your Apps

Once you have bought apps from the App Store you can view details of ones you have purchased and also install updated versions of them.

Even if you interrupt a download and turn off your MacBook you will still be able to resume the download when you restart your computer.

It is always worth updating your apps to improve them and download any security fixes as required.

Don't forget

If there are apps to be updated you can click on the **Update** button to update a specific app, or click on the **Update All** button to update all of the available apps.

UPDATE

UPDATE ALL

Purchased Apps

To view your purchased apps:

1. Click on the **Purchases** button

2. Details of your purchased apps are displayed (including those that are free)

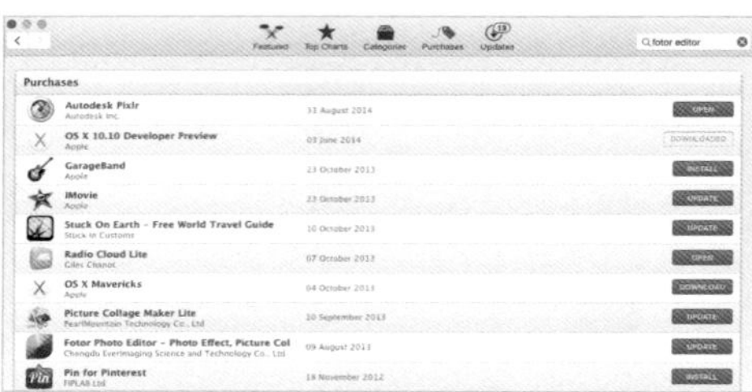

3. If a download of an app has been interrupted, click on the **Resume** button to continue with it

RESUME

Updating Apps

Improvements and fixes are being developed constantly and these can be downloaded to ensure that all of your apps are up-to-date.

1. When updates are available this is indicated by a red circle on the **App Store** icon in the Dock

2. Click on the **Updates** button

3. Information about the updates is displayed next to the app that is due to be updated

8 Internet and Email

This chapter shows how to get the most out of the Internet and email. It covers connecting to the Internet and how to use the OS X web browser, Safari, and its email app, Mail. It also covers Messages for text messaging and FaceTime for video chatting.

Getting Connected

Access to the Internet is an accepted part of the computing world and it is unusual for users not to want to do this. Not only does this provide a gateway to the World Wide Web but also email.

Connecting to the Internet with a MacBook is done through the System Preferences. To do this:

Before you connect to the Internet you must have an Internet Service Provider (ISP) who will provide you with the relevant method of connection, i.e. dial-up, cable or broadband. They will provide you with any login details.

1. Click on the **System Preferences** icon on the Dock

2. Click on the **Network** icon

3. Check that your method of connecting to the Internet is active, i.e. colored green

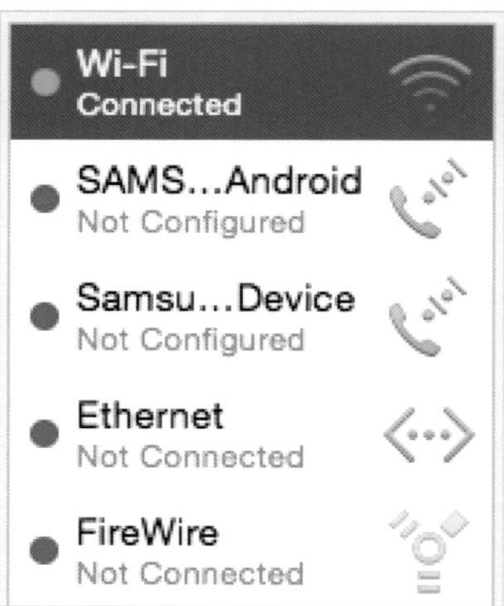

4. Click on the **Assist me...** button to access wizards for connecting to the Internet with your preferred method of connection

Assist me...

5 Click on the **Assistant...** button

Assistant...

6 The **Network Setup Assistant** is used to configure your system so that you can connect to the Internet

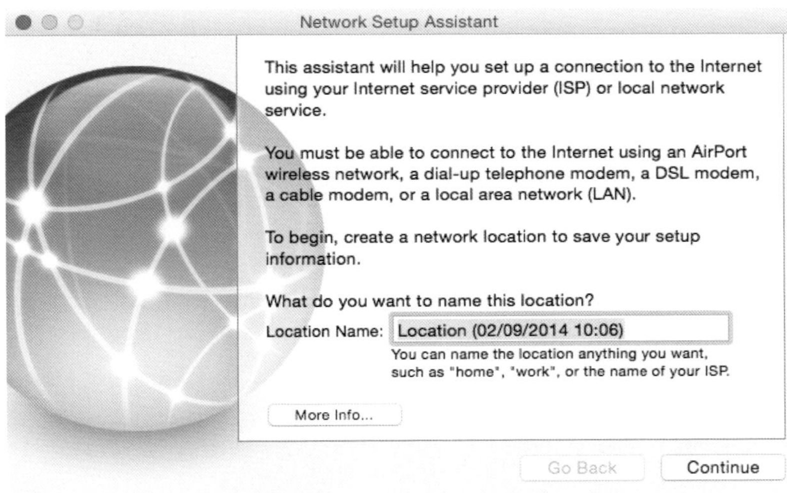

7 Enter a name for your connection

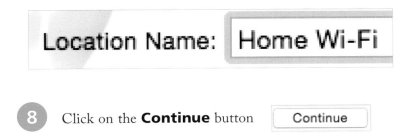

8 Click on the **Continue** button

Continue

...cont'd

9. Select an option for how you will connect to the Internet, e.g. wireless, cable or telephone modem

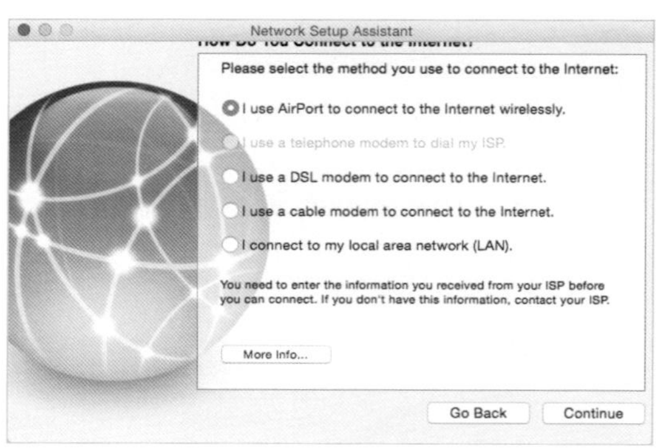

10. Click on the **Continue** button

Continue

11. For a wireless connection, select an available wireless network. This will be the router that is being used to make the connection

Select the wireless network you want to join:

PlusnetWireless792287
virginmedia6249958
Other Wi-Fi Network

12. Enter a password for the router (this will have been created when you connected and configured the router)

Password: Selected network requires a password

••••••••••

13. Click on the **Continue** button

Continue

If you are in range of another wireless router, such as a neighbor's, you will see the router in Step 11. However, you will not be able to use it, unless it is unlocked, i.e. it has not had a password attached to it. Even if it is unlocked you should not use it, unless you get the permission from the owner.

14 The **Ready to Connect** window informs you that you are about to attempt to connect to your network

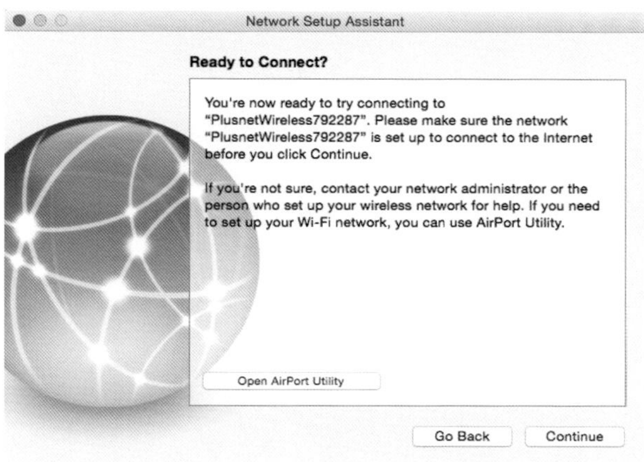

15 Click on the **Continue** button

Continue

16 You are informed if the connection has been successful

Network Setup Assistant
If you're not sure, contact your network administrator or the person who set up your wireless network for help. If you need to set up your Wi-Fi network, you can use AirPort Utility.
Open AirPort Utility
Congratulations! You Are Connected.
You are now connected to the Internet. Your configuration information has been saved in the location you created.
Location Name: Home Wi-Fi
To change your network location, click the Apple menu and choose Location, then choose a location from the submenu.
Go Back
Done

17 Click on the **Done** button

Done

Safari

Safari is a web browser that is designed specifically to be used with OS X. It is similar in most respects to other browsers, but it usually functions more quickly and works seamlessly with OS X.

Safari overview

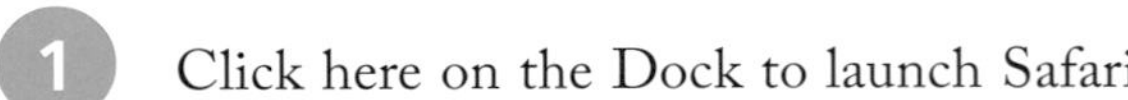

1. Click here on the Dock to launch Safari

2. All of the controls are at the top of the browser

Hot tip

If the Bookmarks Bar is not visible, select **View** from the Menu bar and check on the **Show Bookmarks Bar** option. From this menu you can also select or deselect items such as showing All Tabs, the Status Bar and the Reading List.

Smart Search box

One of the innovations in the latest version of Safari (8) is that the Address bar and the Search box have been incorporated into one item. You can use the same box for searching for an item or enter a web address to go to that page.

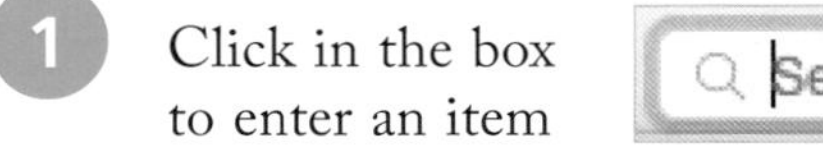

1. Click in the box to enter an item

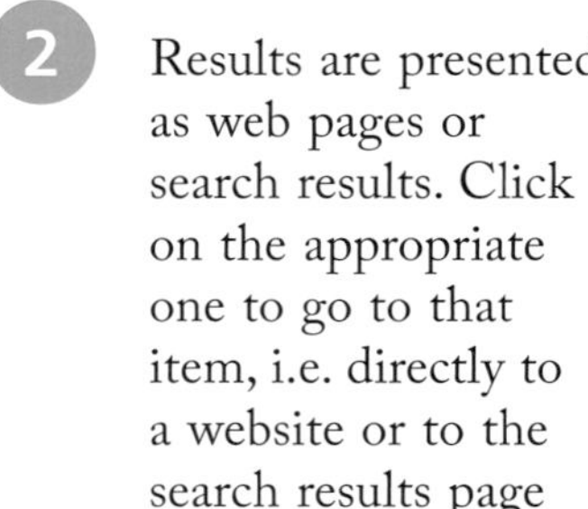

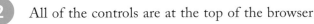

2. Results are presented as web pages or search results. Click on the appropriate one to go to that item, i.e. directly to a website or to the search results page

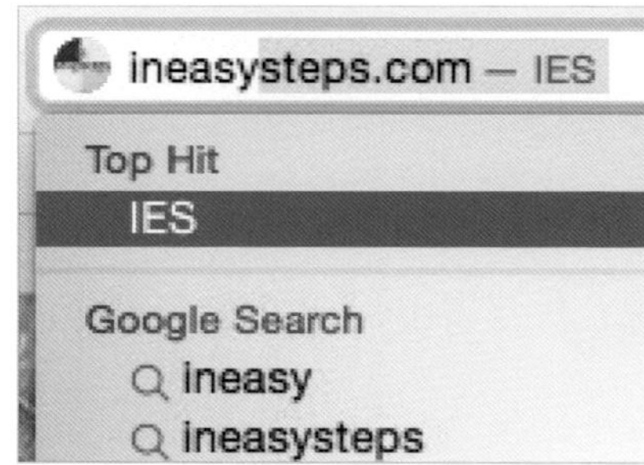

Sharing pages

As with many features in Yosemite, web pages can be shared directly from Safari. To do this, first open a web page.

1. Click on this button and select one of the sharing options

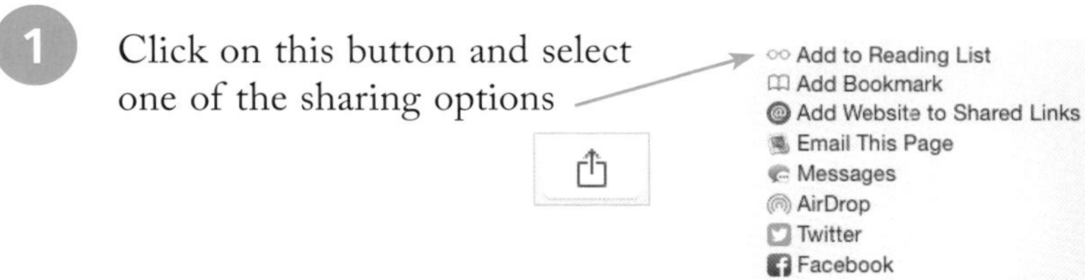

Preferences

Select **Safari > Preferences** from the Menu bar to specify settings for the way Safari operates and displays web pages. This also includes preferences for **Security** and **Privacy** settings.

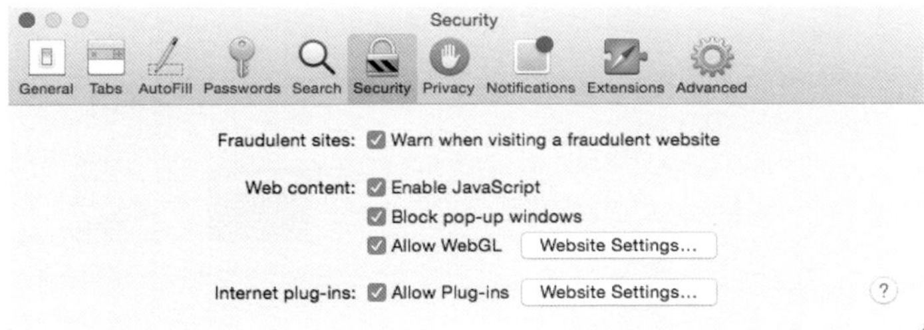

Two useful Safari Preferences are those for **Passwords** and **AutoFill** that can be used to manage your passwords on websites, particularly if it is used in conjunction with iCloud Keychain, see pages 72-75 for more details.

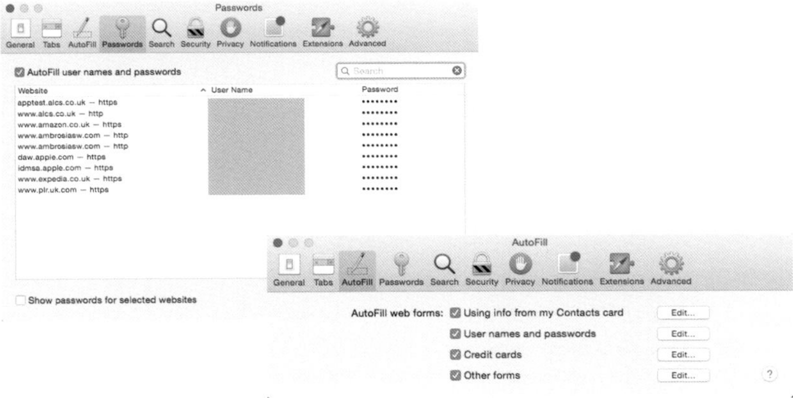

Safari Tabbed Browsing

Tabs are now a familiar feature on web browsers, so you can have multiple sites open within the same browser window.

1. When more than one tab is open, the tabs appear at the top of the web pages

Don't forget

Safari is a full-screen app and can be expanded by clicking the double arrow in the top right corner. For more information on full-screen apps, see pages 116-117.

2. Click on this button next to the tabs to open a new tab

3. Click on one of the Top Sites (see next page) or enter a website address in the Address bar

4. Click on this button next to the **New Tab** button to minimize all of the current tabs

5. Move left and right to view all of the open tabs in thumbnail view. Click on one to view it at full size

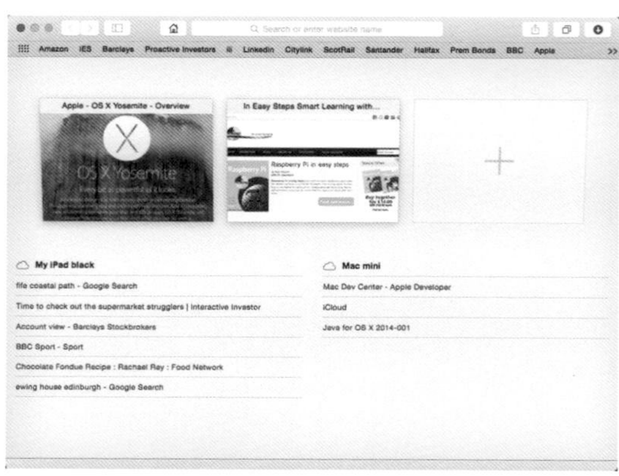

Safari Top Sites

Within Safari there is a facility to view a graphical representation of the websites that you visit most frequently. This can be done from a button on the Safari Menu bar. To do this:

1. Click on this button to view the Top Sites window

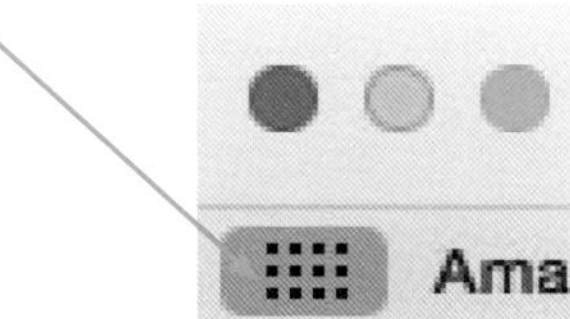

2. The Top Sites window contains thumbnails of the websites that you have visited most frequently with Safari (this builds up as you visit more sites)

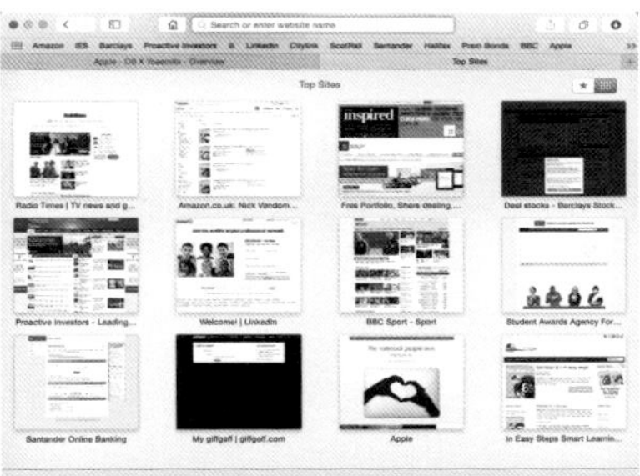

3. Click on the cross to delete a thumbnail from the Top Sites window. Click on the pin to keep it there permanently

4. Click on a thumbnail to go to the full site

5. To add a new site to the Top Sites, open another window and drag the URL (website address) into the Top Sites

The Top Sites window is also accessed if you open a new tab within Safari.

Safari Reader

Web pages can be complex and cluttered at times. On occasions you may want to just read the content of one story on a web page without all of the extra material in view. In Safari this can be done with the Reader function. To do this:

Not all web pages support the Reader functionality in Safari.

1. Select **View > Show Reader** from the Safari menu bar

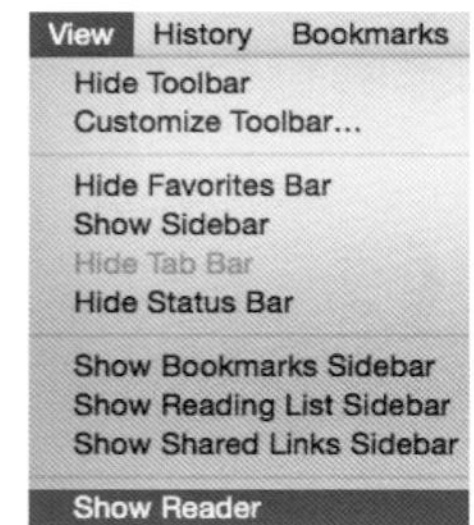

2. Click on the Reader button in the address bar of a web page that supports this functionality

3. The button turns darker once the Reader is activated

4. The content is displayed in a text format, with any photos from the original

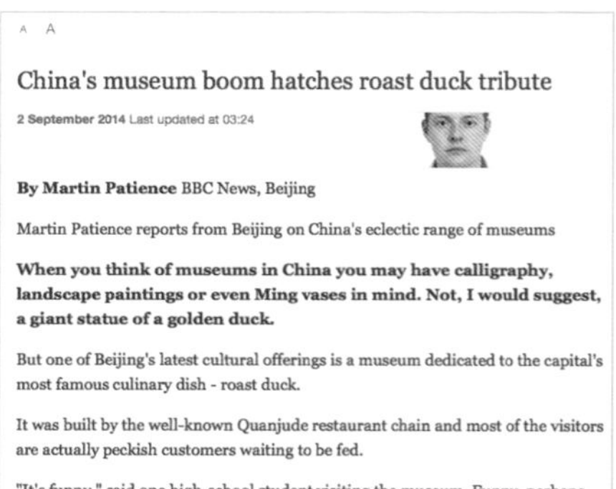

China's museum boom hatches roast duck tribute

2 September 2014 Last updated at 03:24

By Martin Patience BBC News, Beijing

Martin Patience reports from Beijing on China's eclectic range of museums

When you think of museums in China you may have calligraphy, landscape paintings or even Ming vases in mind. Not, I would suggest, a giant statue of a golden duck.

But one of Beijing's latest cultural offerings is a museum dedicated to the capital's most famous culinary dish - roast duck.

It was built by the well-known Quanjude restaurant chain and most of the visitors are actually peckish customers waiting to be fed.

"It's funny," said one high-school student visiting the museum. Funny, perhaps,

Pages that are saved to a Reading List with the button in Step 5 can be read when you are offline, so you do not need to be connected to the Internet.

5. Click on this button on the Safari toolbar if you want to save a page to read at a later date

6. Click on the **Add to Reading List** button to add the page to your Reading List

Adding Bookmarks

Bookmarks is a feature by which you can create quick links to your favorite web pages or the ones you visit most frequently. Bookmarks can be added to a menu or the Bookmarks bar in Safari which makes them even quicker to access. Folders can also be created to store the less frequently used bookmarks. To view and create bookmarks:

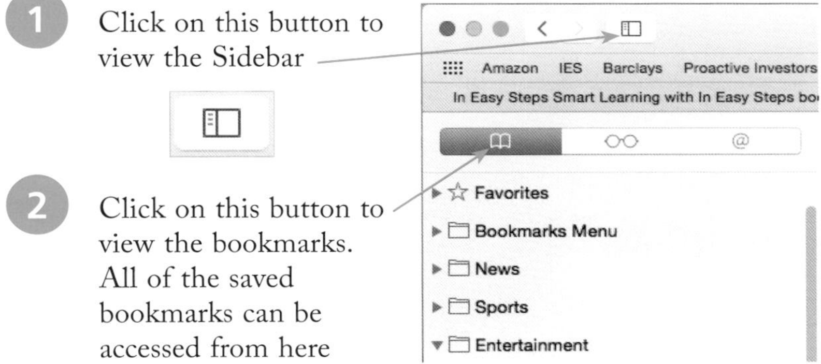

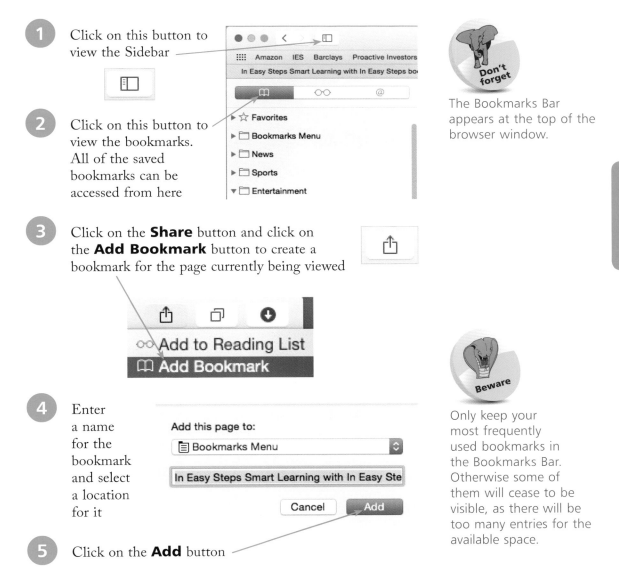

1. Click on this button to view the Sidebar

2. Click on this button to view the bookmarks. All of the saved bookmarks can be accessed from here

The Bookmarks Bar appears at the top of the browser window.

3. Click on the **Share** button and click on the **Add Bookmark** button to create a bookmark for the page currently being viewed

Only keep your most frequently used bookmarks in the Bookmarks Bar. Otherwise some of them will cease to be visible, as there will be too many entries for the available space.

4. Enter a name for the bookmark and select a location for it

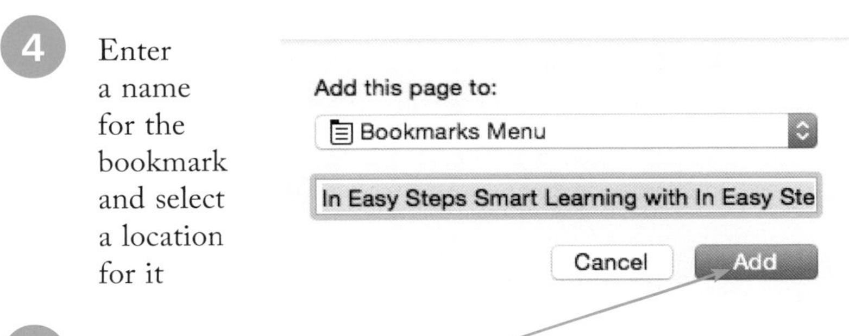

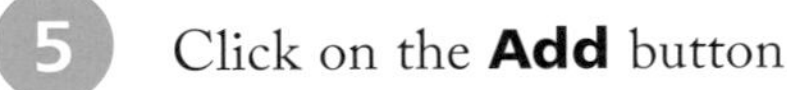

5. Click on the **Add** button

Mail

Email is an essential element for most computer users and MacBooks come with their own email app called Mail. This covers all of the email functionality that anyone could need.

When first using Mail you have to set up your email account. This information will be available from the company which provides your email service, although in some cases Mail may obtain this information automatically. To view your Mail account details:

1. Click on this icon on the Dock

2. Select **Mail > Preferences** from the Menu bar

3. Click on the **Accounts** tab

4. If it has not already been included, enter the details of your email account in the **Account Information** section

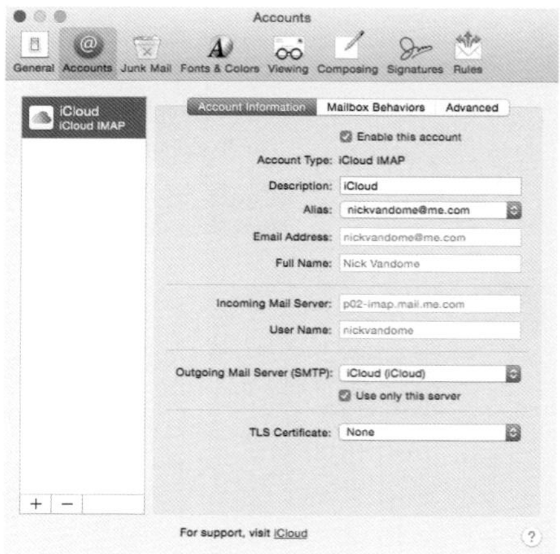
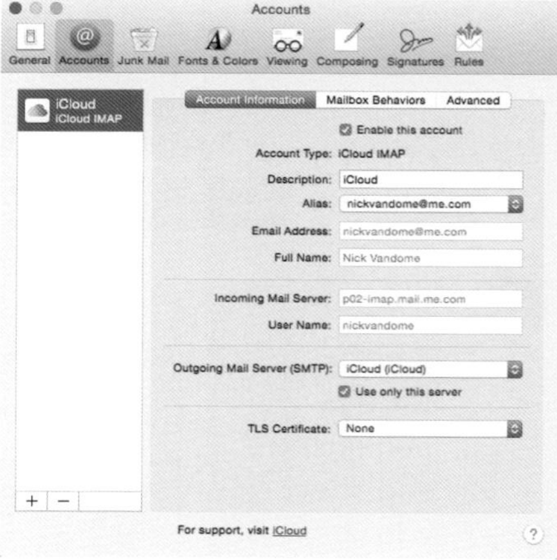

5. Click on this button to add a new email account, using the Mail wizard

Mail can download messages from all of the accounts that you have set up within the Accounts preference.

Using Email

Mail enables you to send and receive emails and also format them to your own style. This can be simply formatting text or adding customized stationery. To use Mail:

To show the text underneath an icon in Mail, Ctrl+click next to an icon and select **Icon & Text** from the menu.

1. Click on the **Get Mail** button to download available email messages

2. Click on the **New Message** button to create a new email

3. Enter a recipient in the To: box, a title in the Subject box and then text for the email in the main window

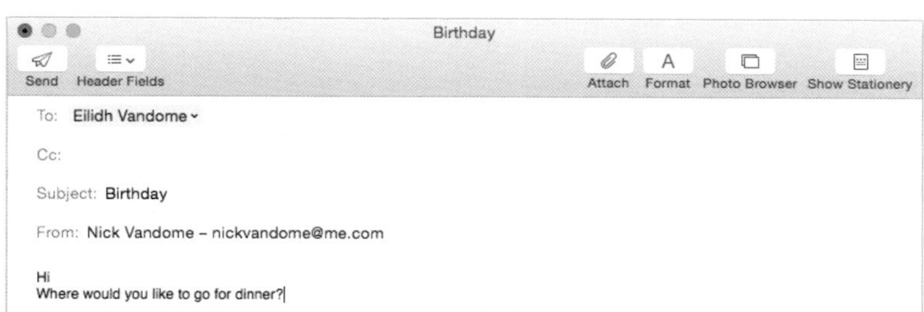

When entering the name of a recipient for a message, Mail will display details of matching names from your Contacts. For instance, if you type DA, all of the entries in your Contacts beginning with this will be displayed and you can select the required one.

4. Click on the **Format** button to access options for formatting the text in the email

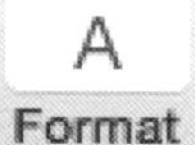

5. Click on these buttons to **Reply** to, **Reply All**, or **Forward** an email you have received

6. Select or open an email and click on the **Delete** button to remove it

If you Forward an email with an attachment then the attachment is included. If you Reply to an email the attachment will not be included.

...cont'd

It is worth occasionally checking in your Junk Mailbox, in case something you want has been put there.

7. Click on the **Junk** button to mark an email as junk or spam. This trains Mail to identify junk mail. After a period of time, these types of messages will automatically be moved straight into the Junk mailbox

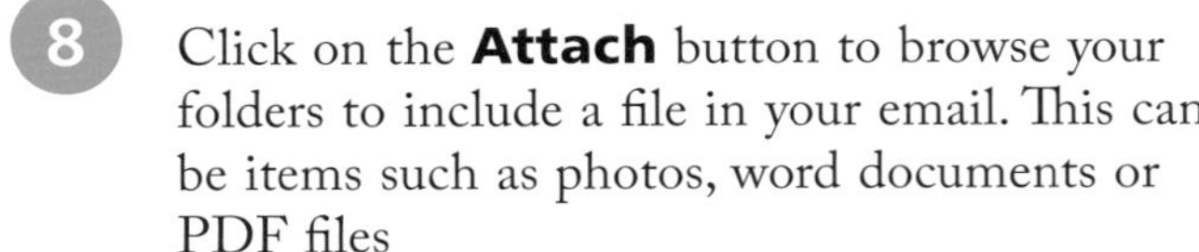

8. Click on the **Attach** button to browse your folders to include a file in your email. This can be items such as photos, word documents or PDF files

9. Click on the **Photo Browser** button to browse photos to add to an email

10. Click on the **Show Stationery** button to access a variety of templated designs that can be added to your email

Do not send files that are too large in terms of file size, otherwise the recipient may find it takes too long to download.

11. Select **View > Organize by Conversation** from the Mail menu bar

12. Emails with the same subject are grouped together as a conversation in the left-hand pane. The number of grouped emails is shown at the right-hand side

13. Click here to view the full list of emails

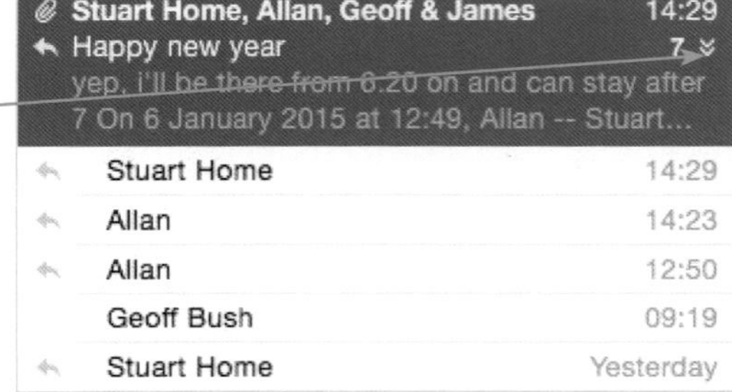

Adding Mailboxes

When you are dealing with email it is a good idea to create a folder structure (mailboxes) for your messages. This will allow you to sort your emails into relevant subjects when you receive them, rather than having all of them sitting in your Inbox. To add a structure of new mailboxes:

1. Click on this button to view your current mailboxes

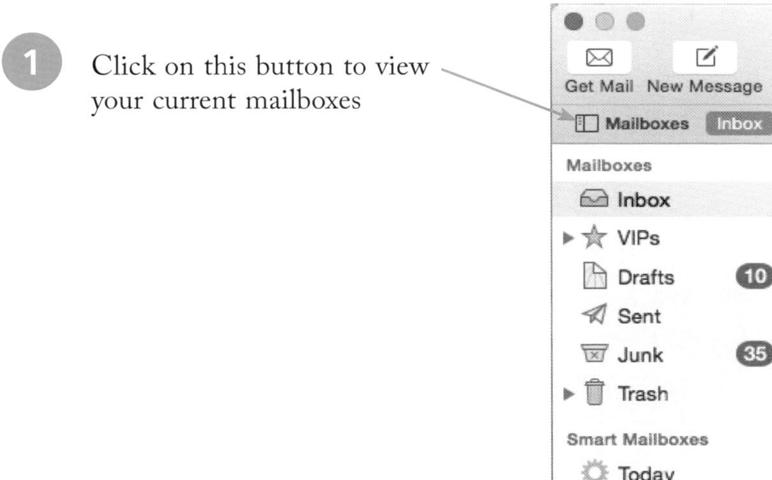

2. Click on the **+** button at the bottom left-hand corner of the Mail window and select **New Mailbox**

3. Enter a name for the Mailbox and a location where you would like it to be stored. Click on the **OK** button

4. The new mailbox is added to the current list

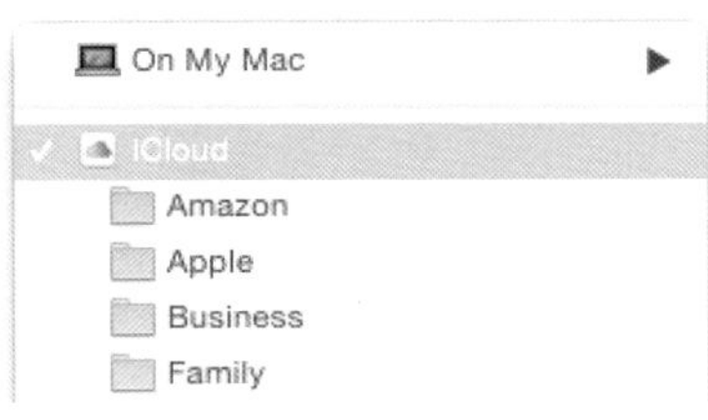

Smart Mailboxes can also be created. These are mailboxes with specific criteria, such as a sender's name or a word in the subject title. Whenever an email arrives which matches this criteria it will be routed into the Smart Mailbox folder.

Messaging

The Messages app enables you to send text messages (iMessages) to other Yosemite users or those with an iPhone, iPad or iPod Touch. It can also be used to send photos, videos and to make FaceTime calls. To use Messages:

Don't forget

You need an Apple ID to use Messages and you will need to enter these details when you first access it. If you do not have an Apple ID you will be able to create one at this point.

1. Click on this icon on the Dock

2. Click on this button to start a new conversation

3. Click on this button and select a contact (these will be from your Contacts app). To send an iMessage the recipient must have an Apple ID

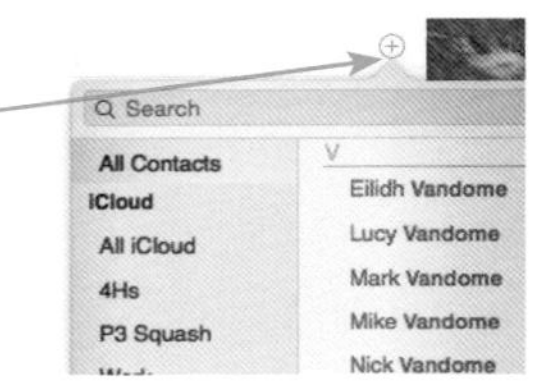

4. The person with whom you are having a conversation is displayed in the left-hand panel

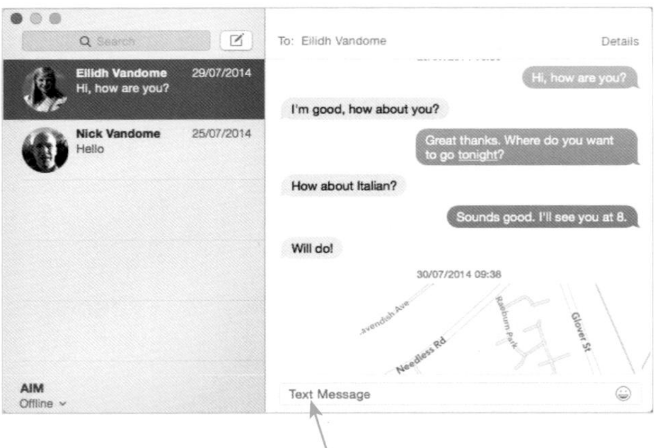

5. The conversation continues down the right-hand panel. Click here to write a message and press Return to send it

Don't forget

To delete a conversation, roll over it in the left-hand panel and click on this cross.

Adding photos and videos

Photos and videos can be added to messages:

1. Select the photo, or video, in the Finder, next to the Messages app

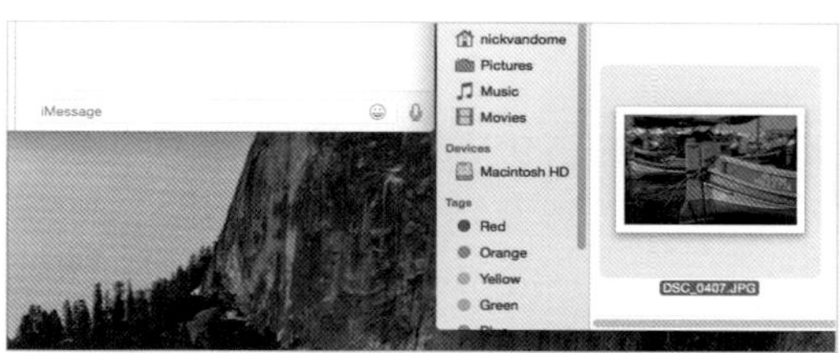

Audio messages can also be included in an iMessage. Click on this icon to the right of the text box and record your message.

2. Drag the photo, or video, into the text box to include it in a message

Text forwarding

If you have an iPhone you can now receive and send SMS text messages, using your MacBook with OS X Yosemite. To use your MacBook and OS X Yosemite to send and receive SMS messages:

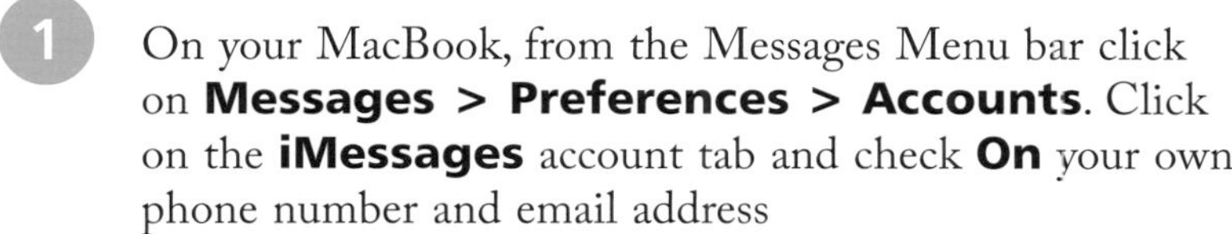

1. On your MacBook, from the Messages Menu bar click on **Messages > Preferences > Accounts**. Click on the **iMessages** account tab and check **On** your own phone number and email address

To use text forwarding you need to have OS X Yosemite on your MacBook and iOS 8.1 on your iPhone, or iPad with cellular capabilities, i.e. the 3/4G version. Wi-Fi also has to be turned on for each device.

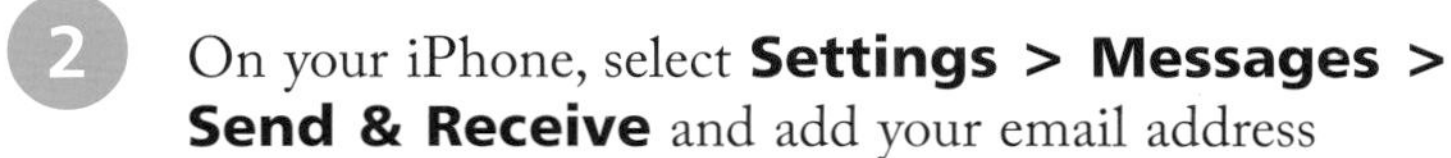

2. On your iPhone, select **Settings > Messages > Send & Receive** and add your email address

3. On your iPhone, select **Settings > Messages > Text Message Forwarding > Turn Text Message Forwarding On**

4. An activation code appears on our MacBook: enter this on your iPhone to enable text forwarding

FaceTime

FaceTime is an app that can be used to make video, and audio, calls to other Macs, iPhones, iPads and iPod Touches. To use FaceTime on your MacBook you must have an in-built FaceTime camera or use a compatible external one.

Don't forget

If you receive a video call, you are alerted to this even if FaceTime is not open and running.

Hot tip

In a similar way to text forwarding, OS X Yosemite on a Mac can also be used for Phone Call Forwarding with your iPhone. Both devices need to have Wi-Fi turned on and be signed into the same iCloud account. On your MacBook, select **FaceTime > Preferences >** and turn **On iPhone Cellular Calls**. Do the same on your iPhone with **Settings > FaceTime > iPhone Cellular Calls**. When you receive a call, it shows up as a notification on your MacBook and you can Accept or Decline it.

1. Click on this icon on the Dock

2. You need an Apple ID to use FaceTime. Enter your details and click on the **Sign in** button

3. Once you have logged in you can make video calls by selecting people from your address book providing they have an Apple ID and a device that supports FaceTime. Click on this button to access your address book

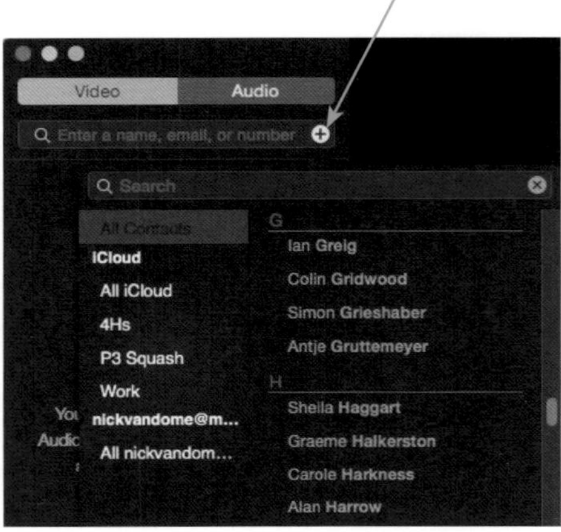

9 Digital Lifestyle

Leisure time, and how we use it, is a significant issue for everyone. This chapter shows how to make the most of your leisure time on your MacBook, using the new Photos app, iTunes for your musical needs and apps for making home movies, music and playing games.

Using the Photos App

For a number of years the photo management and editing tool for OS X has been iPhoto. However, in Spring 2015 the Photos app was introduced. iPhoto can still be used, but the Photos app is designed to mirror the one used on iOS 8 devices and integrate more with iCloud, so that you can store all of your photos in the iCloud and then view and manage them on all of your Apple devices.

If you are using the Photos app, you can specify how it operates with iCloud in the iCloud System Preferences:

Although the iPhoto app can still be used, it may at some point stop being supported by Apple, so it is better to migrate to the Photos app.

1. Click on the **System Preferences** button

2. Click on the **iCloud** button in the System Preferences window

3. Check On the **Photos** checkbox

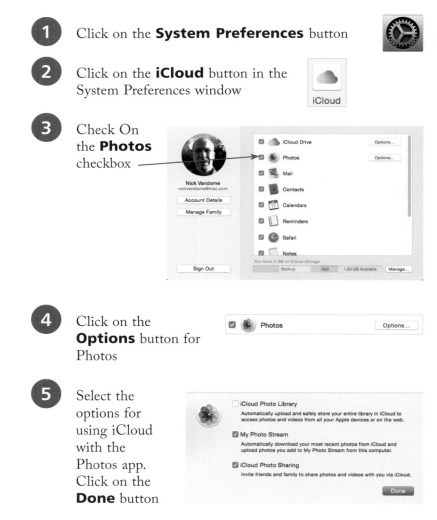

4. Click on the **Options** button for Photos

The iCloud options for the Photos app are: **iCloud Photo Library**, which uploads your entire photo library to the iCloud; **My Photo Stream**, which uploads photos that are added from the device you are using; and **iCloud Photo Sharing**, which enables you to share photos from the Photos app with family and friends.

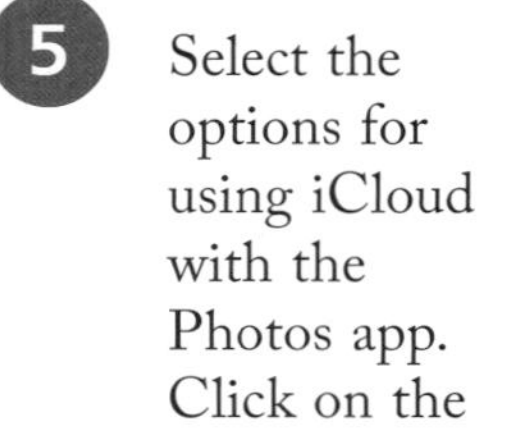

5. Select the options for using iCloud with the Photos app. Click on the **Done** button

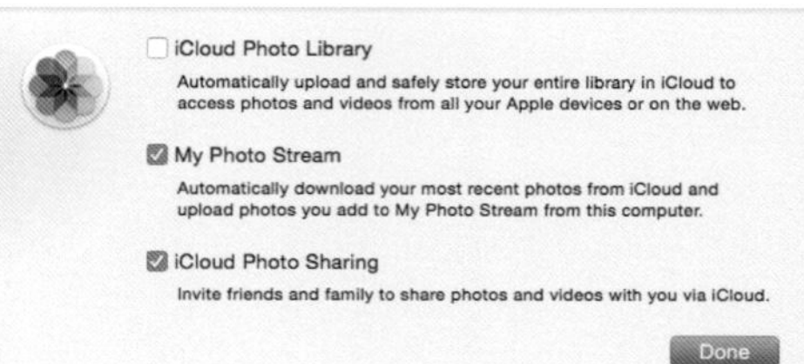

Getting started with the Photos app

If you have previously used iPhoto, you can import your photo library into Photos when you start using it:

1. Click on the **Photos** app in the Dock or from the Launchpad

2. Click on the **Get Started** button in the Welcome window

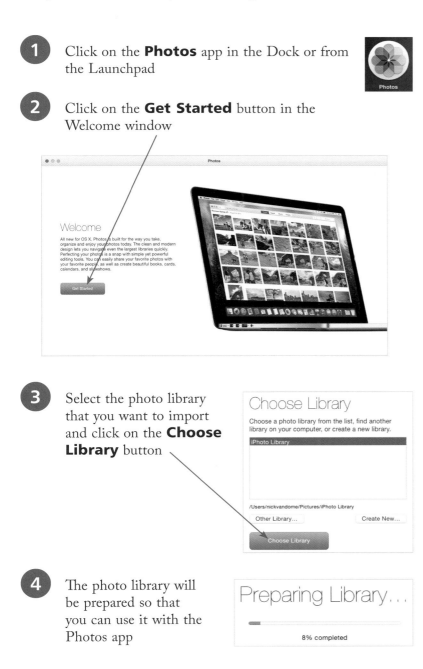

The Photos app is provided as part of a software update to OS X Yosemite. This can be accessed directly through the App Store or from the **App Store** button on the **Apple Menu**.

3. Select the photo library that you want to import and click on the **Choose Library** button

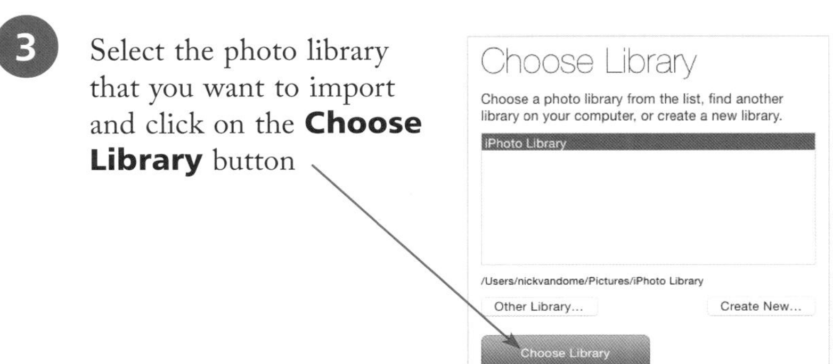

4. The photo library will be prepared so that you can use it with the Photos app

Viewing Photos

The Photos app can be used to view photos according to years, collections, moments or at full size. This enables you to view your photos according to dates and times at which they were taken.

Photos can be imported into the Photos app by selecting **File > Import** from the Menu bar and navigating to the required location within the Finder. This can be used to import photos from your Mac or an external device connected with an USB cable, such as a digital camera, a card reader or a pen drive.

1. Click on these buttons at the top of the Photos window to move between years, collections and moments

2. Click on the left-hand button in Step 1 to move to **Years** view

3. Click and hold on a thumbnail in Years view to enlarge it

4. Click on a photo within the Years section to view the **Collections**. This displays groups of photos (Moments) taken at the same location

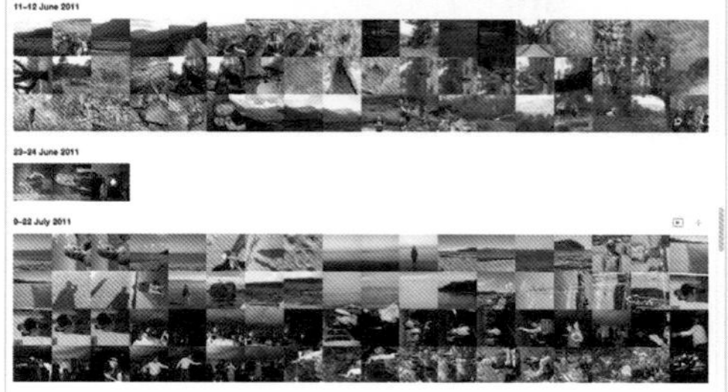

Click on the **Photos** tab at the top of the Photos app window to view your photos in **Years**, **Collections**, **Moments** or full size.

Photos

5. Click on a photo within the Collections section to view specific **Moments**. This displays photos taken at the same time in the same location

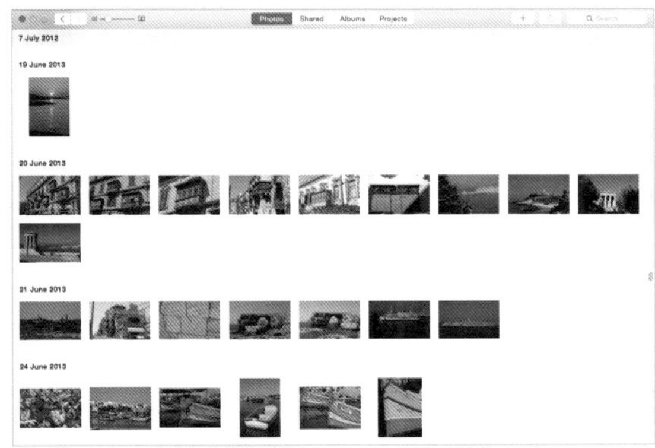

Drag this slider to change the magnification of the photo, or photos, being displayed, in Moments, or at full size view.

6. Double-click on a photo in the Collections or Moments section to view it at full size

Rollover a photo in Collections or Moments view and click on the left-hand icon below to view the relevant photos as a slideshow.

7. For a photo being displayed at full size use these buttons, from left to right, to: add it as a favorite, view information about it, add a new album and create items, share the photo or edit it

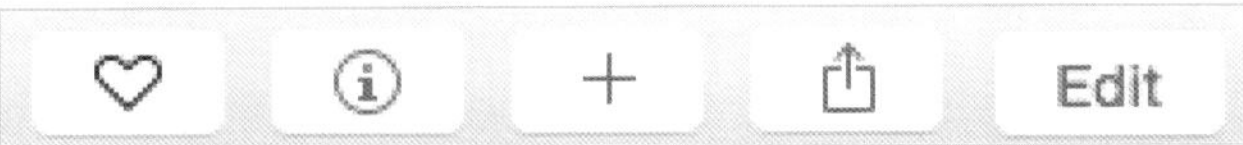

Editing Photos

The Photos app has a range of editing options so that you can fine-tune the appearance of your photos. To do this:

1. Open a photo at full size and click on the **Edit** button

2. The editing options include: **Enhance**, for auto color correction; **Rotate** for rotating the image; **Crop** for cropping the image to remove areas you do not want; **Filters**, for adding effects to the whole image (see Step 3); **Adjust**, for manual color editing (see Step 4); and **Retouch**, for removing unwanted items in an image

3. Click on the **Filters** button and click on one of the filter effects to apply it to the whole image. Click on the **Done** button to apply the effect

4. Click on the **Adjust** button to apply color editing manually. Drag the white bar to apply the adjustments for the required item. Click on the **Add** button to apply the changes

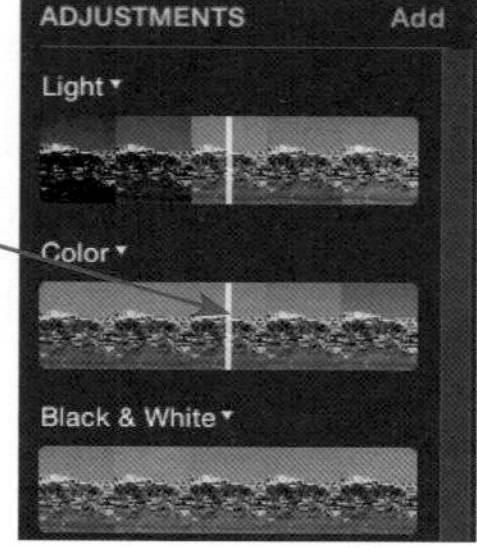

Do not overdo color adjustments as this can create an unnatural effect (unless this is what you are aiming for, as it can be effective in its own right).

Sharing Photos

Individual photos can be shared with the Photos app. Shared albums can also be created and shared using iCloud.

To share specific a photo:

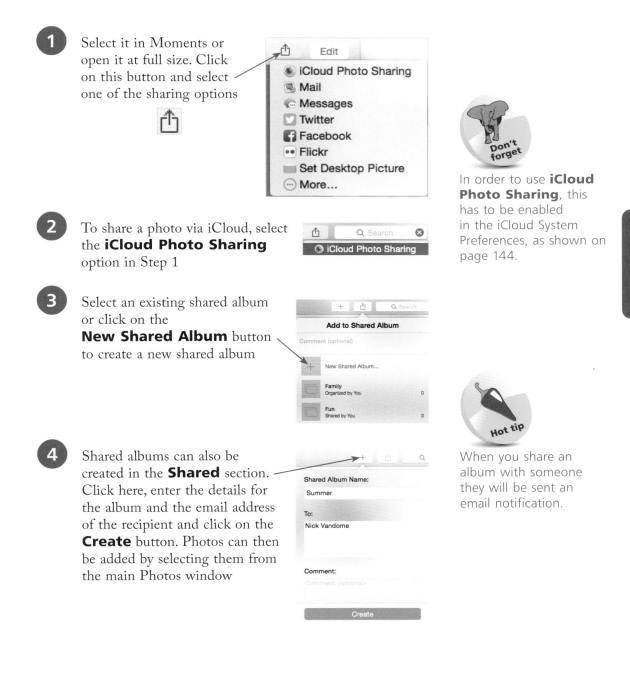

1. Select it in Moments or open it at full size. Click on this button and select one of the sharing options

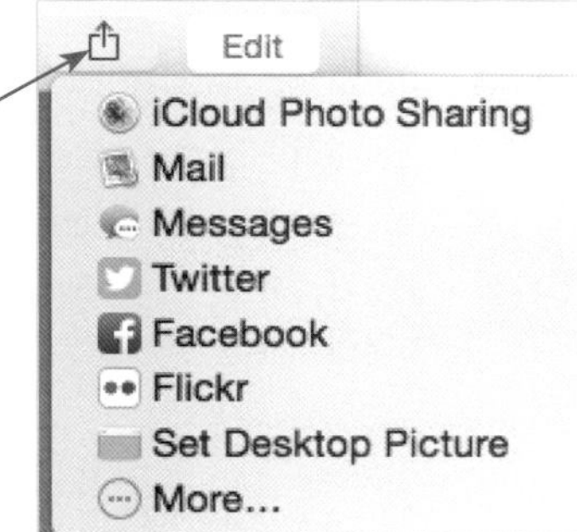

2. To share a photo via iCloud, select the **iCloud Photo Sharing** option in Step 1

3. Select an existing shared album or click on the **New Shared Album** button to create a new shared album

4. Shared albums can also be created in the **Shared** section. Click here, enter the details for the album and the email address of the recipient and click on the **Create** button. Photos can then be added by selecting them from the main Photos window

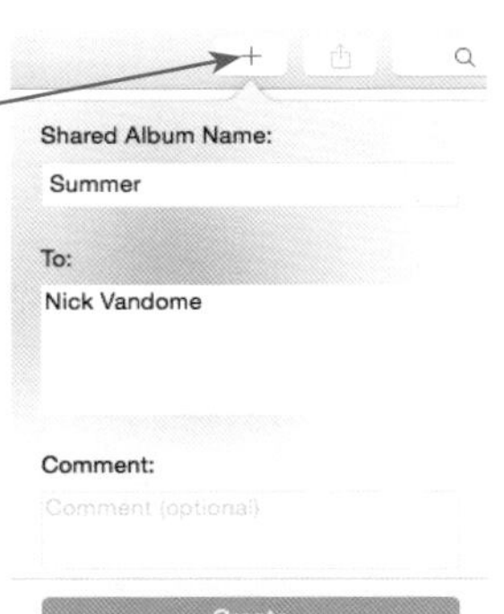

In order to use **iCloud Photo Sharing**, this has to be enabled in the iCloud System Preferences, as shown on page 144.

When you share an album with someone they will be sent an email notification.

iTunes

Music is one of the areas that has revived Apple's fortunes in recent years, primarily through the music player on the iPod, iPhone and iPad, and iTunes and the iTunes music store, where music can be bought online. iTunes is a versatile app but its basic function is to play a music CD. To do this:

1. Click on this button on the Dock and insert the CD in an external CD/DVD drive

2. By default, iTunes will open and display this window. Click **No** if you just want to play the CD

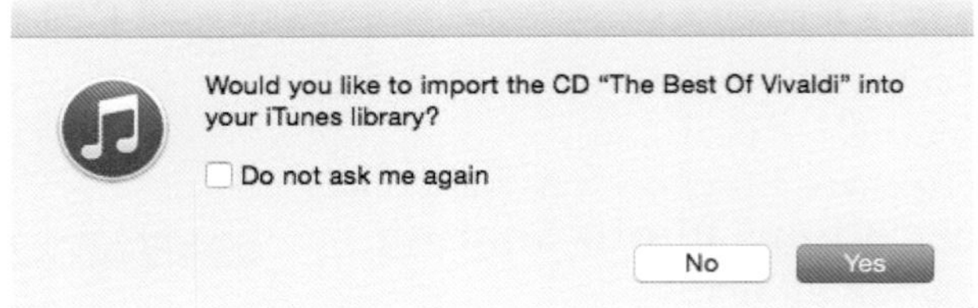

3. Click on the CD name

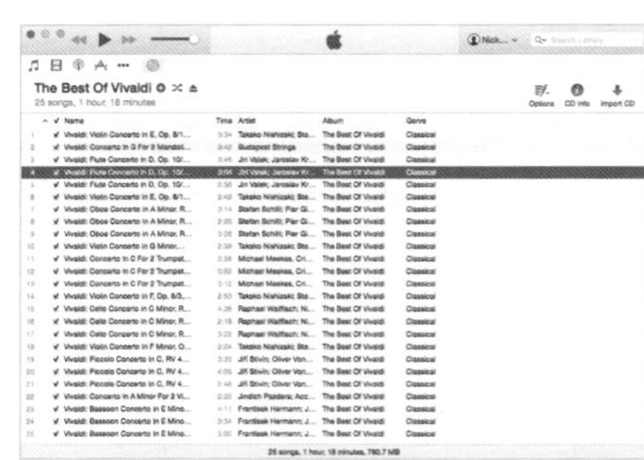

4. Click on this button to play the whole CD

5. Click on the **Import CD** button if you want to copy the music from the CD onto your hard drive

Never import music and use it for commercial purposes as this would be a breach of copyright.

Managing Your Music

iTunes has a variety of ways to display and manage your music:

1. Click on the **Music** button to see the iTunes categories, within a drop-down menu

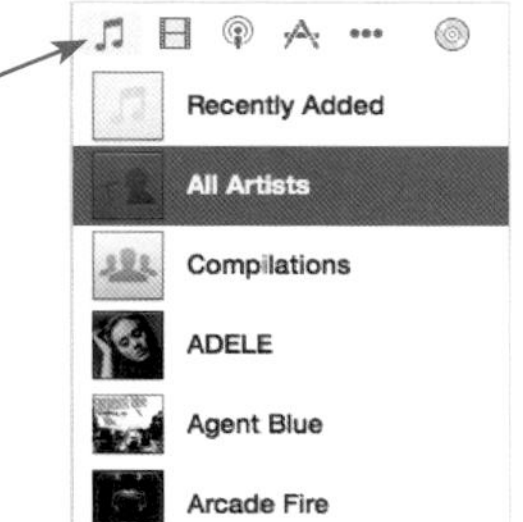

2. Select **View** from the iTunes menu bar to display the left-hand sidebar. Click on the **Music** button to view all of your music content

3. Click on these buttons to view the details of your music according to these headings

4. Within any of the categories in Step 3, click on an item to view the songs within it. Double-click on a track to start playing it

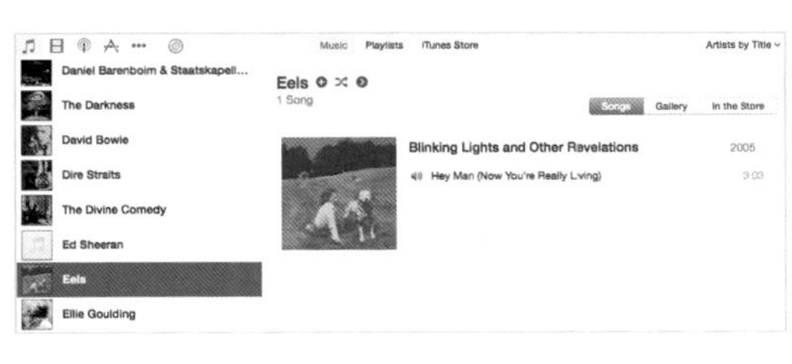

5. When a song is playing it is displayed at the top of the iTunes window, along with controls to move to the next or previous track, pause and play the track and adjust the volume

Don't forget

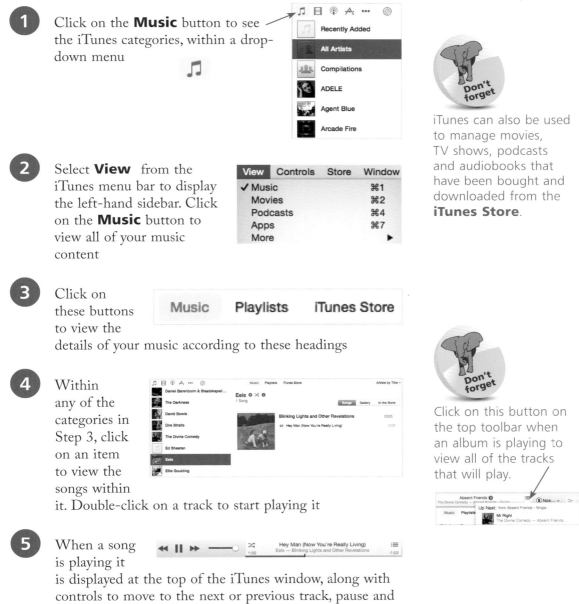

iTunes can also be used to manage movies, TV shows, podcasts and audiobooks that have been bought and downloaded from the **iTunes Store**.

Click on this button on the top toolbar when an album is playing to view all of the tracks that will play.

Purchasing Music

As well as copying music from CDs into iTunes, it is also possible to download a vast selection of music from the iTunes online store. To do this:

Never use illegal music download sites. Apart from the legal factor, they are much more likely to contain viruses and spyware.

1. Click on the **iTunes Store** link to access the online store

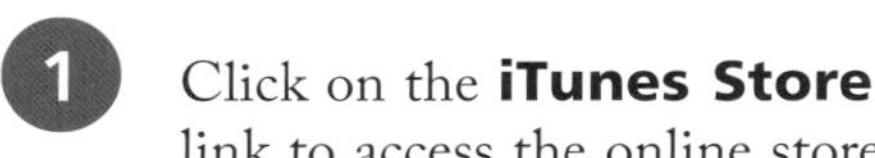

2. Navigate around the iTunes store using the tabs along the top of the iTunes window

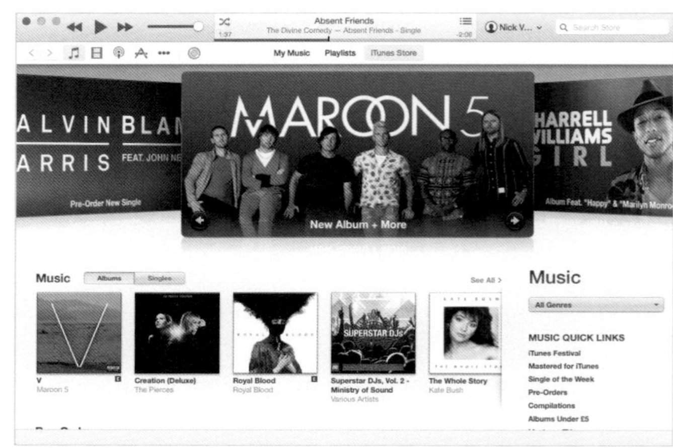

To buy music from the iTunes Store you must have an Apple ID and account.

3. To find a specific item, enter the details in the Search box at the top right-hand corner of the iTunes window

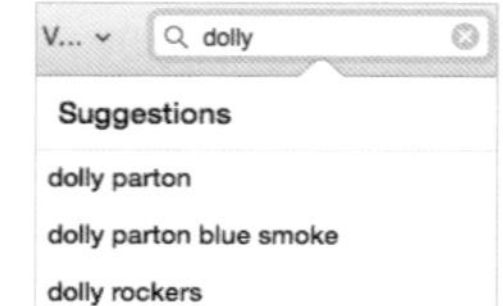

4. Details of the item are displayed within the Store

5. Click on the **Price** button to purchase the item

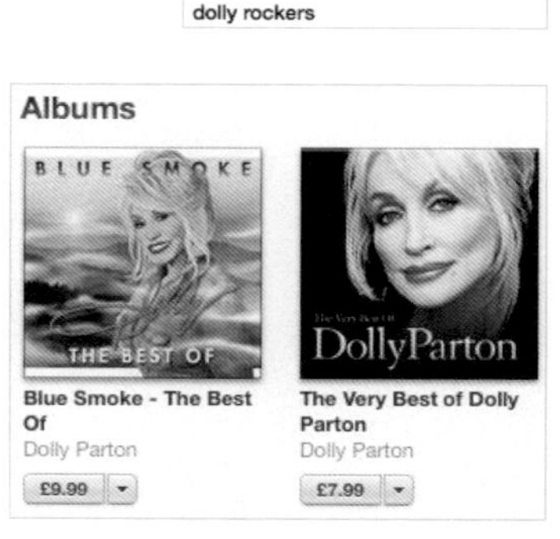

Adding a Mobile Device

With the iPhone, iPad and iPod, Apple has secured a significant foothold in the mobile digital device market. These can also be used in conjunction with a MacBook and iTunes so that you can load your digital devices with content from your MacBook, such as music, videos and books. To do this (this example is for an iPod, but the same applies to iPhones and iPads):

1. Connect your iPod to the Mac with the supplied USB cable

2. iTunes will open automatically and display details about the attached iPod

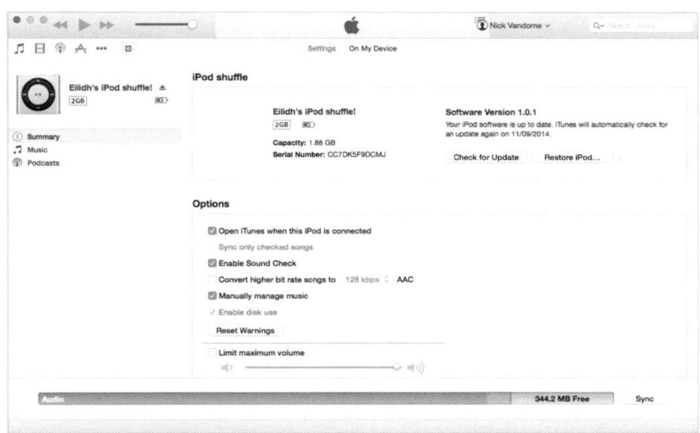

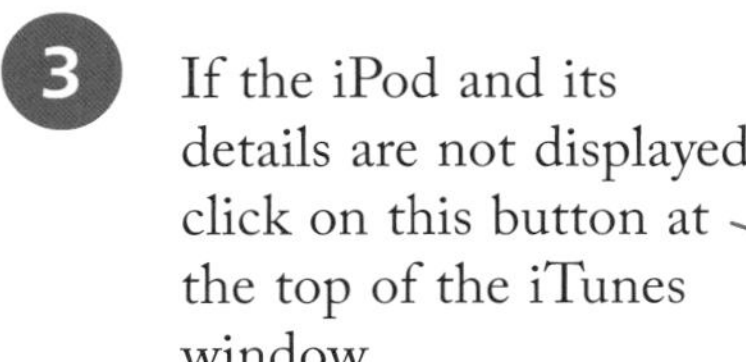

3. If the iPod and its details are not displayed, click on this button at the top of the iTunes window

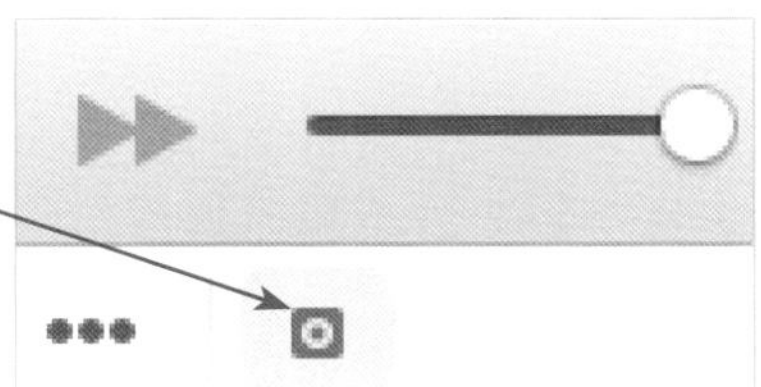

4. Select **File > Sync** from the iTunes Menu bar or click on the **Sync** button to synchronize iTunes and your iPod

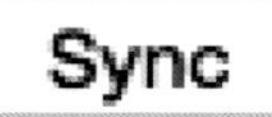

iPods come in a variety of models, colors, sizes and disk capacity. iPhones and iPads can also be added to your Mac and managed in the same way.

iMovie

For home movie buffs, iMovie offers options for downloading, editing and publishing your efforts:

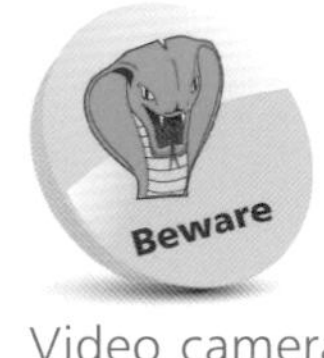

Video cameras can be connected with a USB or Thunderbolt cable. If you have a video camera with a FireWire cable you will need a FireWire adapter.

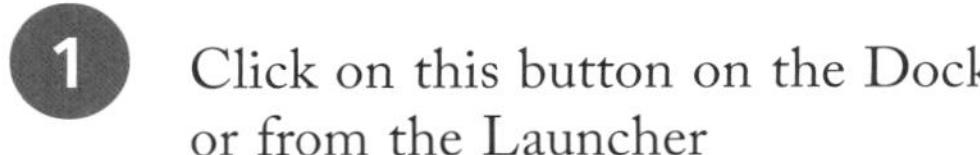

1. Click on this button on the Dock or from the Launcher

2. Click on the **Import Media** button to download video clips into iMovie

3. Select a location from which to download clips. This can be from a video camera, a removable device such as a pen drive, or on your Mac

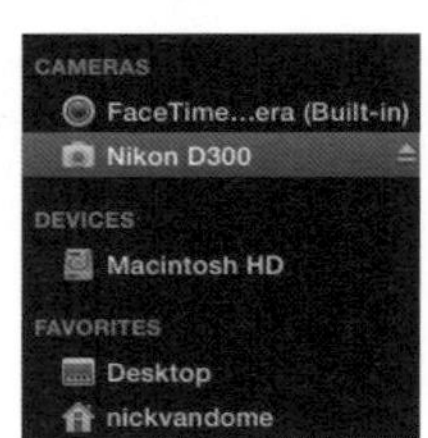

4. Once you have downloaded video clips, click on the **New** button to start your video project

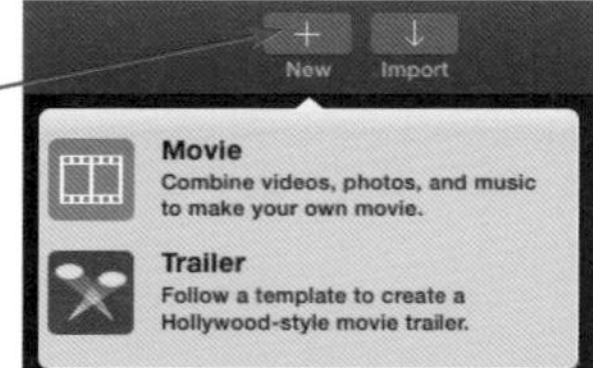

5. Click on the **Theme** for your project and click on the **Create** button

6. Give your project a name and click on the **OK** button

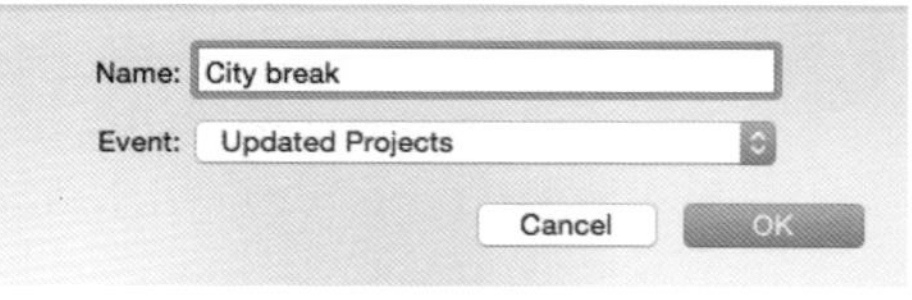

In the past, Apple produced an app called iDVD for creating artistic presentations from your own home moves. However, this has now been discontinued, but other DVD-creation apps can be obtained in the App Store.

7. The video clip selected in Step 3 is added to the iMovie editing window

Video clips for using in projects Preview window

Timeline, where the video project is created and edited. Drag the clip left or right to move it over the Playhead (the orange line). Projects are created in the **Library** area

8. Click on the **Enhance** button to apply editing enhancements to your video project

9. Click on these buttons for options that can be applied to video clips

10. Click on the **Share** button to share a complete movie in a variety of ways

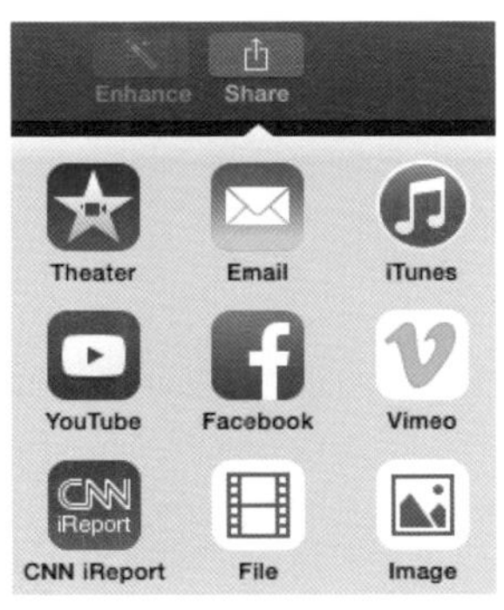

The name of a project is used for the opening title, but this can be changed by double-clicking on it.

Click on a clip on the timeline to trim it by dragging at either end of the yellow box that appears around it.

The **Theater** area displays items that have been shared via iCloud. This can be used to view all of your iCloud video content. Click on this button to access it.

Theater

GarageBand

For those who are as interested in creating music as listening to it, GarageBand can be used for this very purpose. It can take a bit of time and practice to become fully proficient with GarageBand but it is worth persevering with if you are musically inclined and want to compose your own. To use GarageBand:

1. Click on this icon on the Dock or within the Launcher

2. Click on the **New Project** button

GarageBand can appear quite complex at first and it takes a little time to feel comfortable with it.

3. Select an instrument group and click on the **Choose** button

4. Select an instrument within the group

5. Select **Window > Show Keyboard** from the menu bar to display the keyboard for inputting music

6. Click on this button to start recording a track, using the keyboard

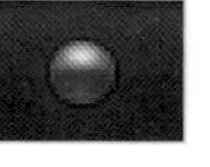

7. Click on the keyboard to record the music

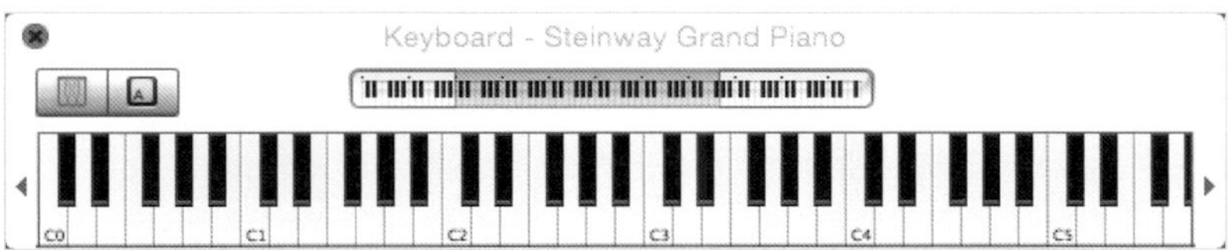

8. The track is placed on the GarageBand timeline

9. Click on this button to view a list of pre-recorded music loops

10. A list of loops is displayed. Select a style and an instrument. The available loops are displayed underneath the **Name** tab

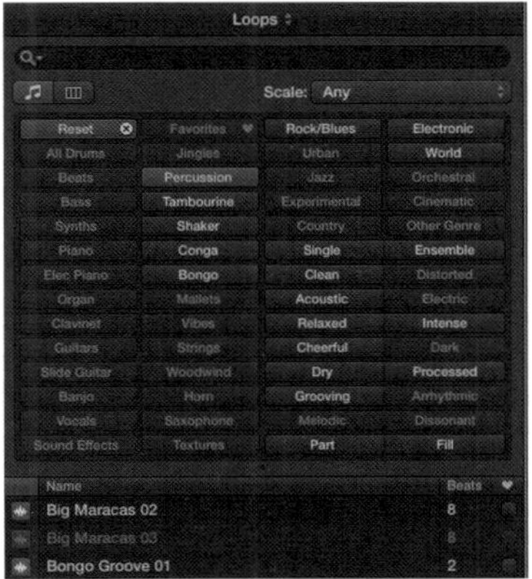

11. Select a loop and drag it onto the timeline to add it to your song

12. The completed song is shown in the timeline. This can consist of several separate tracks

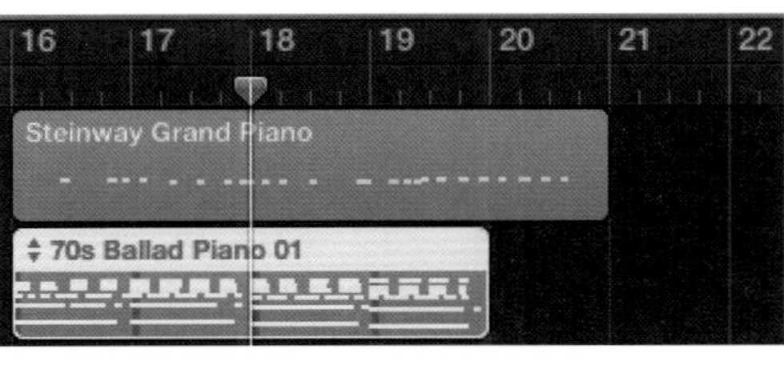

Hot tip

Click on the arrows at either end of the keyboard to access the other sections of it.

Click and drag on tracks on the timeline to move their position.

Game Center

Playing games is one of the most popular pastimes on computers and OS X Yosemite gives you ample opportunity to indulge this with the Game Center. To start playing games:

1. Click on this icon in the Launchpad

2. Enter your Apple ID details and click on the **Sign In** button (or, if you do not have an Apple ID, click on the Create Apple ID button)

3. You can select your own user name and also add a photo for other gamers to see, by clicking on the **Me** icon and selecting a photo from the default menu or select one from your own photos

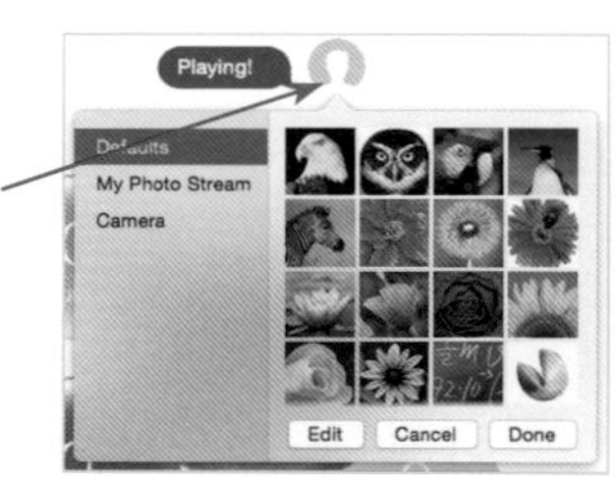

4. Click on **Games** button on the top toolbar

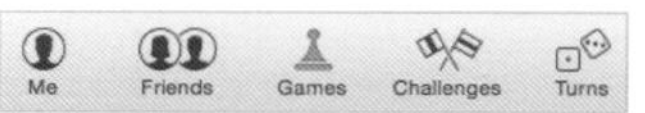

5. Your current games are displayed in the Game Center, including any that you have downloaded on any Apple devices such as iPads, iPhones or iPod Touches

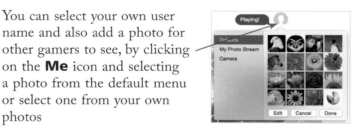

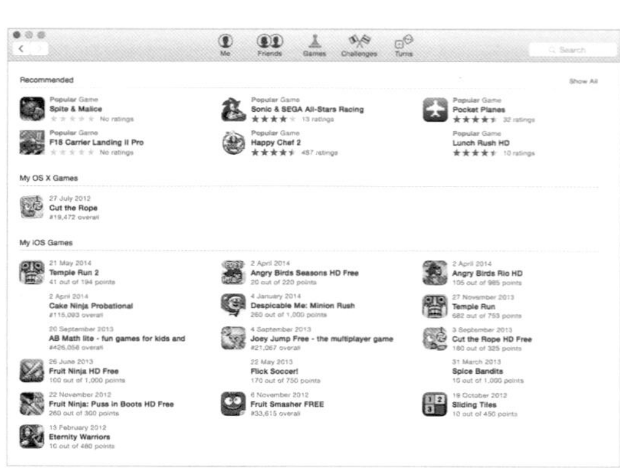

Click on a game to view details about your gaming history and other people's achievements.

10 Sharing OS X

This chapter looks at how to set up different user accounts and how to keep everyone safe on your MacBook using parental controls.

Adding Users

OS X enables multiple users to access individual accounts on the same computer. If there are multiple users, i.e. two or more, for a single machine, each person can sign on individually and access their own files and folders. This means that each person can log in to their own settings and preferences. All user accounts can be password protected, to ensure that each user's environment is secure. To set up multiple user accounts:

Don't forget

Every computer with multiple users has at least one main user, also known as an administrator. This means that they have greater control over the number of items that they can edit and alter. If there is only one user on a computer, they automatically take on the role of the administrator. Administrators have a particularly important role to play when computers are networked together. Each computer can potentially have several administrators.

Don't forget

Each user can select their own icon or photo of themselves.

1. Click on the **System Preferences** icon on the Dock

2. Click on the **Users & Groups** icon

3. The information about the current account is displayed. This is your own account and the information is based on details you provided when you first set up your MacBook

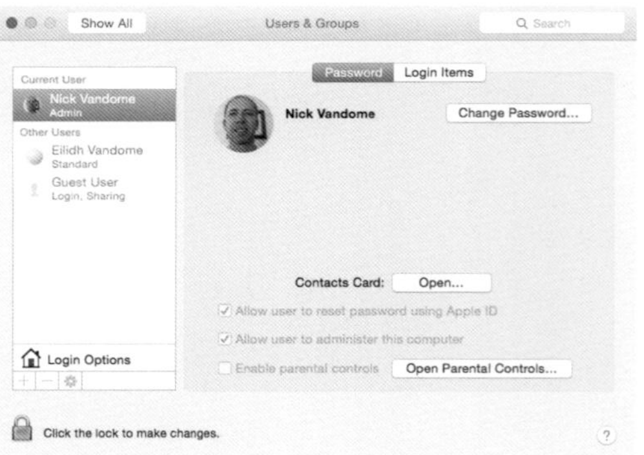

4. Click on this icon to enable new accounts to be added (the padlock needs to be open)

5. Click on the plus sign icon to add a new account 

6. Enter the details for the new account holder

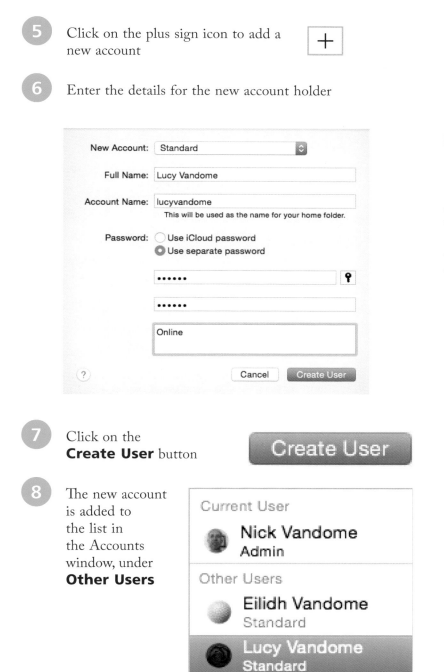

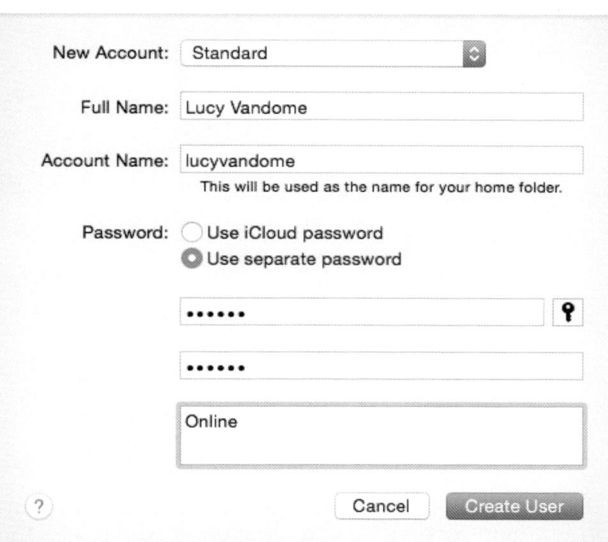

By default, you are the administrator of your own MacBook. This means that you can administer other user accounts.

7. Click on the **Create User** button

8. The new account is added to the list in the Accounts window, under **Other Users**

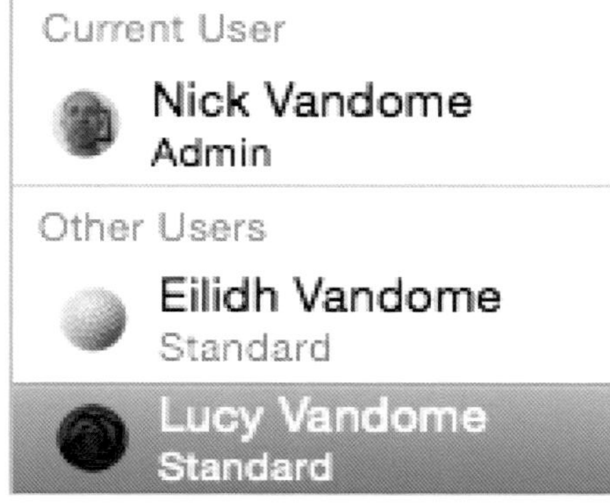

Deleting Users

Once a user has been added, their name appears on the list in the Other Users panel. It is then possible to edit the details of a particular user or delete them altogether. To do this:

Always tell other users if you are planning to delete them from the system. Don't just remove them and then let them find out the next time they try to log in. If you delete a user, their personal files are left untouched and can still be accessed.

1. Within **Users & Groups**, select a user from the list

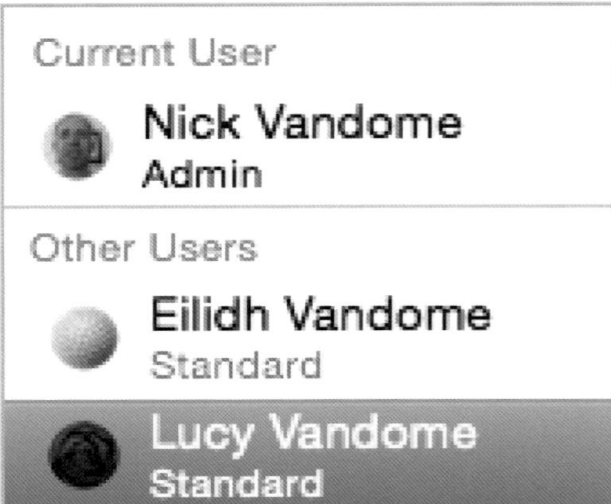

2. Click here to remove the selected person's user account —

3. A warning box appears to check if you really do want to delete the selected user. If you do, select the required option and click on **Delete User**

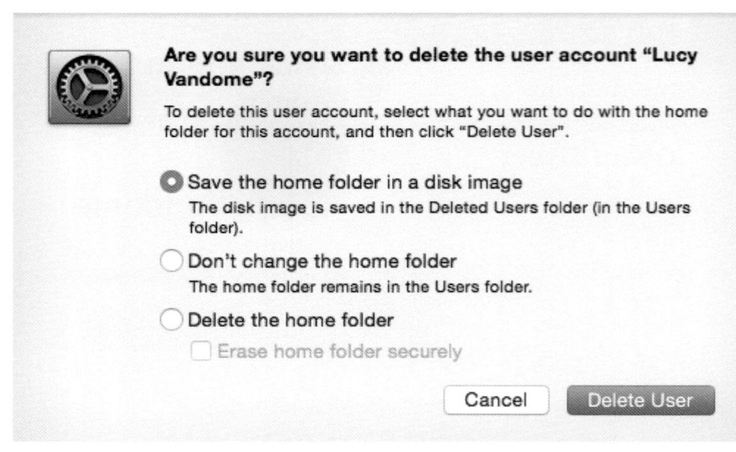

Are you sure you want to delete the user account "Lucy Vandome"?
To delete this user account, select what you want to do with the home folder for this account, and then click "Delete User".
Save the home folder in a disk image
The disk image is saved in the Deleted Users folder (in the Users folder).
Don't change the home folder
The home folder remains in the Users folder.
Delete the home folder
Erase home folder securely
Cancel
Delete User

Fast User Switching

If there are multiple users using OS X it is useful to be able to switch between them as quickly as possible. When this is done, the first user's session is retained so that they can return to it if required. To switch between users:

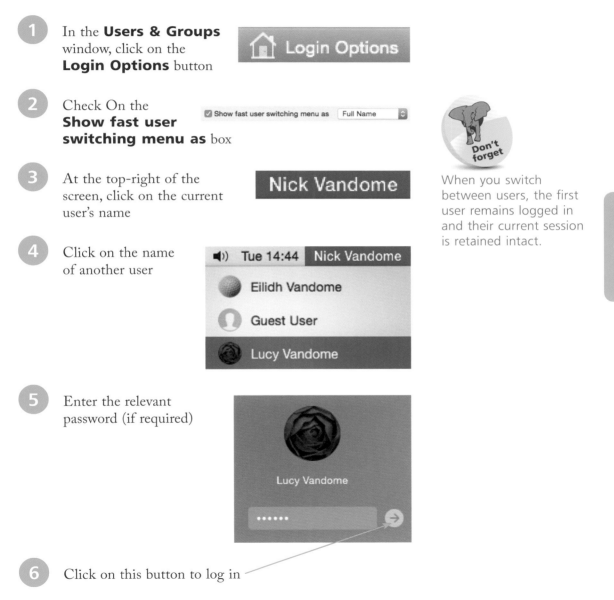

1. In the **Users & Groups** window, click on the **Login Options** button

2. Check On the **Show fast user switching menu as** box

3. At the top-right of the screen, click on the current user's name

4. Click on the name of another user

5. Enter the relevant password (if required)

6. Click on this button to log in

When you switch between users, the first user remains logged in and their current session is retained intact.

OS X for the Family

Many families share their computers between multiple users and, with the ability to create different accounts in OS X, each user can have their own customized workspace. If desired, you can also set up an Apple ID so that other users can access a wider range of products, such as the Apple App Store. To do this:

1.  Access **Users & Groups**

2. Click on the **Apple ID: Set...** button

3. If the user already has an Apple ID, enter it in the appropriate box. If not click on the **Create Apple ID** button to create an account

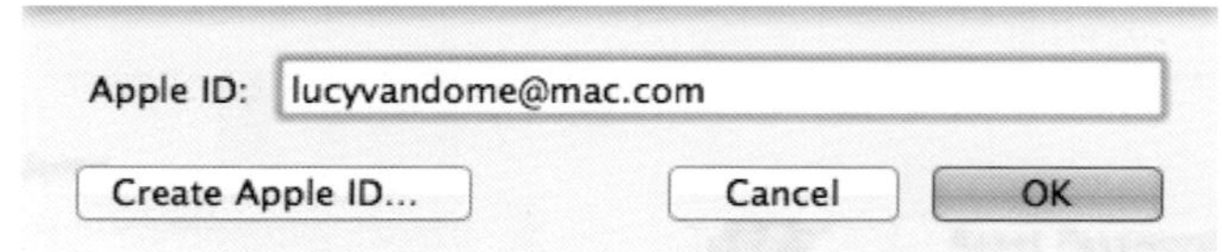

4. A page on the Apple website is accessed. This contains general information about an Apple ID and also a facility for obtaining one

If you give someone an Apple ID, credit card information will have to be given. Therefore, the user will be able to access services such as the iTunes Store and the App Store, where they will be able to purchase a range of items.

Parental Controls

If children are using the computer, parents may want to restrict access to certain types of information that can be viewed, using Parental Controls. To do this:

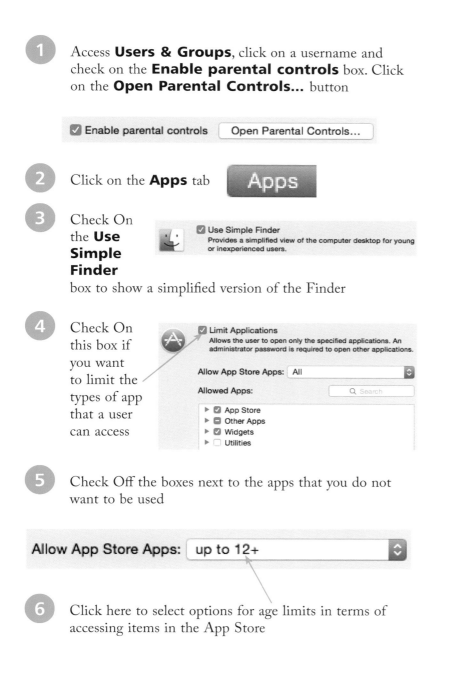

1. Access **Users & Groups**, click on a username and check on the **Enable parental controls** box. Click on the **Open Parental Controls...** button

2. Click on the **Apps** tab

3. Check On the **Use Simple Finder** box to show a simplified version of the Finder

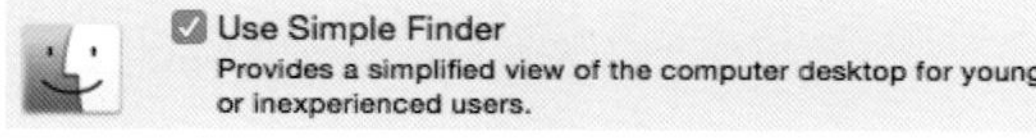

Provides a simplified view of the computer desktop for young or inexperienced users.

4. Check On this box if you want to limit the types of app that a user can access

5. Check Off the boxes next to the apps that you do not want to be used

Allow App Store Apps:

6. Click here to select options for age limits in terms of accessing items in the App Store

...cont'd

Web controls

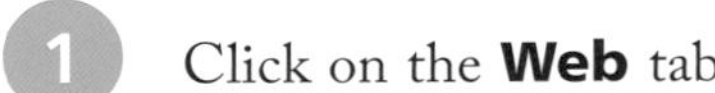

1. Click on the **Web** tab

2. Check On this button to try to prevent access to websites with adult content

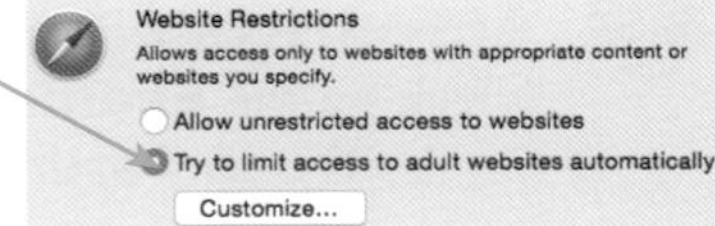

To check which sites have been viewed on a Web browser, check the History menu, which is located on the main Menu bar.

3. Check On this button to specify specific websites that are suitable to be viewed

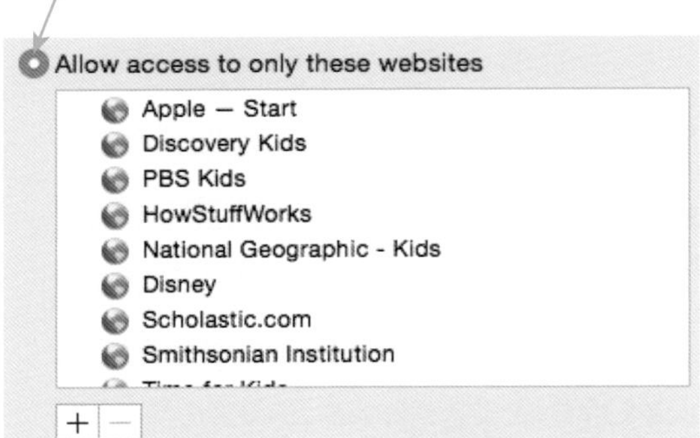

People controls

1. Click on the **People** tab

2. Check On the **Limit** boxes to limit the type of content in email messages, games and text messages

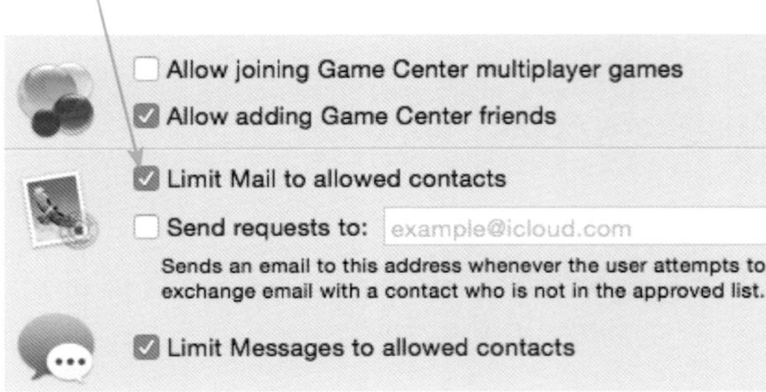

Time Limits controls

1. Click on the **Time Limits** tab Time Limits

2. Check On this box to limit the amount of time the user can use the Mac during weekdays

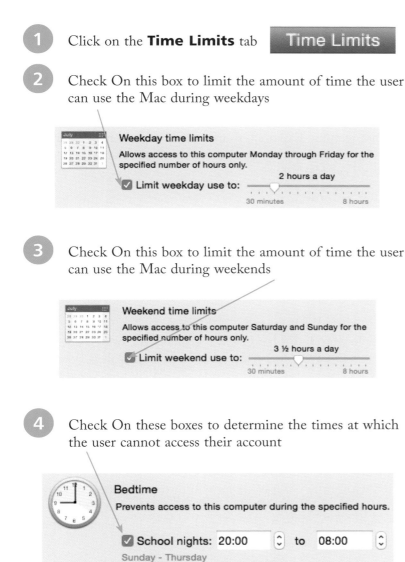

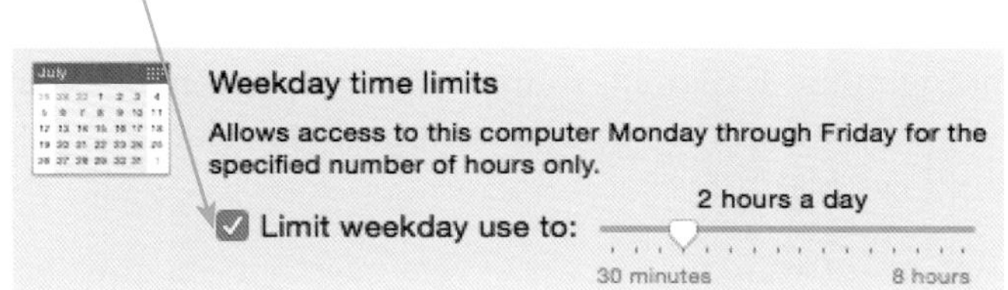

3. Check On this box to limit the amount of time the user can use the Mac during weekends

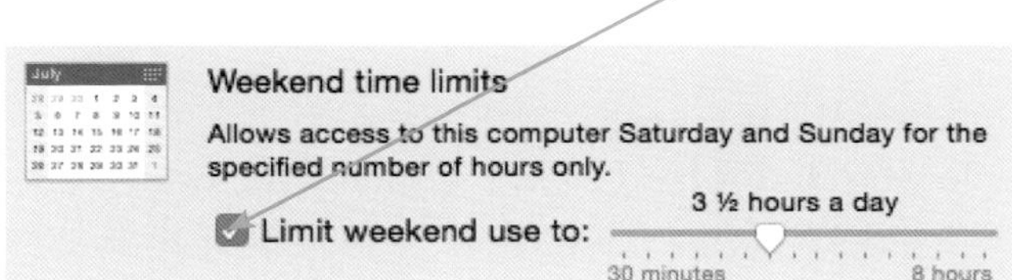

4. Check On these boxes to determine the times at which the user cannot access their account

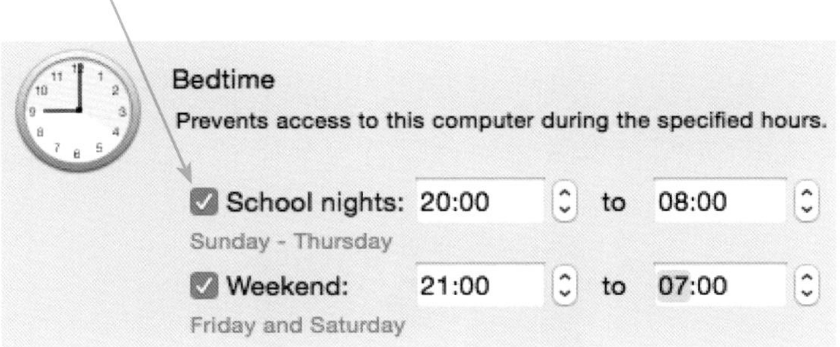

Bedtime
Prevents access to this computer during the specified hours.
School nights: 20:00 to 08:00
Sunday - Thursday
Weekend: 21:00 to 07:00
Friday and Saturday

OS X for Windows Users

General sharing

One of the historical complaints about Macs is that it is difficult to share files between them and Microsoft Windows computers. While this may have been true with some file types in years gone by, this is an issue that is becoming less and less important, particularly with OS X. Some of the reasons for this are:

- A number of popular file formats, such as PDFs (Portable Document Format) for documents and JPEGs (Joint Photographic Experts Group) for photos and images, are designed so that they can be used on both Mac and Windows platforms.
- A lot of software apps on the Mac have options for saving files into different formats, including ones that are specifically for Windows machines.
- Other popular apps, such as Microsoft Office, now have Mac versions and the resulting files can be shared on both formats.

Many file formats can be opened on both Macs and Windows PCs. Even Word, Excel and PowerPoint files can be exchanged, as long as each user has the relevant version of Office.

Sharing with Boot Camp

For people who find it hard to live without Microsoft Windows, help is at hand even on a Mac. Macs have a app called Boot Camp that can be used to run a version of Windows on a Mac. This is only available with Yosemite. Once it has been accessed, a copy of Windows can then be installed and run. This means that if you have a non-Mac app that you want to use on your Mac, you can do so with Boot Camp.

Boot Camp is set up with the Boot Camp Assistant which is located within the Utilities folder within the Applications folder. Once this is run you can then install either Windows XP, Vista, Windows 7, Windows 8 or 8.1 which will run at its native speed.

11 MacBook Networking

This chapter looks at how to use your MacBook to create and work with networks between other computers for sharing information.

Networking Overview

Before you start sharing files directly between computers, you have to connect them together. This is known as networking and can be done with two computers in the same room, or with thousands of computers in a major corporation. If you are setting up your own small network it will be known in the computing world as a Local Area Network (LAN). When setting up a network there are various pieces of hardware that are initially needed to join all of the required items together. Once this has been done, software settings can be applied for the networked items. Some of the items of hardware that may be required include:

- **A network card**. This is known as a Network Interface Card (NIC); all recent MacBooks have them built-in.
- **An Ethernet port and Ethernet cable**. This enables you to make the physical connection between devices. Ethernet cables come in a variety of forms, but the one you should be looking for is the Cat5E type as this allows for the fastest transfer of data. If you are creating a wireless network, you will not require these.
- **A hub**. This is a piece of hardware, with multiple Ethernet ports, that enables you to connect all of your devices together and let them communicate with each other. However, conflicts can occur with hubs if two devices try to send data through it at the same time.
- **A switch**. This is similar in operation to a hub but is more sophisticated in its method of data transfer, thus allowing all of the machines on the network to communicate simultaneously, unlike a hub.

Once you have worked out all of the devices you want to include on your network you can arrange them accordingly. Try to keep the switches and hub within relative proximity of a power supply and, if you are using cables, make sure they are laid out safely.

It is perfectly possible to create a simple network of two computers just by joining them with an Ethernet cable.

Ethernet network

The cheapest and easiest way to network computers is to create an Ethernet network. This involves buying an Ethernet hub or switch, which enables you to connect several devices to a central point, i.e. the hub or switch. All MacBooks, and most modern printers, have an Ethernet connection, so it is possible to connect various devices, not just computers. Once all of the devices have been connected by Ethernet cables, you can then start applying network settings.

AirPort network

Another option for creating a network is using Apple's own wireless system, AirPort. This creates a wireless network and there are two main options used by Apple computers: AirPort Express, using the IEEE 802.11n standard, which is more commonly known as Wi-Fi, which stands for Wireless Fidelity, and the newer AirPort Extreme, using the next generation IEEE 802.11ac standard which is up to five times faster than the 802.11n standard. Thankfully, AirPort Express and Extreme are also compatible with devices based on the older IEEE standards, 802.11b/g/n, so one machine loaded with AirPort Extreme can still communicate wirelessly with an older AirPort one.

Another method for connecting items wirelessly is called Bluetooth. This covers much shorter distances than AirPort and is generally used for items like printers and cellphones. Bluetooth devices can be connected by using the Bluetooth Setup Assistant in the Utilities folder.

One of the issues with a wireless network is security, since it is possible for someone with a wireless-enabled machine to access your wireless network if they are within range. However, in the majority of cases the chances of this happening are fairly slim, although it is an issue about which you should be aware.

The basics of a wireless network with Macs is an AirPort card (either AirPort Express or AirPort Extreme) installed in all of the required machines and an AirPort base station that can be located anywhere within 150 meters of the AirPort enabled computers. Once the hardware is in place, wireless-enabled devices can be configured by using the AirPort Setup Assistant utility found in the Utilities folder. After AirPort has been set up, the wireless network can be connected. All of the wireless-enabled devices should then be able to communicate with each other, without the use of a multitude of cables.

Wireless network

A wireless network can also be created with a standard wireless router, rather than using the AirPort option.

Network Settings

Once you have connected the hardware required for a network, you can start applying the network settings that are required for different computers to communicate with one another. To network two Mac computers:

Beware

If you turn off the Wi-Fi function, this will disconnect you from your network and also the Internet.

1. In **System Preferences,** click on the **Network** button

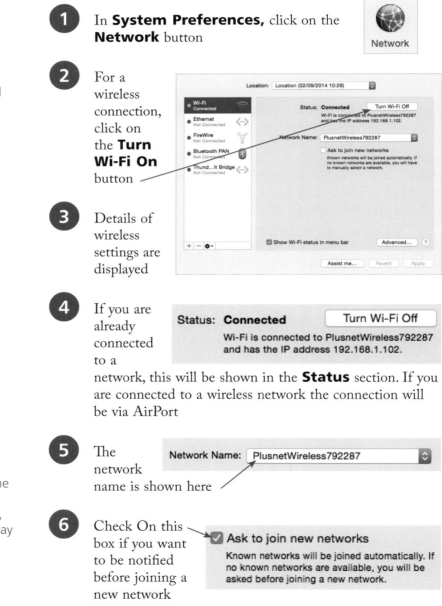

2. For a wireless connection, click on the **Turn Wi-Fi On** button

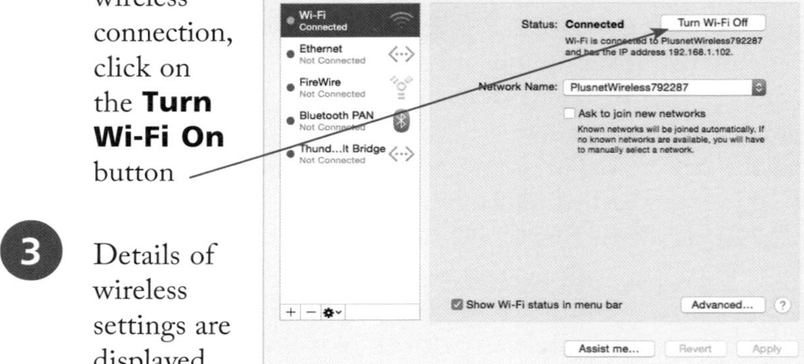

3. Details of wireless settings are displayed

4. If you are already connected to a network, this will be shown in the **Status** section. If you are connected to a wireless network the connection will be via AirPort

Status: Connected Turn Wi-Fi Off
Wi-Fi is connected to PlusnetWireless792287 and has the IP address 192.168.1.102.

If you are asked to join new networks, all of the available networks in range will be displayed, not just the one you may want to join.

5. The network name is shown here

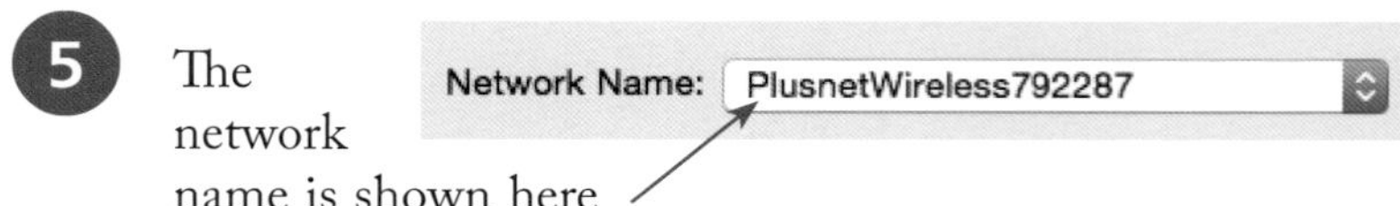

6. Check On this box if you want to be notified before joining a new network

Ask to join new networks
Known networks will be joined automatically. If no known networks are available, you will be asked before joining a new network.

7. For a cable connection, connect an Ethernet cable

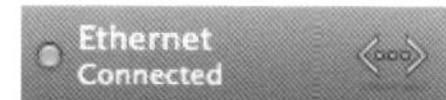

8. Details of the cable settings are displayed

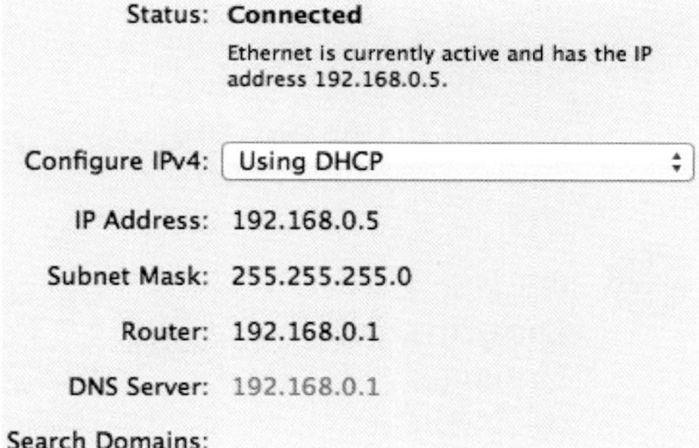

For an Ethernet connection you need to have an Ethernet cable connected to your MacBook and the router.

9. Click on the **Advanced...** button to access a range of options for both Wi-Fi and cable network connections

Advanced...

10. Click on the tabs at the top of the window to view the advanced options for each type of connection

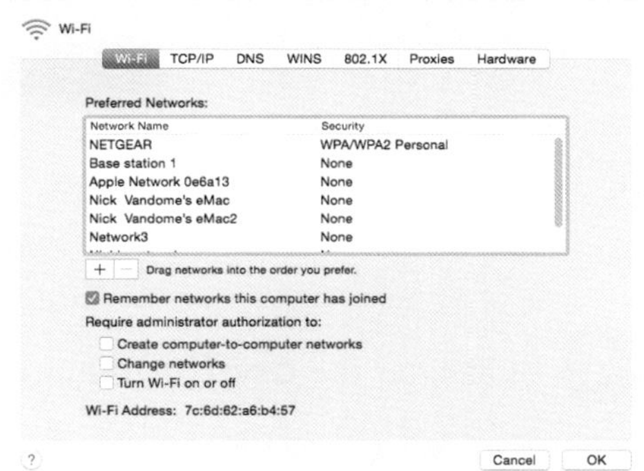

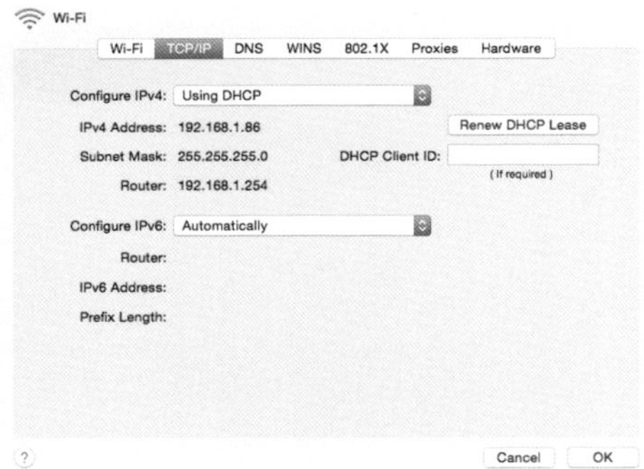

Network Diagnostics

If your network is unavailable you can check to see what the problem is. To do this:

1. If there is a problem connecting to the Internet, click on the **Assist me...** button in the **Network** window

2. Click on the **Diagnostics...** button to troubleshoot a connection problem

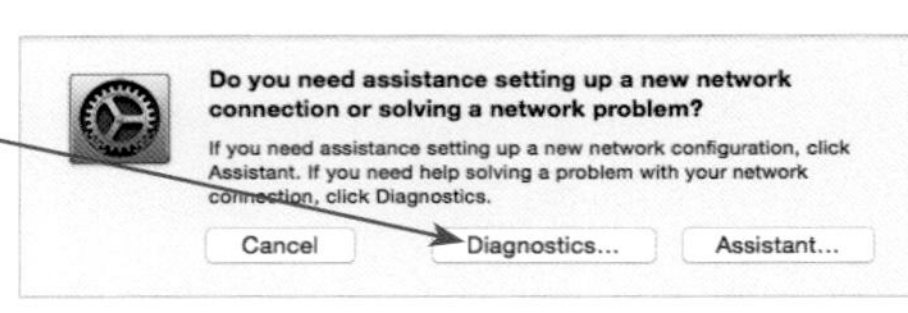

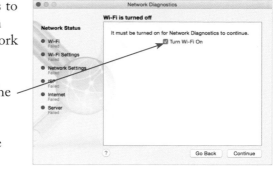

Over time, you may end up with a number of network names, not all of which are still used. Delete any names that are redundant so that the list does not become too long.

3. The status of the network is shown in the left-hand panel. Select the method you want to connect to a network with, e.g. Wi-Fi (wireless)

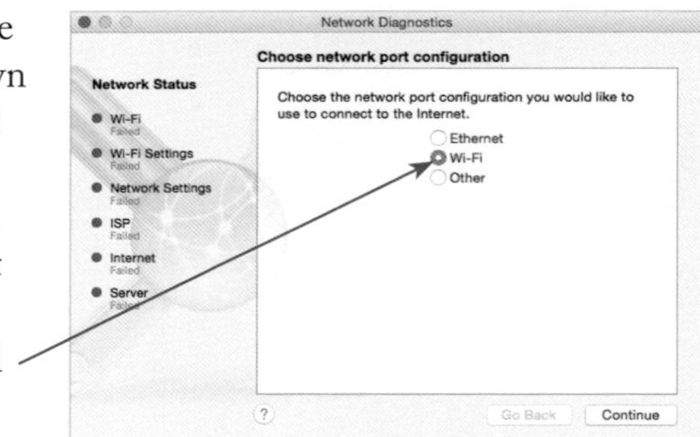

4. Click on the **Continue** button

5. Wi-Fi needs to be turned on for the network diagnostics to continue. Check On the **Turn Wi-Fi On** box and click the **Continue** button

6. Select an available network. The left-hand panel will display the status for each required element

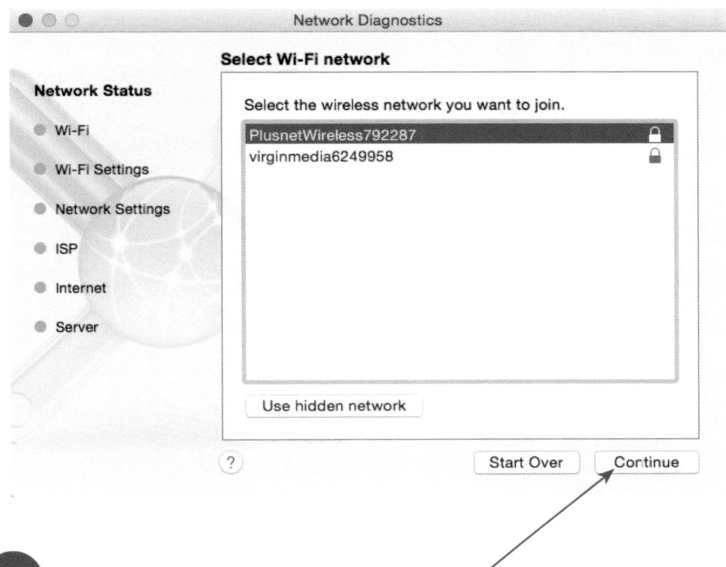

7. Click on the **Continue** button

8. The status of your network is displayed. Click on the **Quit** button to finish the network diagnostics

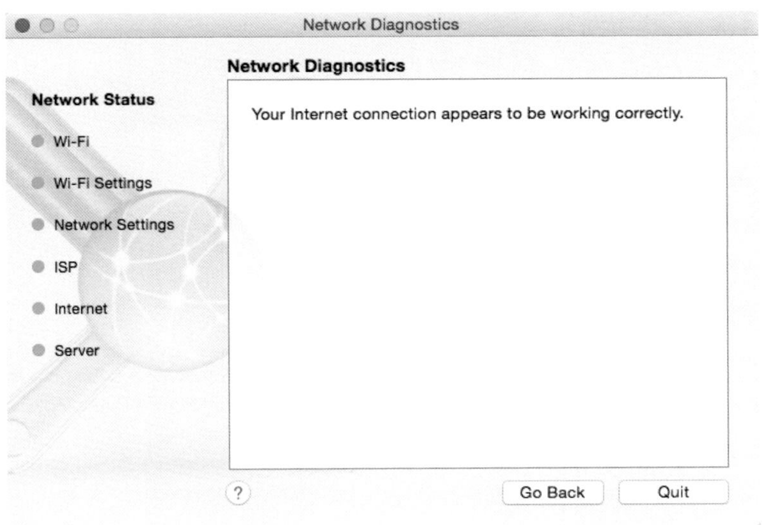

Connecting to a Network

Connecting as a registered user

To connect as a registered user (usually as yourself when you want to access items on another one of your own computers):

Your username and password is specified in the **Accounts** section of System Preferences.

1. Other connected computers on the network will show up in the **Shared** section in the Finder. Click on a networked computer

2. Click on the **Connect As...** button

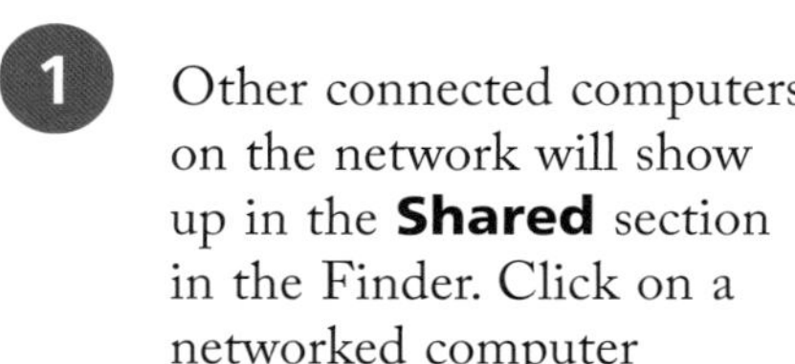

3. Check On the **Registered User** button and enter your username and password

You can disconnect from a networked computer by ejecting it in the Finder, in the same way as you would a removable drive, such as a DVD.

4. Click on the **Connect** button

5. The hard drive and home folder of the networked computer is available to the registered user. Double-click on an item to view its contents

Guest users

Guest users on a network are users other than yourself, or other registered users, to whom you want to limit access to your files and folders. Guests only have access to a folder called the Drop Box in your own Public folder. To share files with Guest users, you have to first copy them into the Drop Box. To do this:

1. Create a file and select **File > Save** from the Menu bar
2. Navigate to your own home folder (this is created automatically by OS X and is displayed in the Finder Sidebar)

3. Double-click on the **Public** folder

4. Double-click on the **Drop Box** folder

5. Save the file into the Drop Box

Drop Box is not the same as Dropbox. Dropbox is a cloud storage facility for documents, photos, etc.

If another user is having problems accessing the files in your Drop Box, check the permissions settings assigned to the files (see page 210 for further details).

The contents of the Drop Box can be accessed by other users on the same computer, as well as by users on a network.

...cont'd

Accessing a Drop Box

To access files in a Drop Box:

1. Double-click on a networked computer in the Finder

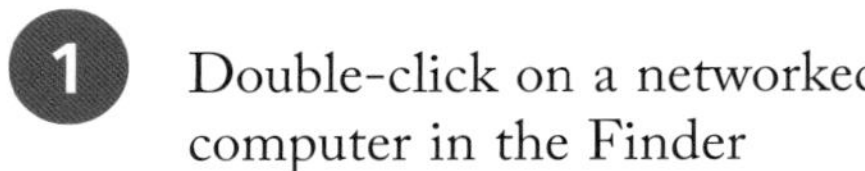

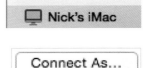

2. Click on the **Connect As...** button in the Finder window

3. Select the **Guest** button

4. Click on the **Connect** button

5. Double-click on the administrator's home folder

6. Double-click on the Drop Box folder to access the files within it

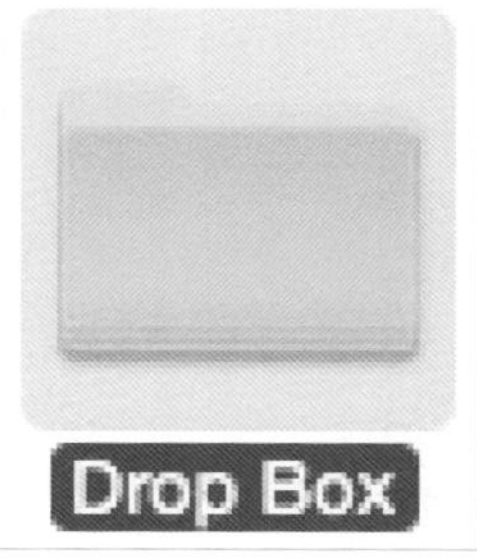

It is better to copy files into the Drop Box rather than moving them from their current location completely.

Set permissions for how the Drop Box operates by selecting it in the Finder and Ctrl+clicking on it. Select **Get Info** from the menu and apply the required settings under the **Ownership & Permissions** heading.

File Sharing

One of the main reasons for creating a network of two or more computers is to share files between them. On networked MacBooks, this involves setting them up so that they can share files and then access them.

Setting up file sharing

To set up file sharing on a networked MacBook:

1. Click on the **System Preferences** icon on the Dock

2. Click on the **Sharing** icon

3. Check the boxes next to the items you want to share (the most common items to share are files and printers)

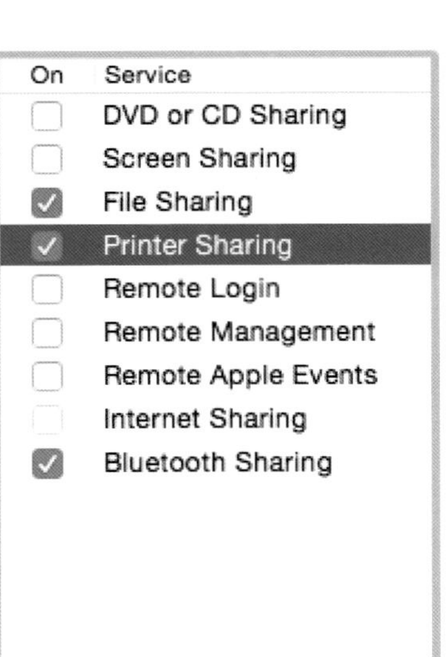

4. Click on the padlock to close it and prevent more changes

If no file sharing options are enabled in the Sharing preference window, no other users will be able to access your computer or your files, even on a network.

Networks can also be created, and items shared, between Macs and Windows-based PCs.

Sharing with AirDrop

Files can also be shared between MacBooks and other compatible Apple devices, such as iPads and iPhones, using the AirDrop feature. This enables the devices to connect wirelessly and you can then share content between them. To do this:

Devices do not have to be on the same network to share content with AirDrop, as a wireless connection is created between the devices.

1. In the Finder Sidebar, click on the **AirDrop** button

2. Other users in range with AirDrop are shown in the main Finder window

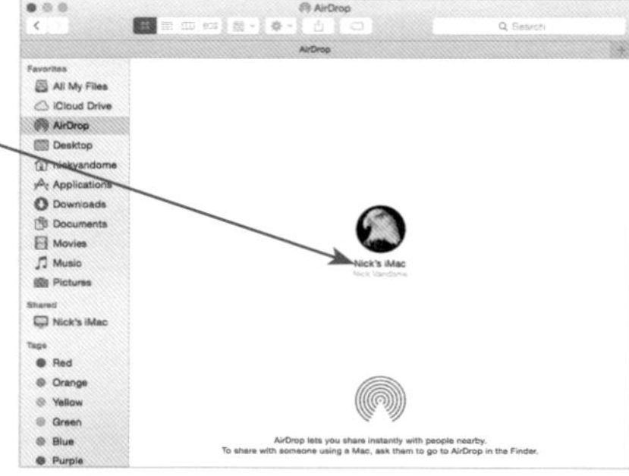

Content can also be shared via AirDrop by selecting it in the Finder and clicking on the **Share** button. Then select **AirDrop** from the options.

3. Drag content from another Finder window (or the Desktop) over the other user's icon to share it with them

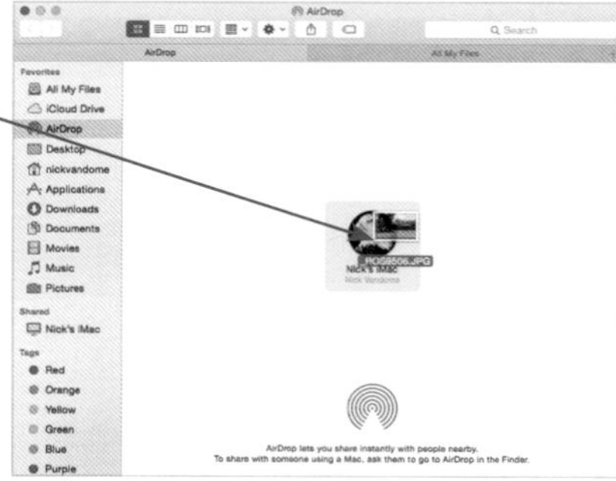

4. Content that has been shared from another device is initially placed in the **Downloads** folder in the Finder. It can then be copied from here and placed in another location, if required

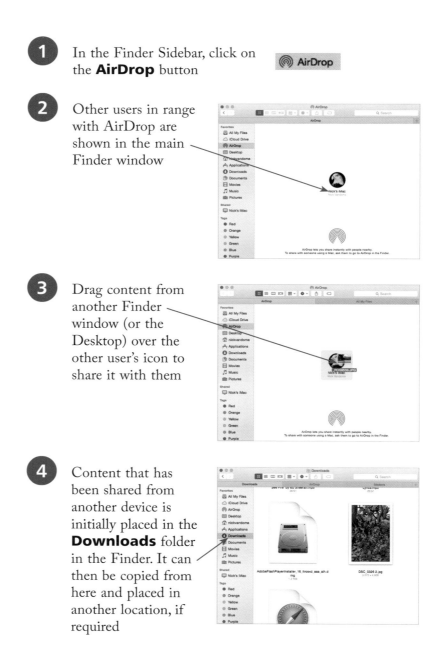

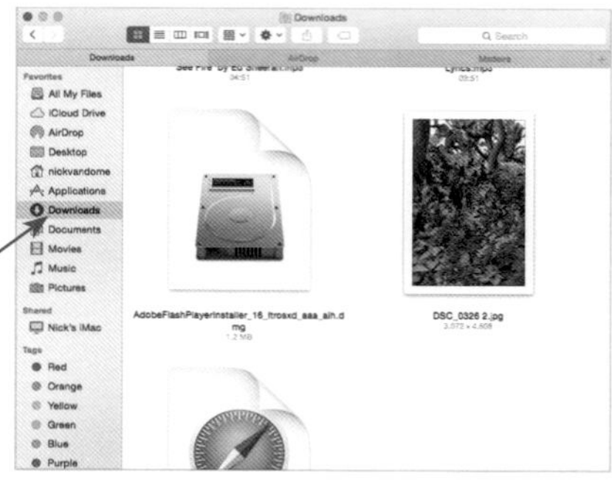

12 MacBook Mobility

MacBooks are ideal for mobile working, for business or pleasure. This chapter looks at being mobile with your MacBook, including protecting it and security concerns.

Transporting Your MacBook

When you are going traveling, either for business or pleasure, your MacBook can be a very valuable companion. It can be used to download photographs from a digital camera, download movies from a digital video camera, keep a diary or business notes and keep a record of your itinerary and important documents. Also, in many parts of the world it can access the Internet via wireless hotspots so that you can view the Web and send emails. However, when you are traveling with your MacBook it is sensible to transport this valuable asset in as safe and secure a way as possible. Some of the options include:

MacBook cases and sleeves

There is a range of MacBook cases and sleeves designed specifically for providing protection for the MacBook. They can be bought from the Apple website or Apple stores.

A backpack for carrying a MacBook can be more comfortable than a shoulder bag, as it distributes the weight more evenly.

Metal case

If you are concerned that your MacBook may be in danger of physical damage when you are on the road you may want to consider a more robust metal case. These are similar to those used by photographers and, depending on its size and design, you may also be able to include any photographic equipment.

Backpacks

A serious option for transporting your MacBook while you are traveling is a small backpack. This can either be a standard backpack or a backpack specifically designed for a MacBook. The latter is clearly a better option as the MacBook will fit more securely and there are also pockets designed for accessories.

Keeping Your MacBook Safe

By most measures, MacBooks are valuable items. However, in a lot of countries around the world their relative value can be a lot more than it is to their owners: in some countries the value of a MacBook could easily equate to a month's, or even a year's, wages. Even in countries where their relative value is not so high they can still be seen as a lucrative opportunity for thieves. Therefore, it is important to try to keep your MacBook as safe as possible when you are traveling with it, either abroad or at home. Some points to consider in relation to this are:

- If possible, keep your MacBook with you at all times, i.e. transport it in a piece of luggage that you can carry rather than having to put it into a large case.
- Never hand over your MacBook, or any of your belongings, to any local who promises to look after them.
- If you do have to detach yourself from your MacBook, put it somewhere secure such as a hotel safe.
- When you are traveling, keep your MacBook as unobtrusive as possible. This is where a backpack carrying case can prove useful as it is not immediately apparent that you are carrying a MacBook.
- Do not use your MacBook in areas where you think it may attract undue interest from the locals, particularly in obviously poor areas. For instance, if you are in a local cafe the appearance of a MacBook may create unwanted attention for you. If in doubt, wait until you get back to your hotel.
- If you are accosted by criminals who demand your MacBook, hand it over. No piece of equipment is worth suffering physical injury for.
- If you are abroad make sure your MacBook is covered by your travel insurance. If not, get separate insurance for it.
- Trust your instincts with your MacBook. If something doesn't feel right, don't do it.

Save your important documents onto a pen drive, or an external hard drive, on a daily basis when you are traveling and keep this away from your MacBook. This way you will still have these items if your MacBook is lost or stolen.

Temperature Extremes

Traveling consists of seeing a lot of different places and cultures but it also invariably involves different extremes of temperature: a visit to the pyramids of Egypt can see the mercury in the upper reaches of the thermometer, while a trip to Alaska would encounter much colder conditions. Whether it is hot or cold, looking after your MacBook is an important consideration in extremes of temperature.

If a MacBook gets too hot it could buckle the casing, making it difficult to close.

Heat

When traveling in hot countries the best way of avoiding any heat damage to your MacBook is to prevent it from getting too hot in the first place:

- Do not place your MacBook in direct sunlight.
- Keep your MacBook insulated from the heat.
- Do not leave your MacBook in an enclosed space, such as a car. Not only can this get very hot, but the sun's power can be increased by the vehicle's glass.

Wrap your MacBook in something white, such as a T-shirt or a towel, to insulate it against extreme heat.

Cold

Again, it is best to avoid your MacBook getting too cold in the first place and this can be done by following similar precautions to those for heat. However, if your MacBook does suffer from extremes of cold, allow it to warm up to normal room temperature again before you try to use it. This may take a couple of hours, but it will be worth the wait, rather than risking damaging the delicate computing elements inside.

Dealing with Water

Water is one of the greatest enemies of any electrical device, and MacBooks are no different. This is of particular relevance to anyone who is traveling near water with their MacBook, such as on a boat or ship, or using their MacBook near a swimming pool or a beach. If you are near water with your MacBook then you must bear the following in mind:

- **Avoid water**. The best way to keep your MacBook dry is to keep it away from water whenever possible. For instance, if you want to update your notes or download some photographs, then it would be best to do this in an indoor environment, rather than sitting near water.
- **Keep dry**. If you think you will be transporting your MacBook near water then it is a good precaution to protect it with some form of waterproof bag. There is a range of "dry-bags" that are excellent for this type of occasion and they remain waterproof even if fully immersed in water. These can be bought from outdoor suppliers.

- **Dry out**. If the worst does occur and your MacBook does get a good soaking, all is not lost. However, you will have to ensure that it is fully dried out before you try to use it again. Never turn it on if it is still wet.

Power Sockets

Different countries and regions around the world use different types of power sockets, and this is an issue when you are traveling with your MacBook. Wherever you are going in the world it is vital to have an adapter that will fit the sockets in the countries you intend to visit. Otherwise you will not be able to charge your MacBook battery.

There are over a dozen different types of plugs and sockets used around the world, with the four most popular being:

North America, Japan

This is a two-point plug and socket. The pins on the plug are flat and parallel.

Power adapters can be bought for all regions around the world. There are also kits that provide all of the adapters together. These provide connections for anywhere worldwide.

Continental Europe

This is a two-point plug and socket. The pins are rounded.

Australasia, China, Argentina

This is a three-point socket that can accommodate either a two- or a three-pin plug. In a two-pin plug, the pins are angled in a V shape.

UK

This is a three-point plug. The pins are rectangular.

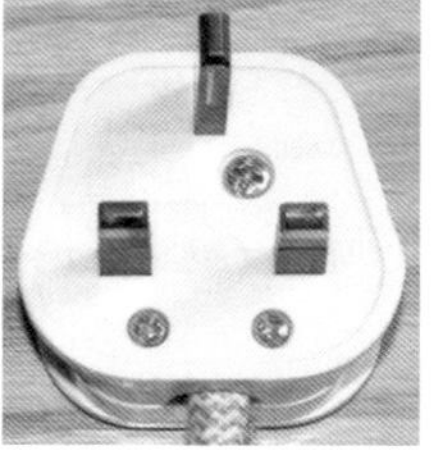

Airport Security

Because of the increased global security following terrorist attacks, such as those of September 11, 2001, the levels of airport security have been greatly increased around the world. This has implications for all travelers, and if you are traveling with a MacBook, this will add to the security scrutiny you will face. When dealing with airport security when traveling with a MacBook, there are some issues you should always keep in mind:

- Keep your MacBook with you at all times. Unguarded baggage at airports immediately raises suspicion and it can make life very easy for thieves.
- Carry your MacBook in a small bag so you can take it on board as hand luggage. On no account should it be put in with your luggage that goes in the hold.
- X-ray machines at airports will not harm your MacBook. However, if anyone tries to scan it with a metal detector, ask them if they can inspect it by hand instead.
- Keep a careful eye on your MacBook when it goes through the X-ray conveyor belt and try to be there at the other side as soon as it emerges. There have been some stories of people causing a commotion at the security gate just after someone has placed their MacBook on the conveyor belt. While everyone's attention (including yours) is distracted, an accomplice takes the MacBook from the conveyor belt. If you are worried about this you can ask for the security guard to hand-check your MacBook rather than putting it on the conveyor belt.
- Make sure the battery of your MacBook is fully charged. This is because you may be asked to turn on your MacBook to verify that it is just that, and not some other device disguised as a MacBook. This check has become increasingly common in recent years due to security threats and for some countries, such as the US, digital devices have to be turned on.
- When you are on the plane, keep the MacBook in the storage area under your seat, rather than in the overhead locker, so you know where it is at all times. Also, it could cause a serious injury if it fell out of an overhead locker.

If there is any kind of distraction when you are going through airport security it could be because someone is trying to divert your attention in order to steal your MacBook.

When traveling through airport security, leave your MacBook in Sleep mode, so it can be powered up quickly if anyone needs to check that it works properly.

Some Apps for Traveling

When you are traveling with your MacBook you can use it for productivity tasks with the iWork suite of Pages, Numbers and Keynote. In addition, Safari can be used to connect wirelessly to the Web and you can use iTunes for listening to music and iPhoto for your photos. There are also some other built-in apps that can be useful when you are traveling:

- **Notes**. Use this to create notes relating to your trip, ranging from Things to Pack lists to health information and travel details such as your itinerary. It is also a good option for keeping track of important items such as passport numbers.

- **iBooks**. Books are an ideal traveling companion and with this app you do not have to worry about being weighed down by a lot of heavy volumes.

- **Maps**. This is the perfect app for researching cities abroad so that you can start to feel at home as soon as you arrive. You can view maps in standard or 3D satellite view and also get directions between two locations.

For some locations, Maps has an automated 3D tour of a city. If this is available for the location being viewed, a **3D Flyover Tour** button will appear. Click on the **Start** button to begin the flyover tour.

3D Flyover Tour of Paris | Start

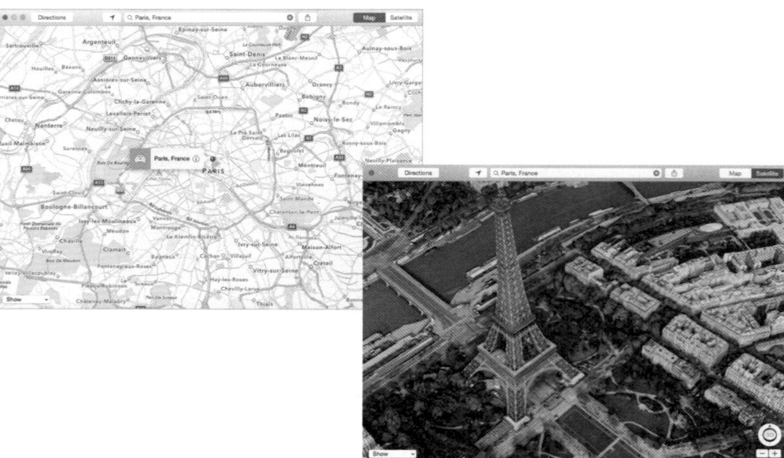

- **FaceTime**. You can use your MacBook to send emails and text messages when you are away from home, but FaceTime allows you to see people too with voice and video calls.

13 Battery Issues

Battery power is crucial to a MacBook. This chapter shows how to get the best from your battery and look after it.

Power Consumption

Battery life for each charge of MacBook batteries is one area that engineers have worked very hard on since MacBooks were first introduced. For the latest models of MacBooks the average battery life for each charge is approximately 8-9 hours. However, this is dependent on the power consumption of the MacBook, i.e. how much power is being used to perform particular tasks. Power-intensive tasks will reduce the battery life of each charge cycle. These types of tasks include:

- Watching a DVD
- Editing digital video
- Editing digital photographs
- Listening to music

Click on the battery icon to show or hide the percentage figure next to it (see next page).

When you are using your MacBook you can always monitor how much battery power you currently have available. This is shown by the battery icon that appears at the top right on the Apple Menu:

As the battery runs down, the monitor bar turns red as a warning:

Because of the vital role the battery plays in relation to your MacBook, it is important to try to conserve its power as much as possible. To do this:

- Where possible, use the mains adapter rather than the battery when using your MacBook.
- Use the Sleep function when you are not actively using your MacBook (see page 25).
- Use power management functions to save battery power (see next page).

Power Management

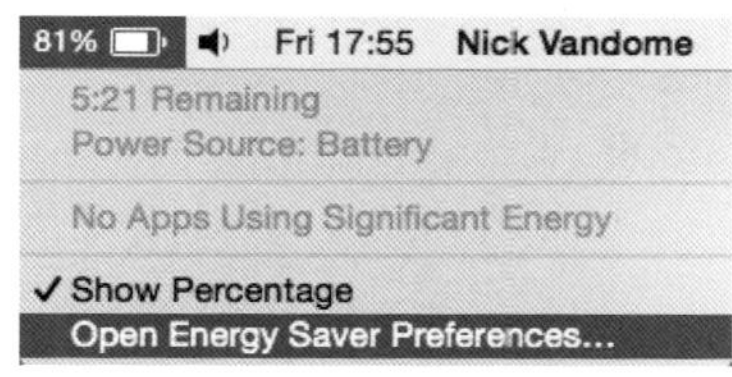

To access power management options, click on the battery icon on the Apple Menu. This shows the current battery source and the amount of power left, or the amount of charge in the battery. Click on the **Show Percentage** link to display or hide the percentage figure for the amount of charge left in the battery. The Energy Saver Preferences can be accessed here by clicking on the **Open Energy Saver Preferences** link or:

1. Access the **System Preferences** and click on the **Energy Saver** button

2. The **Energy Saver** window has a number of settings for the operation of your MacBook battery

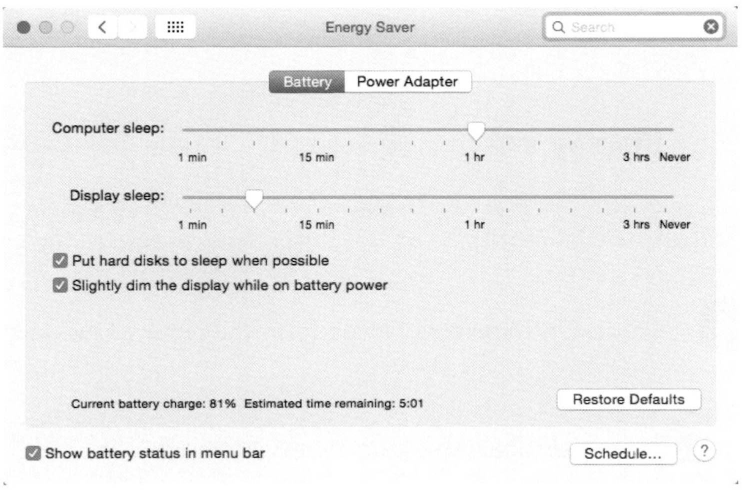

If you are undertaking an energy-intensive task, such as watching a DVD, try to use the external AC/DC power cable rather than the battery, otherwise the battery may drain quite quickly, causing the MacBook to close down completely.

Energy Saver

MacBooks have options for how the battery is managed within the Energy Saver System Preference. These allow you to set things like individual power settings for the battery and to view how much charge is left in the battery. To use the Energy Saver:

1. Access the **System Preferences** and click on the **Energy Saver** button

2. At the top of the Energy Saver window, click on the **Battery** tab. This contains settings for when your MacBook is on battery power alone

Battery

3. Drag the sliders to specify when the computer and the display are put to sleep, i.e. a state of hibernation

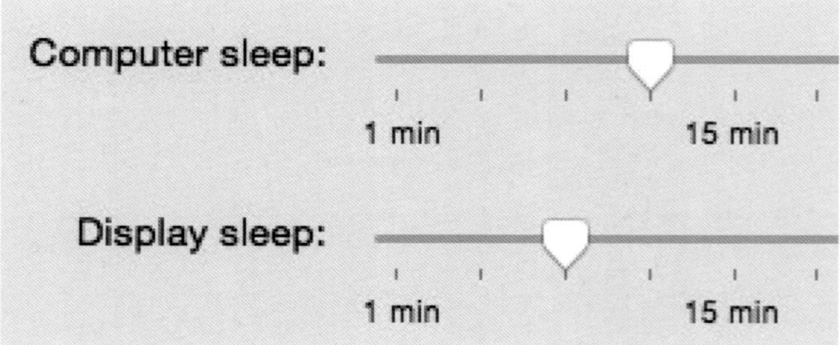

4. Check On these boxes to perform the required tasks

Put hard disks to sleep when possible
Slightly dim the display while on battery power

5 Check On this box to display the battery status at the top right-hand corner of the Apple Menu bar

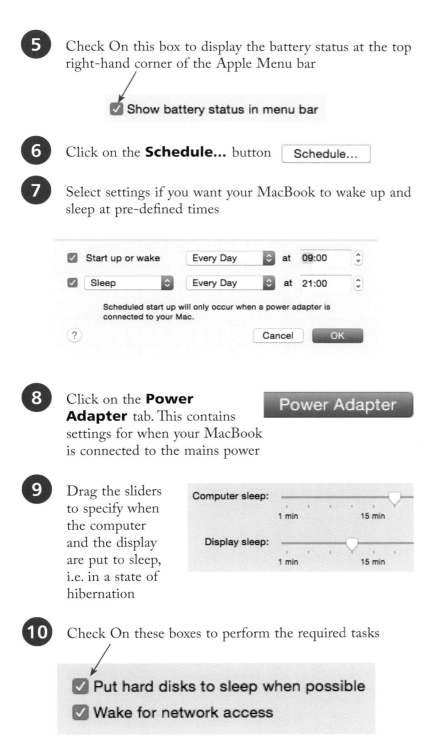

Show battery status in menu bar

6 Click on the **Schedule...** button Schedule...

7 Select settings if you want your MacBook to wake up and sleep at pre-defined times

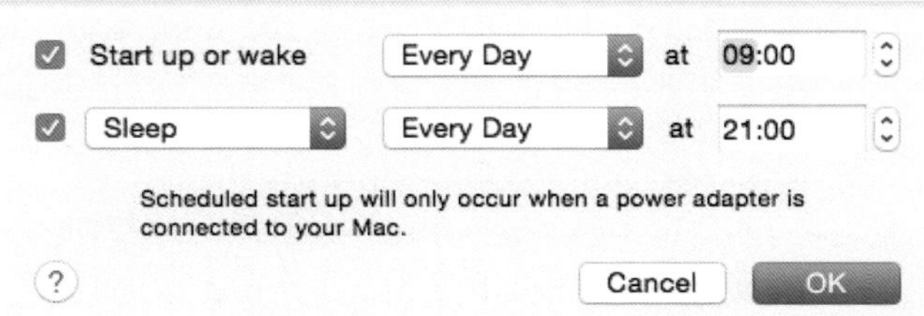

8 Click on the **Power Adapter** tab. This contains settings for when your MacBook is connected to the mains power

Power Adapter

9 Drag the sliders to specify when the computer and the display are put to sleep, i.e. in a state of hibernation

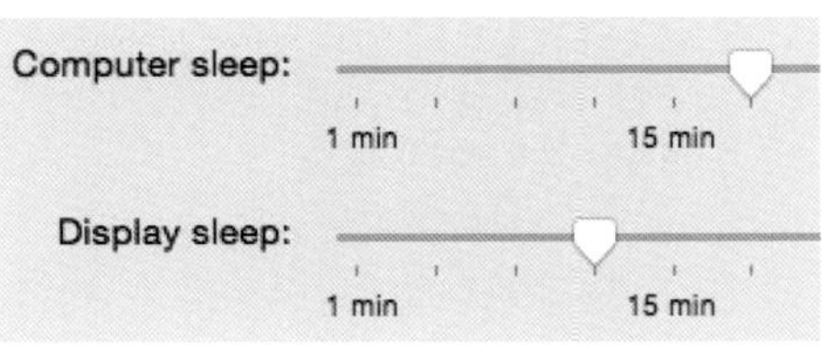

10 Check On these boxes to perform the required tasks

Put hard disks to sleep when possible
Wake for network access

With the power adapter it is acceptable to set longer periods before the computer or the display go to sleep.

Charging the Battery

MacBook batteries are charged using an AC/DC adapter, which can also be used to power the MacBook instead of the battery. If the MacBook is turned on and is being powered by the AC/DC adapter, the battery will be charged at the same time, although at a slower rate than if it is being charged when the MacBook is turned off.

The AC/DC adapter should be supplied with a new MacBook and consists of a cable and a power adapter. To charge a MacBook battery using an AC/DC adapter:

A MacBook battery can be charged whether the MacBook is turned on or off. It charges more quickly if the MacBook is not in use.

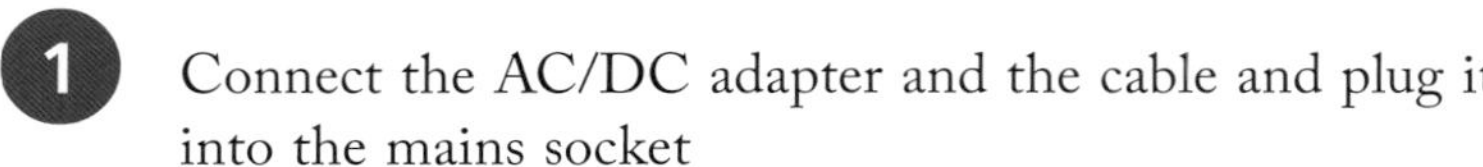

1. Connect the AC/DC adapter and the cable and plug it into the mains socket

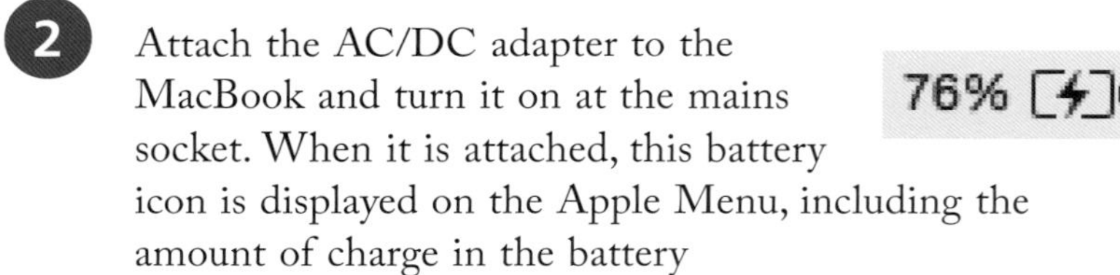

2. Attach the AC/DC adapter to the MacBook and turn it on at the mains socket. When it is attached, this battery icon is displayed on the Apple Menu, including the amount of charge in the battery

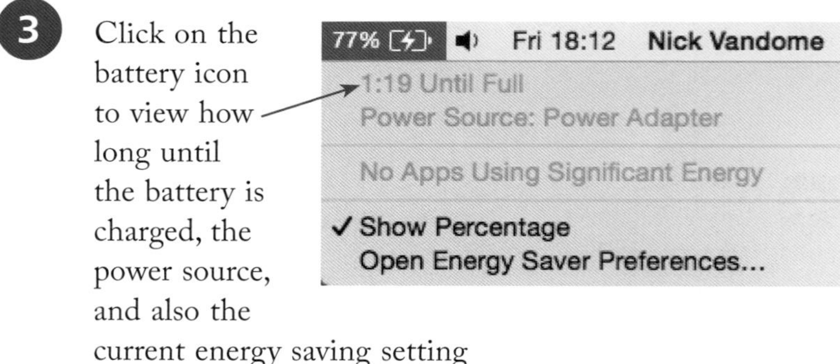

3. Click on the battery icon to view how long until the battery is charged, the power source, and also the current energy saving setting

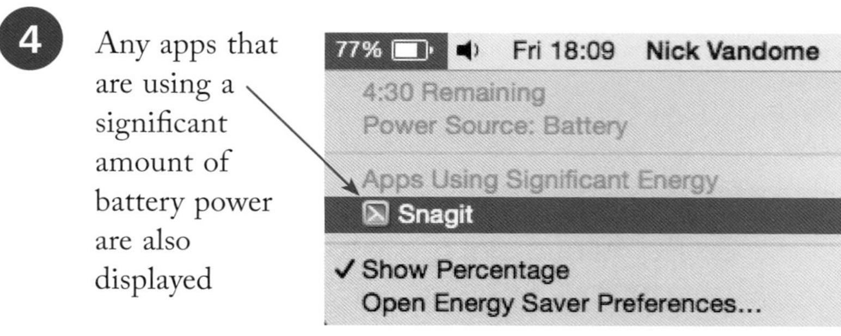

4. Any apps that are using a significant amount of battery power are also displayed

Dead and Spare Batteries

No energy source lasts forever and MacBook batteries are no exception to this rule. Over time, the battery will operate less efficiently until it will not be possible to charge the battery at all. With average usage, most MacBook batteries should last approximately 5 years, although they will start to lose performance before this and become less efficient. Some signs of a dead MacBook battery are:

- Nothing happens when the MacBook is turned on using just battery power.
- The MacBook shuts down immediately if it is being run on the AC/DC adapter and the cord is suddenly removed.
- The following window appears a few minutes or immediately after you have charged the battery and then started to use your MacBook on battery power:

You are now running on reserve battery power.

You need to plug the power adapter into your computer and into a power outlet. If you don't, your computer will go to sleep in a few minutes to preserve the contents of its memory.

OK

Spare battery

Depending on how and where you use your MacBook it might be worth considering buying a spare battery. Although these are not cheap, it can be a valuable investment, particularly if you spend a lot of time traveling with your MacBook and you are not always near a source of mains electricity. In situations like this, a spare battery could enable you to keep using your MacBook if your original battery runs out of power.

MacBook batteries can be bought from the Apple website or from an Apple store. However, they need to be fitted by an Apple store or a recognized Apple reseller.

When you are warned about a low battery, save all of your current work and either close down or switch to using an external AC/DC cable for powering your MacBook.

If you think that your battery may be losing its performance, make sure that you save your work at regular intervals. Although you should do this anyway, it is more important if there is a chance of your battery running out of power.

It is possible to replace a MacBook battery yourself but this is not advised as it would almost certainly invalidate the warranty.

Battery Troubleshooting

If you look after your MacBook battery well it should provide you with several years of mobile computing power. However, there are some problems that may occur with the battery:

- It won't keep its charge even when connected to an AC/DC adapter. The battery is probably flat and should be replaced with a new one. (Even if the battery is flat the MacBook will still operate using the AC/DC adapter).
- It only charges up a limited amount. Over time, MacBook batteries become less efficient and so do not hold their charge so well. One way to try to improve this is to drain the battery completely before it is charged again.
- It keeps its charge but runs down quickly. This can be caused by using a lot of power-hungry applications on the MacBook. The more work the MacBook has to do to run applications, such as those involving videos or games, the more power will be required from the battery and the faster it will run down.
- It is fully charged but does not appear to work at all when inserted. Check that the battery has clicked into place properly in the battery compartment and that the battery and MacBook terminals are clean and free from dust or moisture.
- It is inserted correctly but still does not work. The battery may have become damaged in some way, such as from becoming very wet. If you know the battery is damaged in any way, do not insert it, as it could short-circuit the MacBook. If the battery has been in contact with liquid, dry it out completely before you try inserting it into the MacBook. If it is thoroughly dry it may work again.
- It gets very hot when in operation. This could be caused by a faulty battery and it can be dangerous and lead to a fire. If in doubt, turn off the MacBook immediately and consult Apple. In some cases, faulty batteries can be recalled, so keep an eye on the Apple website to see if there are any details of this if you are concerned. Even in normal operation, MacBook batteries can feel quite warm. Get to know the normal temperature of your battery, so you can judge whether it is getting too hot or not.

If you are not going to be using your MacBook for an extended period of time, turn it off and store it in a safe, dry, cool place.

14 MacBook Maintenance

Despite its stability, OS X still benefits from a robust maintenance regime. This chapter looks at ways to keep OS X in top shape, ensure downloaded apps are as secure as possible and some general troubleshooting.

Time Machine

Time Machine is a feature of OS X that gives you great peace of mind. In conjunction with an external hard drive, it creates a backup of your whole system, including folders, files, apps and even the OS X operating system itself.

Once it has been set up, Time Machine takes a backup every hour and you can then go into Time Machine to restore any files that have been deleted or become corrupt.

Make sure that you have an external hard drive that is larger than the contents of your MacBook. Otherwise Time Machine will not be able to back it all up.

Setting up Time Machine

To use Time Machine it has to first be set up. This involves attaching a hard drive to your Mac. To set up Time Machine:

1. Click on the **Time Machine** icon on the Dock or access it in the **Launchpad**

2. You will be prompted to set up Time Machine

Your Time Machine backup disk can't be found.
Cancel
Set Up Time Machine

3. Click on the **Set Up Time Machine** button

Set Up Time Machine

4. In the Time Machine System Preferences window, click on the **Select Disk...** button

Select Disk...

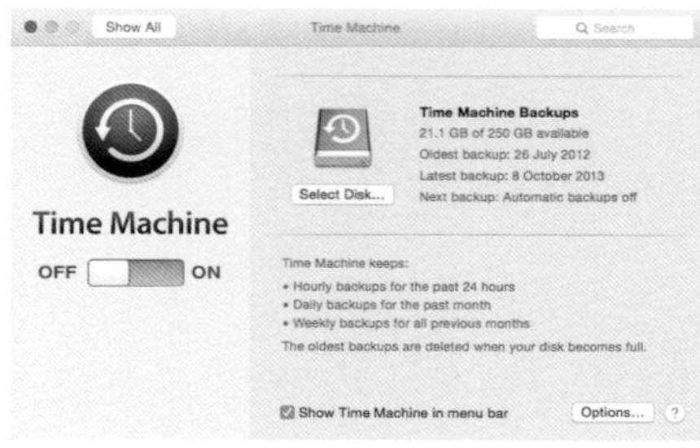

5. Connect an external hard drive and select it

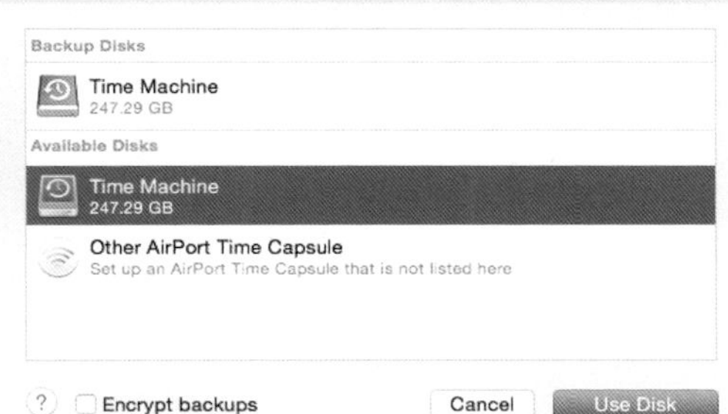

6. Click on the **Use Disk** button

7. In the Time Machine System Preferences window, drag the button to the **On** position

Time Machine

OFF ON

8. The backup will begin. The initial backup copies your whole system and can take several hours. Subsequent hourly backups only look at items that have been changed since the previous backup

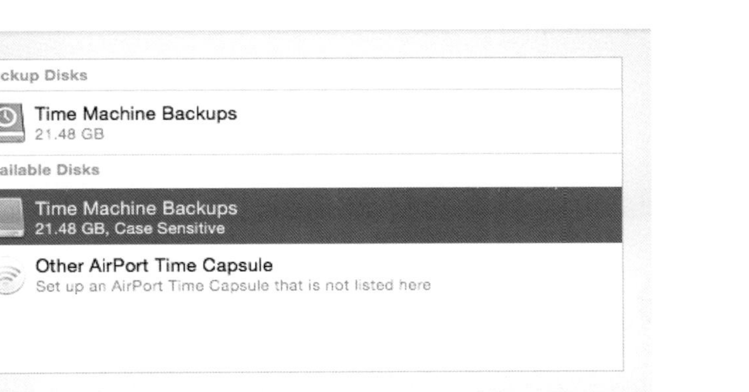

9. 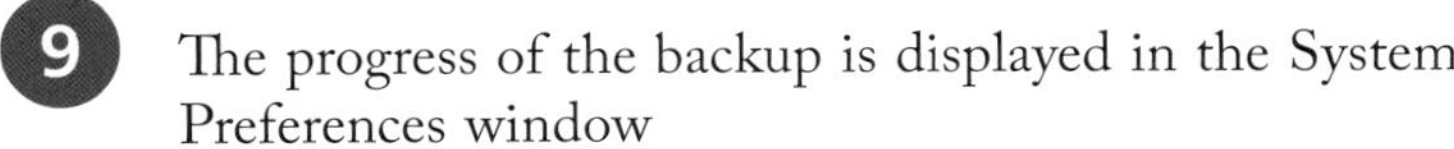

The progress of the backup is displayed in the System Preferences window

When you first set up Time Machine it copies everything on your MacBook. Depending on the type of connection you have for your external drive, this could take several hours, or even days. Because of this it is a good idea to have a hard drive with a Thunderbolt connection to make it as fast as possible.

If you stop the initial backup before it has been completed, Time Machine will remember where it has stopped and resume the backup from this point.

...cont'd

Using Time Machine

Once the Time Machine has been set up it can then be used to go back in time to view items in an earlier state. To do this:

If you have deleted items before the initial set up of Time Machine, these will not be recoverable.

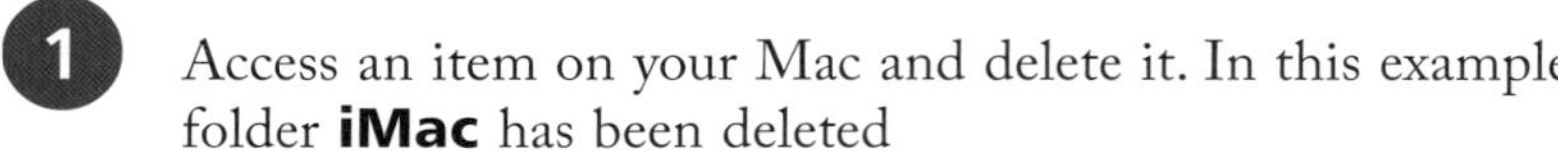

1. Access an item on your Mac and delete it. In this example folder **iMac** has been deleted

2. Click on the **Time Machine** icon

3. The Time Machine displays the current item in its current state (the icon is deleted). Earlier versions are stacked behind it

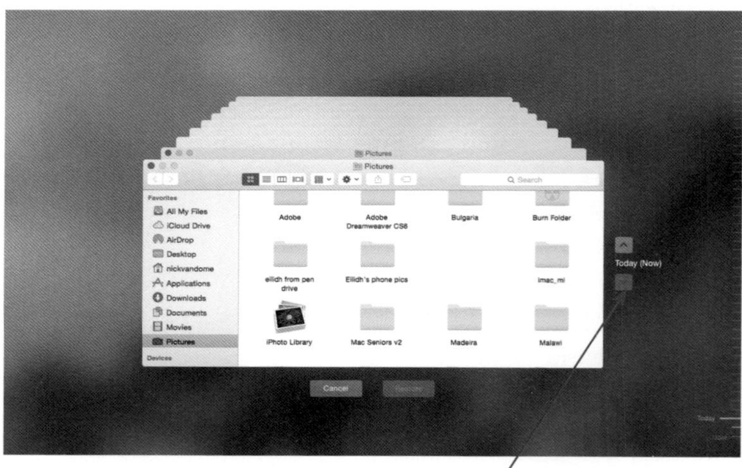

The active item that you were viewing before you launch Time Machine is the one that is active in the Time Machine interface. You can select items from within the active window to view their contents.

4. Click on the arrows to move through the open items or select a time or date from the scale to the right of the arrows

5. Another way to move through the Time Machine is to click on the pages behind the front one. This brings the selected item to the front

6 Click on the **Restore** button to restore any items that have been deleted (in this case the iMac folder)

Restore

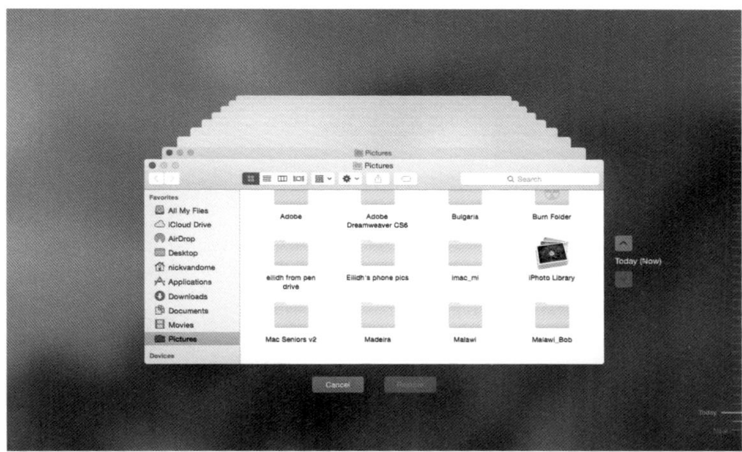

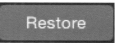

Items are restored from the Time Machine backup disk, i.e. the external hard drive.

7 Click on the **Cancel** button to return to your normal environment

Cancel

8 The deleted folder **iMac** is now restored in its original location

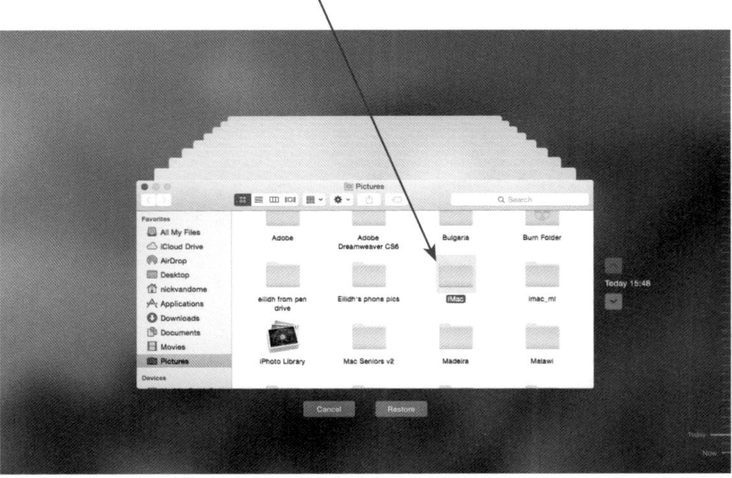

Disk Utility

Disk Utility is a utility app that allows you to perform certain testing and repair functions for OS X. It incorporates a variety of functions and it is a good option for general maintenance and if your computer is not running as it should.

Disk Utility is located within the **Applications > Utilities** folder.

Each of the functions within Disk Utility can be applied to specific drives and volumes. However, it is not possible to use the OS X start-up disk within Disk Utility as this will be in operation to run the app, and Disk Utility cannot operate on a disk that has apps already running. To use Disk Utility:

Checking disks

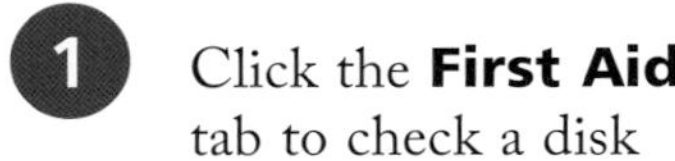

1. Click the **First Aid** tab to check a disk

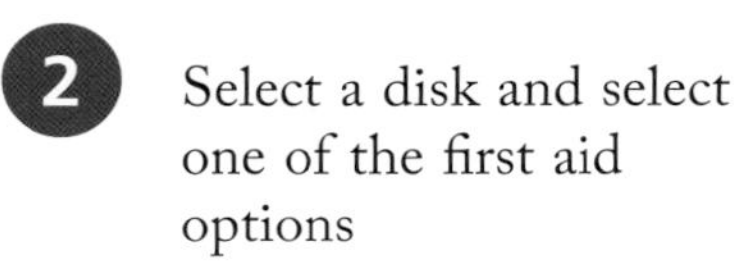

2. Select a disk and select one of the first aid options

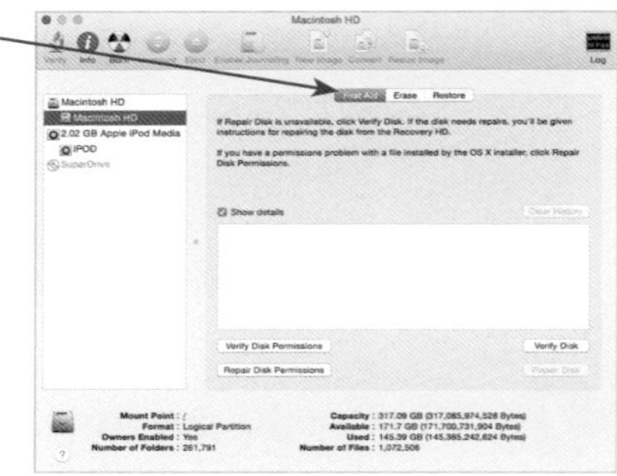

If there is a problem with a disk and OS X can fix it, the **Repair** button will be available. Click on this to enable Disk Utility to repair the problem.

Erasing a disk

To erase all of the data on a disk or a volume:

1. Click on the **Erase** tab and select a disk or a volume

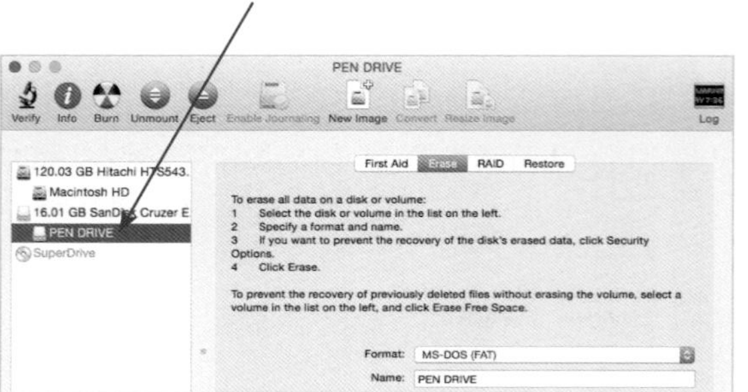

If you erase data from a removable disk, such as a pen drive, you will not be able to retrieve it.

2. Click **Erase** to erase the data on the selected disk or volume

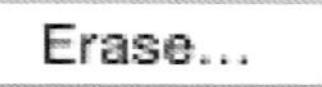

System Information

This can be used to view how the different hardware and software elements on your Mac are performing. To do this:

1. Open the Utilities folder and double-click on the **System Information** icon

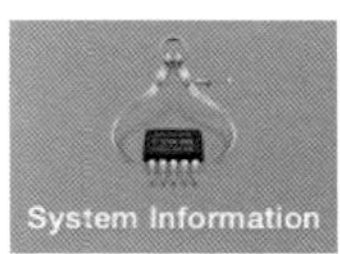

2. Click on the **Hardware** link and click on an item of hardware

System Information is located within the **Applications > Utilities** folder.

3. Details about the item of hardware, and its performance, are displayed

MATSHITA DVD-R UJ-898:

Firmware Revision:	HE13
Interconnect:	ATAPI
Burn Support:	Yes (Apple Shipping Drive)
Cache:	1024 KB
Reads DVD:	Yes
CD-Write:	-R, -RW
DVD-Write:	-R, -R DL, -RW, +R, +R DL, +RW
Write Strategies:	CD-TAO, CD-SAO, DVD-DAO
Media:	To show the available burn speeds, insert a disc and choose File > Refresh Information

4. Click on software items to view their details

Calculator	10.8
Calendar	8.0

Calculator:

Version:	10.8
Obtained from:	Apple
Last Modified:	02/09/2014 21:27
Kind:	Intel
64-Bit (Intel):	Yes
Signed by:	Software Signing, Apple Code Signing Certification Authority, Apple Root CA
Location:	/Applications/Calculator.app
Get Info String:	10.8, Copyright © 2001-2013, Apple Inc.

Activity Monitor

Activity Monitor is a utility app that can be used to view information about how much processing power and memory are being used to run apps. This can be useful to know if certain apps are running slowly or crashing frequently. To use Activity Monitor:

Activity Monitor is located within the **Applications > Utilities** folder.

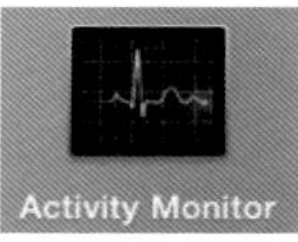

1. Click on the **CPU** tab to see how much processor memory is being used up

System:	1.03%	CPU LOAD	Threads:	719
User:	0.45%		Processes:	187
Idle:	98.51%			

2. Click on the **Memory** tab to see how much system memory (RAM) is being used up

Physical Memory:	4.00 GB	MEMORY PRESSURE	App Memory:	1.19 GB
Memory Used:	3.97 GB		File Cache:	251.3 MB
Virtual Memory:	7.94 GB		Wired Memory:	1.09 GB
Swap Used:	220.0 MB		Compressed:	1.44 GB

3. Click on the **Energy** tab to see how much energy your computer is using and battery performance

ENERGY IMPACT	Graphics Card:	Integrated	BATTERY (Last 12 hours)
	Remaining charge:	100%	
	Battery Is Charged		
	Time on AC:	25:17	

Click on the **Network** tab to see how much data has been sent and received over your network.

4. Click on the **Disk** tab to see how much space and disk usage each app uses

Reads in:	730,337	IO	Data read:	16.51 GB
Writes out:	435,979		Data written:	10.66 GB
Reads in/sec:	3		Data read/sec:	68.0 KB
Writes out/sec:	0		Data written/sec:	5.33 KB

Updating Software

Apple periodically releases updates for its software: both its apps and the OS X operating system. All of these are now available through the App Store. To update software:

1. Open **System Preferences** and click on the **App Store** icon

2. Click here to select options for how you are notified about updates and how they are downloaded

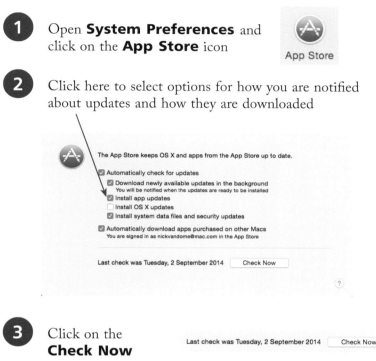

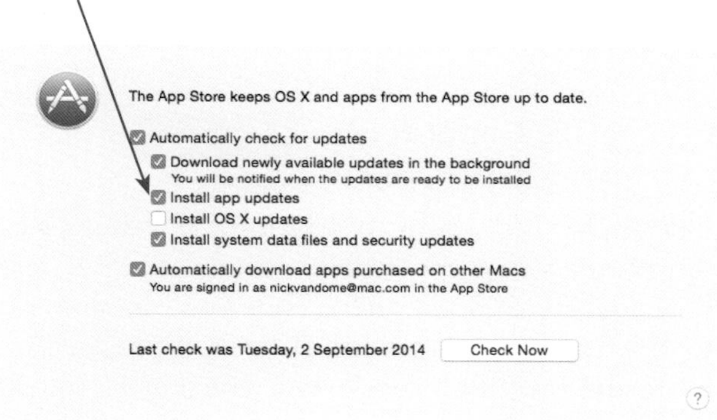

3. Click on the **Check Now** button to check for updates manually

Last check was Tuesday, 2 September 2014 Check Now

4. Available updates are shown in the **Updates** section in the App Store. Click on the **Update** buttons to update

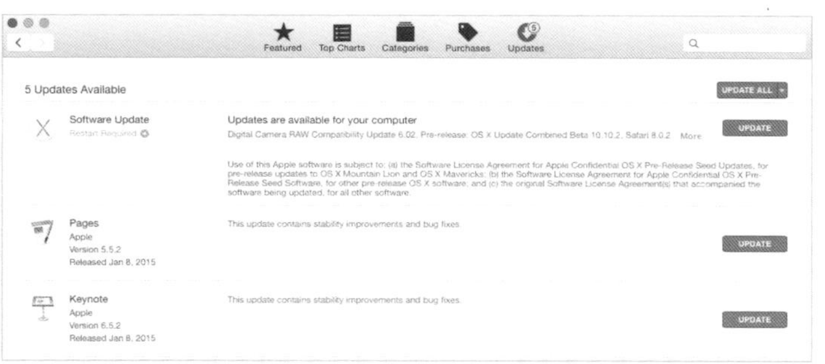

If **Automatically check for updates** is selected, you can specify to be alerted at the appropriate time when updates are available. This is done through the Notification Center.

Check On the **Automatically download apps purchased on other Macs** box if you want to activate this function.

For some software updates, such as those to OS X itself, you may have to restart your computer for them to take effect.

Gatekeeper

Internet security is an important issue for every computer user; no-one wants their computer to be infected with a virus or malicious software. Historically, Macs have been less prone to attack from viruses than Windows-based machines, but this does not mean Mac users can be complacent. With their increasing popularity there is now more temptation for virus writers to target them. Yosemite recognizes this and has taken steps to prevent attacks with the Gatekeeper function. To use this:

To make changes within the General section of the Security & Privacy System Preferences, click on the padlock icon and enter your admin password.

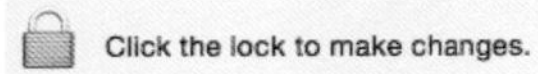

1. Open **System Preferences** and click on the **Security & Privacy** button

2. Click on the **General** tab

3. Check On the buttons to determine which apps can be downloaded. In some earlier versions of OS X, apps were downloaded from anywhere. Now you can also select to only have them from just the App Store, or the App Store and identified developers, which gives you added security in terms of apps having been thoroughly checked

Apple have a very robust checking procedure for apps in the App Store and those produced by identified developers.

4. Under the **General** tab there are also options for using a password when you log in to your account and also if a password is required after sleep or the screen saver

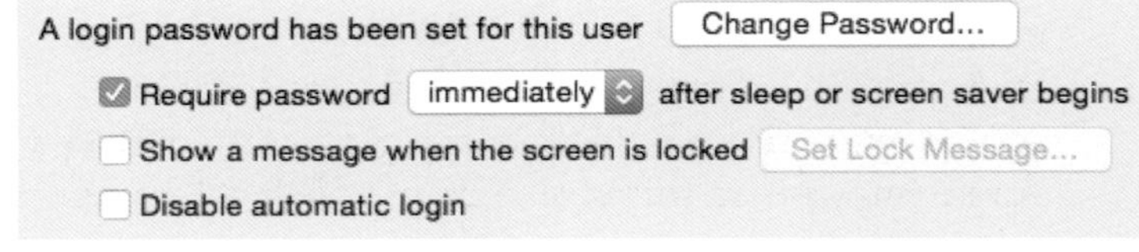

Privacy

Also within the Security & Privacy System Preferences are options for activating a firewall and privacy settings:

1. Click on the **Firewall** tab

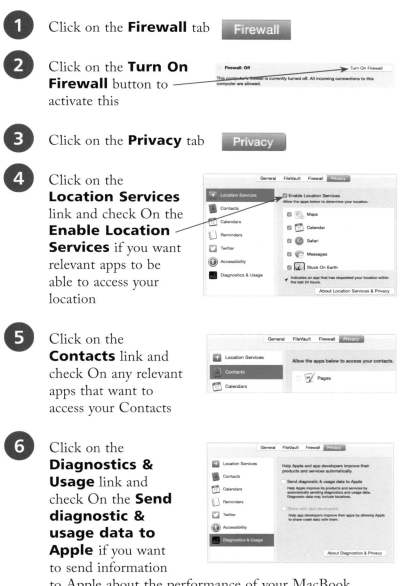

2. Click on the **Turn On Firewall** button to activate this

3. Click on the **Privacy** tab

4. Click on the **Location Services** link and check On the **Enable Location Services** if you want relevant apps to be able to access your location

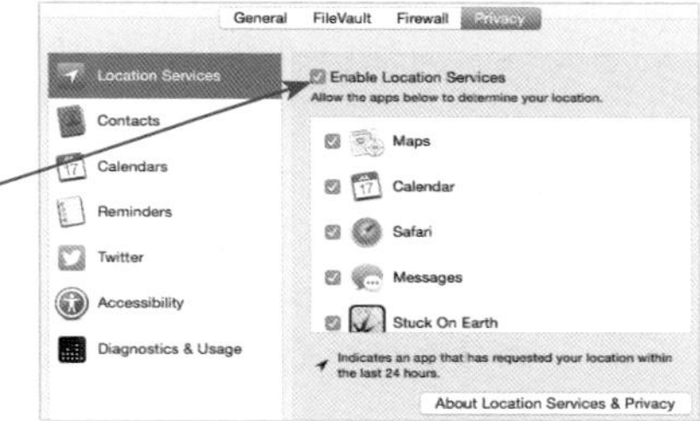

5. Click on the **Contacts** link and check On any relevant apps that want to access your Contacts

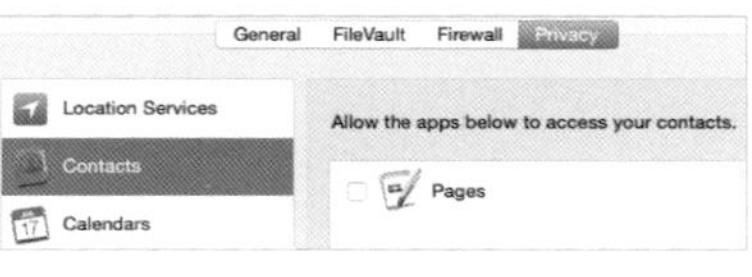

6. Click on the **Diagnostics & Usage** link and check On the **Send diagnostic & usage data to Apple** if you want to send information to Apple about the performance of your MacBook and its apps. This will include any problems and helps Apple improve its software and apps. This information is collected anonymously

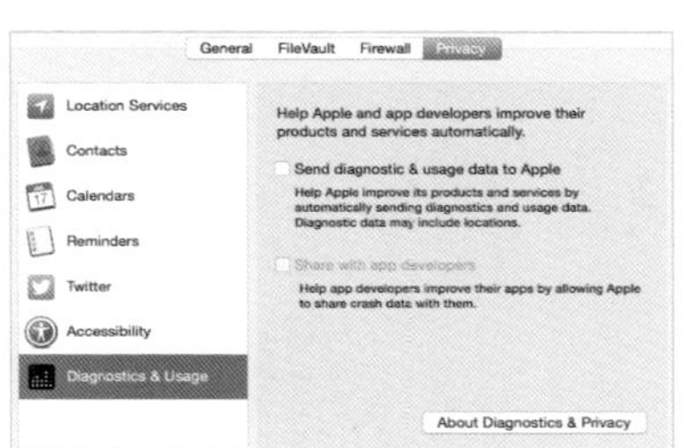

Yosemite apps are designed to do only what they are supposed to, so that they do not have to interact with other apps if they do not need to. This lessens the possibility of any viruses spreading across your MacBook. For instance, only apps that can use Contacts will ask for permission to do this.

Problems with Apps

The simple answer

OS X is something of a rarity in the world of computing software; it claims to be remarkably stable, and it is. However, this is not to say that things do not sometimes go wrong, although this is considerably less frequent than with older Mac operating systems. Sometimes this will be due to problems within particular apps and on occasions the problems may lie with OS X itself. If this does happen the first course of action is to close down OS X using the **Apple menu > Shut Down** command. Then restart the computer. If this does not work, or you cannot access the Shut Down command, try turning off the power to the computer and then starting up again.

Force quitting

If a particular app is not responding it can be closed down separately without the need to reboot the computer. To do this:

1. Select **Apple menu > Force Quit** from the Menu bar

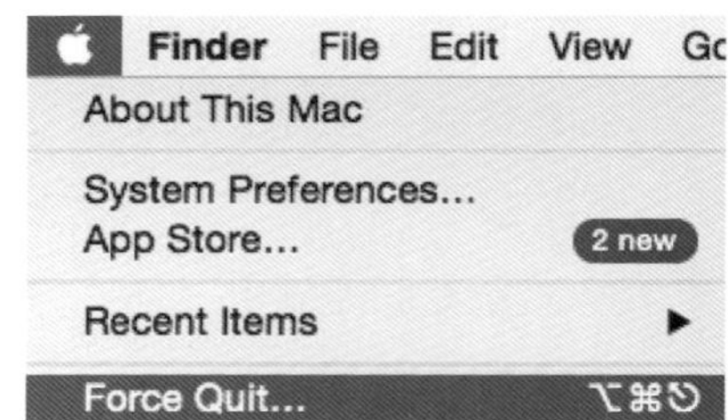

2. Select the app you want to close

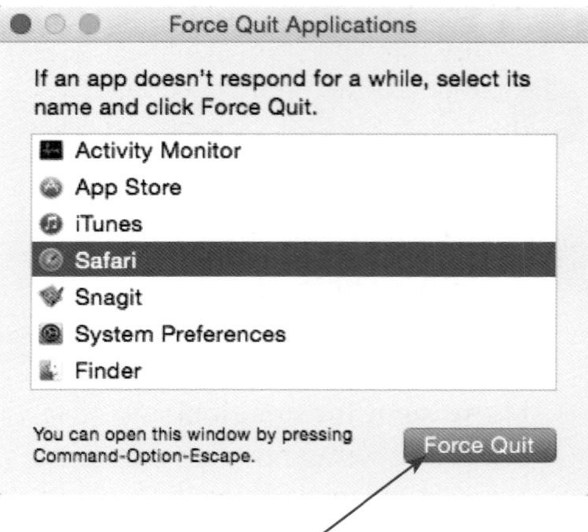

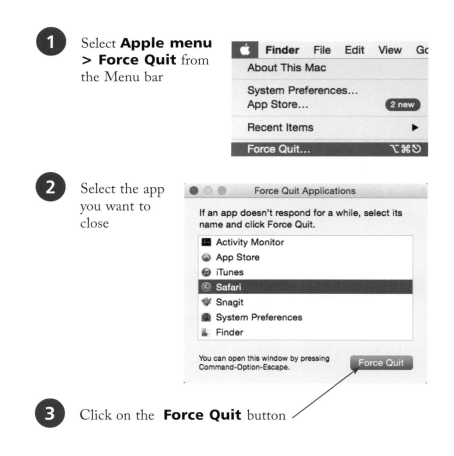

3. Click on the **Force Quit** button

General Troubleshooting

It is true that things do go wrong with OS X, although probably with less regularity than with some other operating systems. If something does go wrong, there are a number of items that you can check and also some steps you can take to ensure that you do not lose any important data if the worst case scenario occurs and your hard drive packs up completely.

- **Backup**. If everything does go wrong it is essential to take preventative action in the form of making sure that all of your data is backed up and saved. This can be done with either the Time Machine app or by backing up manually by copying data to a pen drive, an external hard drive or a CD or DVD, using an external SuperDrive.
- **Reboot**. One traditional reply by IT helpdesks is to reboot, i.e. turn off the computer and turn it back on again and hope that the problem has resolved itself. In a lot of cases this simple operation does the trick but it is not always a viable solution for major problems.
- **Check cables**. If the problem appears to be with a network connection or an externally-connected device, check that all cables are connected properly and have not worked loose. If possible, make sure that all cables are tucked away so that they cannot be pulled out by accident.
- **Check network settings**. If your network or Internet connections are not working, check the network setting in System Preferences. Sometimes when you make a change to one item this can have an adverse effect on one of these settings. (If possible, lock the settings once you have applied them, by clicking on the padlock icon in the Network preferences window.)
- **Check for viruses**. If your computer is infected with a virus this could affect the efficient running of the machine. Luckily this is less of a problem for Macs as virus writers tend to concentrate their efforts towards Windows-based machines. However, there are plenty of Mac viruses out there, so make sure your computer is protected by an app such as Norton AntiVirus which is available from **www.symantec.com**

In extreme cases, you will not be able to reboot your computer as normal. If this happens, you will have to pull out the power cable and reattach it. You will then be able to reboot, although the computer may want to check its hard drive to make sure that everything is in working order.

...cont'd

- **Check Login items**. If you have set certain items to start automatically when you log in to your MacBook, this could cause certain conflicts within your computer. If this is the case, disable the items from launching during the login process. This can be done within the **Users & Groups** preference of System Preferences by clicking on the **Login Items** tab, selecting the relevant item and clicking on the minus button.

- **Check permissions**. If you, or other users, are having problems opening items this could be because of the permissions that are set. To check these, select the item in the Finder, click on the File button on the Finder toolbar and select **Get Info**. In the Sharing & Permissions section of the Info window you will be able to set the relevant permissions to allow other users, or yourself, to read, write or have no access.

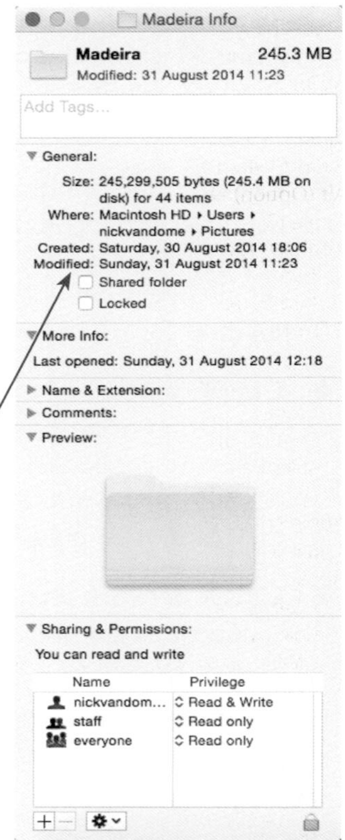

Click here to view permissions settings

- **Eject external devices**. Sometimes external devices, such as pen drives, can become temperamental and refuse to be ejected, or even show up on the Desktop or in the Finder. If this happens you can try and eject the device by clicking the trackpad when the Mac chimes are heard during the booting up process.

- **Turn off your screen saver**. Screen savers can sometimes cause conflicts within your computer, particularly if they have been downloaded from an unreliable source. If this happens, change the screen saver within the **Desktop & Screen Saver** preference of the System Preferences or disable it altogether.

Index

A

B

C

D

E

F

G

H

I

J

K

L

M

N

O

P

Q

R

S

T

U

V

W

Z